THE CENTAUR GUIDE TO

Bermuda, The Bahamas, Hispaniola
Puerto Rico and the Virgin Islands

Companion volume to:
THE CARIBBEAN & EL DORADO

ATLANTIC

OCEAN

BERMUDA

UNITED STATES

BAHAMAS

CUBA

JAMAICA

HISPANIOLA

PUERTO RICO

UANA I.
CAICOS IS.
TURKS IS.

50 0   100   200   300 MILES

Mona Passage

PUERTO RICO

BR. VIRGIN IS.

U.S. VIRGIN IS.

ANGUILLA

BARBUDA

ANTIGUA

DOMINICAN REPUBLIC

niola

Leeward Is.

GUADELOUPE

DOMINICA

S E A

MARTINIQUE

ST. LUCIA

ST. VINCENT

Windward Is.

BARBADOS

GRENADA

TOBAGO

TRINIDAD

VENEZUELA

GUYANA

THE CENTAUR GUIDE TO

Bermuda
The Bahamas
Hispaniola
Puerto Rico
and the
Virgin Islands

by JOHN CROCKER

CENTAUR PRESS LTD.
FONTWELL   SUSSEX

*First published 1968 by the Centaur
Press Ltd., Fontwell, Sussex, and 11-14
Stanhope Mews West, London, SW7
Printed in Great Britain by
Clarke, Doble & Brendon Ltd.,
Cattedown, Plymouth*

CONTENTS

LIST OF ILLUSTRATIONS

LIST OF MAPS

vii

ACKNOWLEDGMENTS

For pictures and information the author would like to thank the Bermuda Trade Development Board, the Bahamas Government Information Services, the Puerto Rico Commonwealth Department of Tourism, and the Department of Commerce of the United States Virgin Islands. Thanks are also given to the British and United States Embassies in Santo Domingo, to the British Embassy in Port-au-Prince, the British Consul in St. Thomas, the office of the Administrator in the British Virgin Islands, Pan American World Airways, the United States Travel Service, and the Central Office of Information, London.

INTRODUCTION

The islands described in this book are noteworthy for two main reasons. The first concerns the effect on them of the "wind of change" which has been altering the political structure of many nations and territories since the war. The second is that they are being increasingly visited by foreigners who know little, if anything, of their past histories and present aspirations; the average visitor, sipping a frozen daiquiri or rum punch beneath a gaily coloured umbrella on a sun-drenched, white sand beach, is unaware of the thoughts and ambitions of the "native" waiter who serves him.

One cause of this unawareness has been the tendency of some guide books to give an impression of static societies in the islands, yet the fact that these do not now exist was clearly shown by the result of the Bahamas elections of January 1967, when the white European stock "Establishment", which had ruled the islands for more than 300 years, suffered a rebuff at the polls by a predominantly Negro party. To many people this was both a shock and a surprise. In the same context the assassination in 1961 of the ruthlessly corrupt dictator who had ruled the Dominican Republic for 31 years was a shock to more people in the United States than would care to admit it; and the surprise occasioned by the ousting in 1959 of Cuba's equally ruthless and corrupt dictator was yet another example of myopic wishful thinking. The truth is that these islands are all politically and economically on the move; and, once this is understood, they become more, not less, attractive to the visitor, to the settler, and even to those considering investing money in them.

A guide book which is still in circulation contains the following phrase in English and in Russian: "Stationmaster, kindly tell me the time of the next train to St. Petersburg". There is a similar outmoded approach in many publications which seek to help visitors to the islands described in this book and in its companion piece which deals with the Caribbean area further south. This is a pity, if only because mass tourism, which forms a highly significant aspect of present-day international relations, could have just as much influence on the future of these islands as the introduction of sugar or piracy to the Caribbean area had in the seventeenth and eighteenth centuries. The fact that a Negro became head of the Bahamas government for the first time in 1967 is directly attributable to the fact that some 800,000 white North Americans and British had been deciding each year that they liked to go there either for a holiday, to settle, or to "develop" a piece of property.

This is not to suggest that the new Premier, Mr. L. O. Pindling, is in any way anti-American or anti-British (this has been made clear by my talks with him in Nassau), but it is very much to suggest that many Bahamians were not satisfied with the way in which their affairs were being conducted by what they regarded as a closed circle of white people who, supposedly, got most of the pickings from the money which had been pouring in from the United States, Canada and Britain.

Similar residual effects of mass tourism have been coming to the surface in Bermuda, Puerto Rico and the American Virgin Islands. These effects formed a part also of the post-Trujillo turbulence in the Dominican Republic where one of the world's most plush hotels contrasts its splendour with some of the world's greatest poverty. In Haiti, where the tourist plushness is less, but the poverty even greater, the contrast is equally evident. Yet, without exception, all the islands described in this book rely to a greater or less extent, as Cuba once did, on the money brought in by tourism to develop their economies and improve their standards of living. By and large the inhabitants are happy that this should be so even though, like the Jamaicans described in the companion volume, some tend to look with something approaching contempt on the people who come and "chuck their money around."

Figures dealing with the amount of money spent by tourists make interesting reading. In Bermuda and the Bahamas combined, during the second half of the nineteen sixties, the annual amount was about $130,000,000, and this takes no account of the money invested to provide accommodation and entertainment for the visitors. Perhaps even more significant is the number of visitors in relation to inhabitants; the figures here for the two groups of islands combined are 183,000 inhabitants and 1,000,000 visitors. In other words, at any given moment foreigners outnumber native Bermudians and Bahamians by about six to one; and it is anticipated that these figures will be doubled by the end of the next two decades. The United States Virgin Islands have a population of about 42,000, yet 250,000 visitors go there each year and spend $50,000,000. In Puerto Rico the number of visitors is not so large relative to the population—about 620,000 compared with 2,750,000— but the amount of money brought in is of a similar large order, about $120,000,000 annually.

The British Virgin Islands are only just beginning to attract visitors in large numbers, but their population is so small that they will soon be swamped. The Dominican Republic entered a period of tourist doldrums due to the violence which followed Trujillo's assassination and, as late as 1967, there was scarcely a tourist in sight there. The political situation in Haiti during the fifties and sixties has not been such as to attract large numbers of visitors. It is perfectly possible, however, that both these countries, which have all the basic attributes which a tourist seeks, will become booming resorts by the end of this century. It is in any case certain, not merely possible, that facilities for air travel from both North America and Europe to these islands will be vastly better in the eighties decade than they were in the sixties; and from this it follows that all, not merely some, of the islands will have an annual influx of visitors, not perhaps as numerically great relative to the inhabitants as has been the case in Bermuda and the Bahamas, but certainly in highly significant numbers.

The panegyrics about sun, sand and palm which appear ever more frequently in the North American and British newspapers and magazines only give part of the picture of what is going on in these islands; the field is much wider, the situation more fluid. Fluidity, indeed, is the main problem of any book which attempts to describe a locality and the way of life of the people who live in it. Place names, political alignments and economic factors can, and do, change suddenly. For all anybody knows the capital of the Dominican Republic, now known by its original title, Santo Domingo, but for long called Ciudad Trujillo, may change its name again. In this context the writer of the Russian guide cannot be blamed for using the name St. Petersburg, but the fact that he did so, presumably with absolute confidence about its immutability, is a good example of the guide books' tendency to treat their subjects as static.

When I was last in Haiti Dr. Francois Duvalier was President and he, like the late Rafael Trujillo in the neighbouring Dominican Republic, has had such an important effect on his country that his policy and activities have to be recorded. He is, of course, no more a permanent fixture than is the man who was Governor of the United States Virgin Islands at the time of my last visit there in 1967—Mr. Ralph M. Paiewonsky. These contemporary—more or less—personages have to be mentioned in the same sense as Bermuda's first "Governor", Sir George Somers, or Blackbeard the pirate, have to be mentioned; they are all responsible for making the islands the absorbingly interesting and attractive places which they now are.

* * *

In dealing with hotels it is perhaps wise to remember Oscar Wilde's definition of a cynic : "A man who knows the price of everything and the value of nothing." Some hoteliers in the Caribbean, though not many in the islands mentioned in this book, are even worse than cynics because they have little understanding of any relationship between price and value, being of the opinion, presumably, that all tourists have untold wealth and that they ought to be only too delighted to spend it in such a charming part of the world. Where such an attitude does exist the reason usually is that the hotelier is totally inexperienced about what goes on elsewhere in the world and is ignorant about the true value of the goods and services which he has to offer.

The hotels in this book are classified according to a simple rule : value for money. In the top category, which I have called A-plus, are those hotels whose owners, whether big corporations or private individuals, have set out to offer their guests all the amenities which high prices demand. These must include such things as swimming pools, beaches, air conditioning, a wide range of sports facilities and evening entertainment, first-class food and service and an attractive decor. It may well be that some people consider one particular decor more, or less, attractive than another, one beach more suited to their recreational desires than another. The bartender, possibly, at a given hotel may not be able to produce the simplest —and in many ways the best—of all drinks, a Scotch whisky and water, to the complete satisfaction of the connoisseur; a French visitor may scoff at the way a steak is cooked by a chef conditioned by North American taste. Such guests should go somewhere else. If the hotel they are in has an A-plus rating, they may rest assured that all reasonable requirements will be met; the beach, of course, cannot be altered, but the Scotch and water can be, and will be, mixed differently to suit individual taste. If you pay good money, you should expect good value for it.

And so the classification goes on down the scale. An A-minus hotel has not all the facilities of an A-plus hotel and you are therefore not expected to pay as much money to stay there. An hotel in the B category has even fewer facilities to offer the visitor; but it does not follow in any way that the B class hotel is a bad one. On the contrary, it may be extremely good if it corresponds with the requirements of the guests in terms of what he wants to spend and what he wants to get for his expenditure. In this sense a C category hotel or guest house can be just as "good" as one in the A-plus bracket if it gives the value for money which the guest expects. Every now and then one does come across an hotel which is so good in its own way—food, service, civility, situation, architecture, and so on— as to suggest fitness for top classification; but, if it has not got the stipulated qualifications in the way of facilities, it is not eligible.

With the proliferation of tourist agencies all over the world and the frequency with which airlines alter their schedules and expand their points of call, it is pointless to attempt to give any detailed information about how to get from one place to another. All that has been done is to give a rough idea of how accessible a place is by air or sea. Transport, like social and political conditions, is essentially a fluid and variable factor in the islands which I have tried to describe.

JOHN CROCKER

THE QUONDAM ISLE OF DEVILS

Bermuda

"The biggest small place in the world."—Mark Twain

"I shan't be in to lunch, but I'll see you for dinner this evening." These words spoken to me by the owner of the charming old-modern house where I was staying in the Tucker's Town parish of Bermuda would not be worth repeating except that it later became apparent that the man was having lunch in New York.

There are many fascinating aspects of Bermuda, but not the least of them is that nowadays residents of, or visitors to, this semi-tropical group of lovely islands can get from Kindley Field airport to downtown Manhattan in not much more than $2\frac{1}{2}$ hours. Another interesting fact is that in 1959 Bermuda celebrated its three hundred and fiftieth anniversary of being a British territory. A third fact is that in the second half of the sixties' there were signs that although almost all Bermudians wanted to remain under the Union Jack, a lot wanted—and got—a change from the paternalistic rule of two dozen or so prominent Bermudian families.

These families, commonly known as "The Front Street Boys" because their prosperous and entrenched businesses are on the waterfront of that name, in 1965 began to become aware that the time had come for them to get in step politically with the second half of the twentieth century. In February of that year there was a riot in the trim, spotlessly clean and flower-decked streets of the capital city, Hamilton, and seventeen policemen were injured in a scuffle with picketing trade unionists. The leader of the trade unionists, no dark-skinned Bermudian, but a small, white, woman doctor, Dr. Barbara Ball, was later tried and acquitted on all counts including assaulting a policeman and inciting others to obstruct the police.

How could this have happened in a small, smug island group where there was virtually no unemployment (nor is there now) and where nobody but a moron could fail to earn, if he or she wanted to, a minimum of $40 a week? It was so difficult for some Bermudians to believe that riots and a trial of this nature could occur in a territory which had hitherto been happily shared between some 17,500 whites and 30,500 people of Negro stock, that they sought refuge in the belief that there was a plot afoot initiated by "international Communism," helped by racialists of the American Black Moslem type, to take over power by disrupting Bermuda's economy, which is almost totally dependent on the 200,000 tourists (90% of them North American) who come to Bermuda each year and spend something like $30 million.

In fact the riots did not represent an attempt to get rid of the established Government. They were based on a move, largely initiated by the Negro population, to get rid of the anachronisms with which the governmental system was surrounded. There may have been no poverty in Bermuda, but equally there was no universal suffrage; the minimum voting age was 25; and there was also a property qualification to be met before anybody could vote.

All this was, to say the least, anomalous in an age when a man in Bermuda's upper stratum of society could leave his home, have lunch in New York, and be back in time for dinner. Other anomalies were that the executive branch of government was not responsible to the elected House of Assembly. Even the oddly named Legislative Council—actually an Upper House, or Senate, consisting of nominated or ex-officio members—had little power. Real executive power lay in the hands of a number of "Boards", presided over by senior and respected members of the community. And the paterfamilias was the senior member of Bermuda's leading family, Sir Henry (Jack) Tucker, head of the Bank of Bermuda and director of several companies in the Front Street hierarchy.

Probably most Bermudians were content enough to have men of stature and integrity like Sir Henry, and others, in charge of their affairs. But the advocates of change were

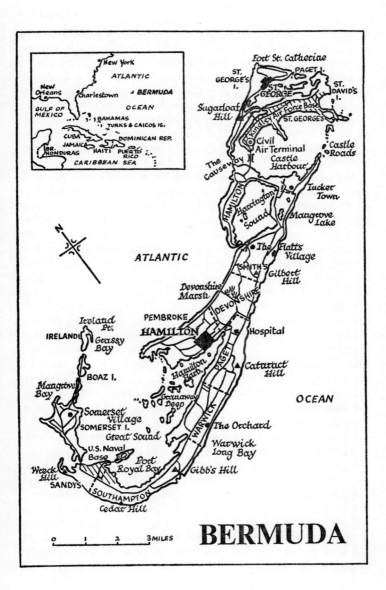

BERMUDA

0 1 2 3 MILES

strengthened in their cause by the fact—which must be unique
in British colonial history—that there has been until recently
no serious attempt by the Government to train local people for
positions of responsibility in the Civil Service. The apologists
for this state of affairs in Bermuda maintained that the average
Bermudian, white or Negro, would not consider entering
Government employment simply because he, or she, could do
so much better in private business. But this, in the view of
most intelligent Bermudians, neither was nor is a satisfactory
answer.

Bermuda is a mid-Atlantic paradise of yellowish-pink sand,
golf, and good living; and it is certainly not even remotely true
that changes designed to bring it more politically up-to-date
will have an adverse effect on its charms. It is true that at, for
example, a barbecue picnic party on the small beach of the
Mid-Ocean Club (in one of the most exclusive areas of Bermuda) you do get the feeling of being among an Anglo-
American group which wants to stick to itself. And why not?
There are plenty of other clubs and hotels where other groups
can go and stick to themselves also. There is cash for every-
one in Bermuda, thanks to the money which comes in from
abroad; and, with the abolition of political anachronisms,
there is no reason why the aura of paradise should be removed.
The "Establishment" and the "Front Street Boys"—with the
exception of a few, who, as a senior civil servant told me, are
only concerned with "scraping in money from the tourists"—
are not now political reactionaries, though they do want to
keep their group of islands unspoilt.

Politics, indeed, in the modern sense of the word, have only
recently come to Bermuda, the two-party system having only
been started after the 1963 elections; and, at any rate up to
early 1967, the basic difference in aims between the major
parties was never great. The minority party in the House of
Assembly, the Progressive Labour Party, which has the support of most Negroes, has always sought to achieve constitutional reforms such as universal suffrage over the age of 21,
the abolition of property qualifications for voting, the adoption
of the ministerial system, and the training of more local people

for the civil service, with particular reference to the police. Their view has been that it would be a luxury, to say the least, for 47,000 Bermudians to seek to commit themselves to a demand for total independence from Britain, though the position should be kept constantly under review. The ruling (1967) United Bermuda Party now has similar views. Both parties have fully accepted the principle of collective bargaining by organised trade unions; both parties are opposed to racialism of any sort; both want to remain under the Union Jack, with Britain retaining responsibility for foreign affairs, internal security and defence.

So it is possible, indeed right, for the visitor to Bermuda to relax on one of its lovely beaches, within sight perhaps of a delightful eighteenth-century coral limestone house, and substitute thoughts of Shakespeare for those of politics. Much has been written about the connections of one of his plays, *The Tempest*, with Bermuda; and it is not only pleasant but historically accurate to imagine that Shakespeare got some of his plot from the adventures of Admiral Sir George Somers and his passengers and crew, who spent nine months there in 1609 when their ship, the *Sea Venture*, was wrecked off the coast in a storm on its way to the new North American colony of Virginia. Two accounts of the episode were published in London by two of the survivors, Silvanus Jourdain and William Strachey, the first in 1610 and the second in 1612. *The Tempest* was produced in November, 1611. In those days London was a small place and it is only too likely that William Shakespeare and William Strachey (who went to live in Blackfriars, not far from the Globe Theatre) met and talked about the episode. It is even possible that Shakespeare assisted Strachey in the preparation of his account before publication. Obviously, too, this highly newsworthy shipwreck story was the gossip of all the taverns; and there is also the fact that the Earl of Southampton, Shakespeare's patron, was a member of the Company of Adventurers and Planters of the City of London who sponsored Admiral Somers' voyage; so were a number of other prominent men with whom Shakespeare is known to have been associated. That this much-publicised "story of the year"

seemed an ideal basis for a play can hardly be doubted; and
there is the further consideration that the Bermuda islands
had a reputation among seamen—including Sir Walter Raleigh
—of being the abode of spirits and demons ideally suited for
Ariel, Caliban and Prospero.

In both *The Tempest* and Strachey's account there are
several analogous passages. For example, Strachey says : "Sir
George Somers had an apparition of a little round light like a
faint star trembling and streaming along with a sparkling
blaze, half the height upon the maine mast and shooting sometimes from shroud to shroud, tempting to settle upon one of
the four shrouds, and for three or four hours together or rather
more, half the night, it kept with us running sometimes along
the maineyards to the very end and then returning. . . ."

In *The Tempest* Prospero says to Ariel : "Hast thou, spirit,
performed to point the tempest that I bade thee?"

Ariel, who had been posing as St. Elmo, replies :

> *To every article.*
> *I boarded the King's ship; now on the beak,*
> *Now in the waist, the deck, in every cabin,*
> *I flamed amazement; sometimes I'd divide*
> *And burn in many places; on the topmast,*
> *The yards, the bowsprit, would I flame distinctly,*
> *Then meet and join. . . .*

There are other similarities in Shakespeare's and Strachey's
texts : a butt of sack "cast overboard"; "a plague upon this
howling;" "the sea mounting to the welkin's cheek". The
evidence is incontrovertible and I maintain that there is little
to be said for those of the anti-Shakespeare/Bermuda lobby
who quote the following passage as proof that *The Tempest*
wreck was nowhere near Bermuda. Ariel, in reply to a question
by Prospero about the ship, says :

> *Safely in harbour*
> *Is the King's ship; in the deep nook where once*
> *Thou call'dst me up at midnight to fetch dew*
> *From the still-vexed Bermoothes. . . .*

Shakespeare's *Tempest* was supposed to take place somewhere
between Tunis and Naples, both of which cities are in the

Mediterranean, not the Atlantic. To the purist it must seem wrong, therefore, that the following enchanting lines should be found in the play :

> *Full fathom five thy father lies;*
> *Of his bones are coral made. . . .*

There is no coral in the Mediterranean; and in any case Ariel's cousin, Puck, in *A Midsummer Night's Dream* "put a girdle round about the earth in forty minutes." Shakespeare could distort geography even quicker. The point is that both the site and the plot of *The Tempest* are imaginary; but the evidence is that Bermuda contributed greatly to the image.

The visitor to Bermuda, therefore, after playing a round of golf on one of the finest courses in the world, or having visited one of several houses built about 1700—the one called Inwood, for example, in the parish of Paget East—can well afford to lie back under the sun on the beach and think he hears Ariel say :

> *Come unto these yellow sands,*
> *And then take hands;*
> *Curtsied when you have, and kiss'd*
> *The wild waves whist. . . .*

After all, there was less than a hundred years interlude between Shakespeare's writing these lines and the still-preserved deeds of the sale of Inwood to one Francis Jones "in the Twelfth year of the raigne of our Soveraigne Lord William the third. . . ." This is the sort of atmosphere which Bermuda has; and you can lunch in Manhattan next day.

HISTORY

Bermuda's claim to historical distinction is twofold : first, unlike almost all the other Western Atlantic and Caribbean islands which have now become tourist playgrounds, it was *not* discovered by Christopher Columbus; and, secondly, as I have tried to demonstrate, it is almost certain that this "Isle of Devils", as the famous navigator, Sebastian Cabot, called it in his map published in 1544, largely inspired a work of one of the world's greatest poets and playwrights.

It was first referred to in writing, so far as is known, by a Spaniard called Oviedo, who was a passenger in a ship called *La Garza* (The Heron), commanded by one Juan de Bermudez, which in 1515 sailed close to the islands with the intention of landing and putting some hogs ashore which would multiply and provide food for subsequent visits. They were prevented by a gale from landing, but they did, according to Oviedo's account, anchor for some hours off this group of islands, whose name, Bermuda, is referred to with familiarity, thereby suggesting that Bermudez had been there before. For more than a century after this visit Bermuda was regarded as a place to be avoided by mariners and neither the Spanish nor the Portuguese made any attempt to settle there.

In 1603 another Spaniard, Luis Ramirez de Cordova, whose ship went aground there in 1603, reported graphically on the thousands of seabirds which shrieked around him and his men when they went ashore : "These are the devils reported to be about Bermuda. The sign of the Cross at them ! We are Christians !" But, before Ramirez's enforced visit, an Englishman, one Henry May, had had to brave the Bermuda "devils" for several months in 1594. He was making a passage from Santo Domingo to England in a French warship whose pilot and crew, thinking they had passed the perilous Bermudas, indulged in a drinking bout. Nobody was keeping a proper watch, and shortly after midnight on 17 December 1593, the ship struck the rocks off Bermuda's northwest coast. May and some two dozen of the crew managed to get ashore where they lived, largely off fish and birds, until the following May when they sailed for Cape Breton in a boat which they had managed to build of local cedar. The report which May wrote about his adventures when he got back to England did little to improve Bermuda's reputation.

In 1609 a squadron of nine British ships was sailing from England to the new Virginia colony in North America, and on 24 July one of them, the *Sea Venture*, got separated from the others in a storm and sprung a leak. She was the flagship of the squadron commanded by Admiral Sir George Somers, and among the passengers was Sir Thomas Gates, the newly appointed Deputy-Governor of Virginia, and William Strachey, who was going to take up an appointment as Governor's secretary. Another was Sylvanus Jourdain. Both men wrote accounts of the four-day storm, and a third account, published in Virginia, described it as "three daies perpetual horror." Strachey said: ". . . the storme was fury added to fury . . . the sea swelled above the clouds and gave battell unto Heaven. . . ." Admiral Somers reported that on 28 July "wee sawe the land of Bermuda wheare our ship lieth upon the rocke a quarter of a mile from the shoare. . . ." He said that all lives were saved and "much of our goods" by landing in the ship's boats after the storm had abated. The Admiral took possession of the island in the name of the King.

The party remained nine months on Bermuda living off hogs (which by then had become plentiful), fish, turtles and birds. Using some of the wood of the *Sea Venture* and some local cedar, the party managed to build two small ships, and in May, 1610, they sailed for Virginia; but they left two men behind, Christopher Carter and Robert Waters, who elected to stay rather than face a trial in Jamestown under Sir Thomas Gates for some unspecified crimes which they had committed. On his arrival in Virginia Admiral Somers found the colonists there very short of food and so he sailed again in May for Bermuda, ostensibly to get supplies (presumably hogs), but in reality, one or two historians have suggested, to see how Carter and Waters were getting on. He found them in fine fettle and delighted with what the island had to offer in the way of fertile soil and "development potentials," to use a modern phrase. He decided, therefore, to return to England to raise money for establishing a plantation and a proper settlement. He died, however, in November before he could get away and was buried in what is now Somers Garden in the parish of St. George.

Carter and Waters decided once again to remain behind when the dead Admiral's ship, now commanded by Captain Mathew Somers, Sir George's nephew, sailed for England; and a third man, Edward Chard, decided to remain also. For two years these three men lived and worked together, tilling the soil and building themselves better places to live in; they quarrelled of course, particularly over a valuable find of ambergris; they got on each others nerves and came to blows; but just as they had decided to build a boat and sail to the American mainland a ship called *The Plough* arrived from England carrying a group of settlers under a man named Richard Moore who held a commission as Governor from "The Company of Adventurers and Planters of the City of London for the Colony of Virginia" whose Charter had been extended to include Bermuda in 1612.

Though Carter and Waters, and later Chard, might be considered to be Bermuda's first settlers, it is really from the arrival of Moore and his group that the islands' colonisation should be dated. Moore was an able and energetic man; he founded the first permanent township at St. George; he built fortifications and a church; he planted tobacco; he set up a firm administration; but he became disillusioned by, among other things, frequent letters of complaint from London, and he returned to England in 1615. For about a year Bermuda was left in the hands of half a dozen men, including Carter, Waters and Chard, who alternated in the governership; but it was a period of idleness and drunkenness.

In 1615 the Virginia Adventurers Company sold the islands of Bermuda for £2,000 to "the Governor and Company of the City of London for the Plantation of the Somers Islands," and the new charter included authority to form a General Assembly with powers to pass laws. In May 1616, Captain Daniel Tucker, a man who had spent some years as a planter in Virginia, took over the post of Governor. He was a man of dictatorial character and he harshly drove the settlers to work clearing ground and planting and felling timber. He frequently used the whip and the cudgel on recalcitrants and exercised his power of hanging. But he did make money for the Company. Finally, however, so many letters of complaint reached London that the Company recalled Tucker and appointed a new Governor, Captain Nathanial Butter, who arrived in Bermuda in 1619 bringing more colonists with him. The following year the first meeting of the General Assembly was held and it is from this fact that Bermuda claims to be the first self-governing British Colony, though in practice the Company retained the power of altering or rejecting any law which the Assembly might pass. Nevertheless, Butter's administration was on the whole just and beneficial to the colony, but he retired to England after three years feeling that he had been badly treated by the money-grabbing Company.

From the 1620's the Company became an even harsher taskmaster; it was becoming evident that both ambergris and tobacco were not anything like as profitable as had been anticipated; and various restrictions were placed upon Bermudians to make them work harder and solely in the Company's interests. Successive Governors became more and more tyrannical, and discontent was rife. The Bermudians at this time were beginning the process of welding themselves into a distinct and determined group opposed to arbitrary domination from London. When King Charles I was beheaded and England became a Comonwealth under Oliver Cromwell they proclaimed Charles II King and refused to accept the authority of the English Parliament. There is an interesting early parallel here with Rhodesia's unilateral declaration of independence in 1965 under which Queen Elizabeth II was acknowledged Sovereign but the authority of Prime Minister Wilson's Government rejected. In 1652, however, Bermuda was forced—along with Barbados, which had made a similar U.D.I. declaration—to acknowledge the Cromwell Government. Conditions, however, went from bad to worse in Bermuda, and there was much suffering. In the 1670's the Company became completely disillusioned with Bermuda and began selling out its land to the tenants. In 1684 the Company's charter was annulled, and government of the colony passed to the Crown. In 1687 the first General Assembly met under the new dispensation which provided for four men to be elected from each of the nine parishes; and it is really from this date—there had been no Assembly meetings in the last year of the Company's rule—

that representative government in Bermuda can be said to have started.

The island now entered a period of prosperity under a Governor named Robinson. Its inhabitants were freed from the restrictions imposed by the Company, and with their skill in shipbuilding and sailing they soon became one of the most important trading communities in the western hemisphere. Salt for North America was taken in their ships from the Caribbean; they would sail with rum and sugar from the West Indies to England; they would bring back either money or goods; their crews became well known in ports as far north as Nova Scotia. Unfortunately, little agricultural work was done and Bermuda relied almost entirely for food on the North American colonies, so that with the advent of the American Revolutionary War and the resulting ban on trade, the island once again entered a period of something like famine. However, despite the efforts of an unpopular Governor, George Bruere, it was not long before trade was resumed with America. Many Bermudians were sympathetic to the revolutionary cause and a plot was hatched to rifle the magazine at St. George and ship its contents to the armies of General Washington which were known to be suffering from a severe shortage of gunpowder. Several prominent Bermudians were involved in the plot, the upshot of which was that the United States Congress arranged for an immediate shipment of food to be sent to Bermuda, and the regular two-way interchange trade of food and salt was soon resumed; the Governor, fulminating impotently against this illegal trade, could do nothing to stop it.

One result of this highly successful incursion into the realms of contraband trade was that the Bermudians turned in the 1780's to privateering, an activity in which they proved to be highly successful. This was the beginning of a long period of war, mainly between Britain and France, and Bermuda grew rich with the prizes and prize-money brought in by the able and adventurous captains who sailed under "letters-of-marque" which theoretically entitled them to capture any ship belonging to, or even trading with, a nation with which their country was at war. This was an arrangement which could be made to cover a multitude of sins, and Bermuda had the ships (more than 200 in 1793) and the men to take full advantage of it. Money began to pour in and acted as a catalyst for the expansion of trade and business in general. Many of the large, elegant houses which are a feature of today's Bermuda scene were built during this period. An aggressive captain would return to harbour with twenty or more ships taken as his prizes. It was a time for making quick fortunes, perhaps even more than was the case further south in the Bahamas and the Caribbean.

Prosperity lasted till the early 1820's, athough in later years it was based not so much on privateering as on shipping goods between North America and the Caribbean where British ports were closed to U.S. ships till 1822.

Slavery was abolished in 1834 and this did nothing to help the island's poor agricultural production because the Negroes, pretty well the sole tillers of the soil, refused to work even for money. Some help to the economy had been given by the British Government's decision to build a large naval base on Ireland Island at the entrance to Great Sound, which led, incidentally to the transference of the capital in 1815 from St. George to Hamilton because of the better harbour facilities. But it was not until 1861, with the outbreak of the American Civil War, that Bermuda had another burst of prosperity. Once again her ships were active, this time in running the blockade with transhipped cargoes from England to the southern states and returning with cotton for Liverpool. This boom lasted for four years; then the island sank once more into a state of lethargy which lasted until the advent towards the end of the nineteenth century of a new source of income.

Tourism, as it is known today, did not begin to come to Bermuda until the twentieth century was well established. This statement is made in the same context as would apply to, say, Monte Carlo, meaning that in the turn-of-the-century years it was the visitor, more often than not rich and seeking exclusiveness, who went there. The "masses" had not yet begun to penetrate so far afield; the modern giant hotels had not been built. Mark Twain, a devotee of Bermuda, described it as "tranquil and contenting." Woodrow Wilson, before he became President of the U.S., said it was "one of the last refuges" in the world where one could escape from the extravagant and sporting set. Rudyard Kipling was fond of Bermuda, and later authors such as Eugene O'Neill and James Thurber used to go there to write and read. A furore was created when it was first suggested in the early years of the twentieth century that Bermuda needed a railway. (The first train did not run till 1931.) Nevertheless, the ships carrying visitors were beginning to enter Hamilton's harbour in increasing numbers; the yachts of American millionaires could be seen lying at anchor; the palatial type of hotel was being constructed.

Then, in 1941, an event occurred which put Bermuda very much on the twentieth-century map—the Churchill-Roosevelt destroyers-for-bases deal. The result of this was that some 7,000 Americans came to live on the island of St. David's (Kindley Air Force Base) and at the King's Point Naval Base. During the war Bermuda played a vital part in the Anglo-American western hemisphere defence system. (It still does, for that matter, though from the defence point of view it is now largely an American "sphere of influence," the British garrison having been withdrawn in 1957 and the Royal Navy using it only for visits of the one or two frigates stationed in the area.) At the end of the war, partly, no doubt, as a result of the U.S. servicemen stationed there going home and telling of the island's attractions, Bermuda entered the properly so-called tourist era and by 1967 some 200,000 visitors were going there each year, mostly from North America, and spending something like $30 million annually. Bermuda is now very much in the "big league" tourist business and there is an interesting analogy here with the historical experiences of the Bahama islands which went through similar periods of wealth and poverty to emerge into the post-war boom era of tourism.

Motorcars—they have to be small and are not allowed to travel at more than 20 miles an hour—were allowed to be imported into Bermuda for the first time in 1947, much to the horror of many Bermudians, and in the same year the railway was scrapped; but it is by no means true to say that the advent of the "horseless carriage" and the construction of large tourist hotels totally changed the Bermuda pattern of life. A great deal of life on the island can still be described as "exclusive", as I have tried to indicate in the first part of this chapter. This exclusiveness is indicated by the fact that in a pamphlet put out by the British Colonial Office in 1965, only four points of constitutional change are mentioned between the years 1684, when the charter of the "Somers Islands Company" was annulled, and the year 1964. These are that in 1888 a Legislative Council was introduced; in 1944 the franchise was extended to women with the necessary property qualifications; in 1963 the formation took place of the first political party, the Progressive Labour Party; and in 1964 the United Bermuda Party was formed. This is a period of 280 years during which constitutional changes hardly occurred at all. Here again there is a parallel with the Bahamas.

ECONOMY

In the early days Bermuda earned its living like so many Caribbean islands—of which group it has always insisted it is not a part—by growing tobacco and sugar; there was also a considerable ship-building industry, and there was a bonanza period of privateering. Since the beginning of the twentieth century however, and even more so since the beginning of the second half of the century, the islands' economy has been almost entirely dependent upon tourism. This now brings in well over $30 million each year, having grown from about 71,000 visitors in 1950 to more than 200,000 in 1967. More than 90% come from the United States and Canada and about 4% from Britain. The result has been "overemployment" in the sense that there are more jobs open to Bermudians than there are Bermudians seeking jobs. A higher standard of living than exists in most Caribbean countries has also been created; as early as 1960, for example, 96% of the population owned refrigerators and 94% had either a gas or electric cooker.

Another source of income is the fact that Bermuda is a tax haven which attracts many international companies for registration purposes, and there is a flourishing banking trade. There is a free-port on Ireland Island which has attracted more than thirty companies. On the face of it Bermuda's exports and re-exports do not amount in terms of money to even as much as two-thirds of its imports (about $64 million annually) but in fact, due to the "invisibles" provided by tourism, the activities of international companies, and by the U.S. bases, Bermuda's overall balance of payments is very favourable and puts her in the position of being among the largest earners of dollars in the sterling area.

Bermuda buys almost 50% of her imports from the United States and about 20% from Britain, the main items being food, timber, footwear, textiles, machinery, hardware, chemicals and electrical supplies. The main "visible" export earnings come from drugs and essences, but bunkering facilities (re-exports) are easily the main source of the islands' revenue in this field.

With the rapid growth of the tourist industry and the construction of hotels and houses, land available for agriculture in Bermuda is now minimal—probably a little less than 1,000 acres. Vegetables, fruit and flowers are grown on about 500 acres and the rest are either used for pasture or left fallow. About two million pounds of fish and crustaceans are caught annually, with a value of around $640,000.

The government has a policy of tax concessions to promote the growth of small manufacturing industries and among the most important now in existence are ship repairing, small boat building, cedar woodwork, and the manufacture of souvenirs, perfumes, pharmaceuticals and mineral water extracts. A Central Planning Authority has been in existence since 1965 for the hotel and guest house business, and its purpose is to aid growth in this field, but a non-Bermudian who wants to buy land in the islands has normally to go through a searching period of character (and finance) investigation. The Bermud-

1.   Bermuda's Easter Lilies in full bloom

2. Secret coves and small quiet beaches are among the main attractions of Bermuda

ians are determined that their islands shall not lose the unique attractions for the tourists which they now possess.

Currency is the Bermuda pound sterling, though the U.S. dollar is accepted everywhere.

SIGHTSEEING

Hamilton, Bermuda's capital, is an attractive enough small town, but once you have strolled up and down the waterfront area there is little of interest to see. Front Street (a dull name if ever there was one) has a row of pleasant early nineteenth-century buildings directly overlooking the harbour where the big tourist liners berth only a few yards away. It is Bermuda's main shopping street and throughout the year it is a hub of gay, sunlit activity. The busiest point of Front Street is at its junction with Queen Street, known as Heyl's Corner, where a policeman stands, pith-helmeted in a "birdcage", directing the traffic. The Visitor's Service (information) Bureau is here and it is worthwhile looking in to get maps and brochures which are helpful in sightseeing. Between it and the sea is a pretty little public park called Albouy's Point, adjacent to the Royal Bermuda Yacht Club, from which you get a good view of the harbour, with its dozen or more small islands, ferry-boats bustling hither and yon, dinghies with white sails, and speedboats churning up the clear water. Walk up Queen Street —the streets leading off the waterfront slope steeply upwards —and on your left you see two buildings which are probably Hamilton's greatest claim to architectural distinction. They were both built in the first decade of the nineteenth century by the Perot family. The first is the Perot Post Office, which has been well restored and is now open for postal business. Postmaster William Perot made philatelic history in 1848 when he issued "stamps" signed by himself. Next door is the building which now houses the Public Library and Historical Museum. This was built in 1807 by the father of the famous Postmaster William and is a charming period house with a fine cedar staircase and many interesting prints and historic Bermudiana, including a replica of Sir George Somers' ship,

C

the *Sea Venture*. Behind these two buildings are the Par-la-
Ville Gardens which are attractively laid out with colourful
trees (some rare, it is said), shrubs and flowers.

At the top of Queen Street is the impressively modern, supposedly Swedish-style, Town Hall, which contains an art gallery and a theatre. Turning right along Church Street, you
come to the Anglican Cathedral which was completed in 1894
in—as the date suggests—somewhat ponderous Victorian gothic
style. After this you should turn right down Parliament Street
past the House of Assembly and Supreme Court (very late Victorian) and the Post Office (about 1869), and arrive once more
on Front Street where, on your left, you see the Colonial
Secretariat, the main part of which is a well-designed building with a columned portico dating from about 1830. Now
turn right and stroll back westward along Front Street, pausing a few yards up Burnaby Street for refreshment at the Hog
Penny Inn. This is a tropical version of the English pub and
is named after the coinage with which the early seventeenth-
century Governor, Daniel Tucker (his descendants are one of
the most important families in Bermuda), paid his labourers.
A hog was stamped on one side of the brass coins in memory,
presumably, of the wild hogs which had been put on the island
by early Spanish or Portuguese mariners to proliferate. Tucker's
labourers treated the coins with scant respect; hence the name.
And so back to Heyl's Corner. The brochures of the Visitor's
Service Bureau list other points of interest to visit in Hamilton,
but the circular walk described above gives a good impression
of the most important part of the city.

There are any number of organised tours round Bermuda
lasting a day or half a day, about which the hotel people will
be only too delighted to tell you. But there are two points to
bear in mind, assuming the place of departure to be Hamilton
—which is by no means necessarily the case, as there are many
hotels in other parts. The first is that the old capital, St.
George, must be visited; and the second is that you must go
to the westernmost part of the island. Most of the rest of Bermuda can be taken in on these two trips. To get to St. George
and back in a day, the best thing to do is to set off northward

through Hamilton to the North Shore Road, which you join near the Ducking Stool where the eighteenth-century Bermudians used to express communal displeasure of minor miscreants by immersing them in the same warm sea-water for the pleasure of swimming in which North Americans, and others, today pay large sums of money. Nearby is Government House, big, impressive, on the top of a hill. You drive for about three miles along the North Shore Road and note that, though this is perhaps Bermuda's least attractive coast from the bathing point of view, advantage has been taken of every tiny bay or inlet to build an attractive house. (There is not much land left anywhere in Bermuda of reasonable house-building quality which is available to the newcomer.) You then arrive at the delightful village of Flatts built on the edges of an inlet where small boats and yachts of every description are moored. Eighteenth-century buildings indicate that Flatts was an important small harbour in the days of sail; today, with its cleanly painted houses and small bridge over the narrow point where the inlet enters Harrington Sound, it is one of Bermuda's biggest small beauty spots.

Near the bridge is the Aquarium and Museum, plus a small zoo; and it is essential that a stop should be made there. All sorts of colourful—and some not so colourful—tropical fish are to be seen swimming, apparently happily, in tanks. There is a fine display of sea shells and coral. In the museum next door there is a fascinating and, I imagine, extremely valuable collection of treasure trove recovered in the post-war years from a Spanish ship which was wrecked probably in the last decade of the sixteenth century. Among the items on display— obviously part of a cargo being shipped from the Americas to Spain—is an unusually fine gold cross set with emeralds which dates from the late sixteenth century. This collection is a "must" for any visitor to Bermuda; and it was recovered by a man with a famous Bermudian name, Mr. Teddy Tucker.

Continue along North Shore Road to Bailey's Bay where you can pause for a swim on an excellent beach. Turn south past the Perfume Factory and make a stop at one of the caves —Crystal Cave and Leamington Cave are the best known, though Prospero's Cave has the best name—which contain impressive crystal stalactite and stalagmite formations gleaming under electric light. You now cross the causeway to St. George's Parish, past the air terminal and the northern end of the U.S. Kindley Air Force Base and across the Swing Bridge to Mullet Bay—full of fishing boats and yachts—and so to the ancient town of St. George.

The inhabitants of Jamestown, Virginia, claim that their's is the most ancient Anglo-Saxon settlement in the western hemisphere, dating from 1607; Bermudians, on the other hand, point to the fact that, whereas the early Virginians had to give up their settlement for a period, St. George has been inhabited without a break since 1612. Fortunately its period buildings are in an excellent state of preservation; it is today, in fact, a town which is very much alive and has nothing of the flavour of a museum piece. The best thing to do is to get out of the car in King's Square and walk around. On the eastern side of the square is the Town Hall which is not, unfortunately, the original building constructed on this site in 1782, but it is a very ably reconstructed replica. Just off the northeastern corner of the square is the Old State House, which, dating from 1619, is the oldest building in Bermuda and among the oldest in the hemisphere. For 200 years it was the site of Assembly meetings and of the Assize Courts; it is now a masonic lodge and not open to the public. On the north side of the square is a model of a stocks and pillory, and on the square's southwest corner is the old White Horse Tavern. The square is not a large one, as squares go, but it is certainly one of the most architecturally satisfying and historically interesting in the western hemisphere.

On Duke of York Street, just north of King's Square, is St. Peter's Church, a spreading, whitewashed edifice at the top of a broad flight of brick steps, which claims, probably with justification, to be the oldest site of Anglican worship in the hemisphere. The present building dates largely from 1713, but it is on the site of the one erected by Governor Moore in 1612. This early building was replaced by another two or three years later and some of the material of this second church was used in the 1713 structure. The tower was added in 1814. The original altar, constructed to Moore's specifications, dates from 1624. The Communion plate was presented to the church by King William III and is dated 1684; and there is a silver chalice dating from about 1625. Even older is the font which dates from as far back as the fourteenth century (brought out by the first settlers) and which must surely be one of the earliest pieces of European church furniture to be seen anywhere in the western hemisphere. The churchyard has some interesting inscriptions. One of them reads :

> Here lieth the Body of
> Mrs Mary Bell, Wife of Dr. Richard Bell
> Who departed this life the
> 13th of March, 1783,
> Aged 17 years.

There is also an inscription to their two daughters who died in April, 1783, one aged two years, the other three weeks. Obviously longevity was not a feature of Bermudian life in those days.

Opposite St. Peter's is the house which Governor Samuel Day built for his private residence in 1700. It is now known as the Confederate Museum (arms, prints, coins, etc.), as it was the headquarters during the American Civil War of Confederate blockade runners. Turn left off Duke of York Street up Duke of Clarence Street and you see on the right a charming early eighteenth-century house, now maintained as the St. George Historical Museum, which contains a good collection of old furniture, china, prints, clothes and early Bermudian household equipment. The old Rectory (you are still close to St. Peter's) is reached by turning left off Duke of Clarence Street into Church Street and then right up the alley opposite the churchyard gate. This is one of the best examples of an early eighteenth-century house to be seen anywhere in Bermuda, and it could be put to no better use than it has been : it is the town's Public Library. Across Queen Street from the old Rectory is Stockdale House where the colony's first newspaper was printed as long ago as 1784. Walking back down Queen Street and across Duke of York Street you should turn right on Water Street and visit Tucker House which was the home of various members of the Tucker family from 1770 till 1950 when it was acquired by the Historical Monuments Trust of Bermuda; it has a good collection of furniture, portraits, china and silver. Also on Water Street is the Carriage Museum which houses a private collection of pre-motorcar Bermudian transport vehicles.

Stroll back along Water Street to King's Square and across it, past the State House, to Somers Garden where you can sit for a while beneath the palms and contemplate the fact—or, perhaps, well-based belief—that this garden is the burial place of the heart of Sir George Somers, Bermuda's "founder", who died in 1610. You may have heard of a minor, but gifted and dashing, Irish poet called Tom Moore, who spent about four months in St. George in 1804, probably in Old Maid's Lane, and fell in love with 17-year-old Nea Tucker, wife of William Tucker. Moore wrote some delightful verses about the beauties of both Bermuda and Nea :

> Oh ! could you view the scenery, dear,
> That now beneath my window lies,
> You'd think that nature lavish'd here
> Her purest wave, her softest skies,
> To make a heaven for love to sigh in,
> For bards to live and saints to die in !

And :

> Nay, tempt me not to love again,
> There was a time when love was sweet;
> Dear Nea ! Had I known thee then,
> Our souls had not been slow to meet !

Shakespeare's *The Tempest* and Moore's *Odes to Nea* make ideal reading while sitting in Somers Garden.

It is now a good idea to get back into the car and drive round the outskirts of the town and the headlands of St. George's promontory. You come first to Gates Fort, named after Sir Thomas Gates who was in the famous shipwreck with Sir George Somers, and go on past Buildings Bay where the two ships were built in 1610 which took the survivors on to Virginia. On St. George's northeast point is Fort St. Catherine which is now a museum with dioramas displaying the important episodes of Bermuda's history. From there you turn left along the north coast past Loot Pond and Tobacco Bay where the stolen gunpowder was embarked on its way to General Washington's armies. You re-enter St. George by driving along Artillery Road, pausing on the way at Gunpowder Cavern (now a restaurant) from whose magazines the powder was removed. And so out of St. George's Parish across the Causeway.

To return to Hamilton via the south coast you turn left into Harrington Sound Road and proceed on to Tucker's Town, which is actually a Parish. It got the name "town" because Governor Daniel Tucker had visions of it becoming an important settlement based on whaling and pearl fishing in the early seventeenth century. Nothing much seems to have happened in the area until about 300 years later when it became the exclusive habitat of the rich who were attracted by its lovely unspoilt scenery and by the opening of the Mid-Ocean Club and golf course. Some of the finest modern houses in Bermuda—some of them big, some of them small, but nearly all in good taste—have been built round this golf course and on the southern shores of Castle Harbour. There is nothing to stop you walking over the golf course and enjoying the scenery. One cannot help feeling that Daniel Tucker would have been pleased with this very posthumous development; but it is unfortunate that hardly any evidence remains of buildings put up in his day.

In Tucker's Town you join the South Road and turn right past Trott's Pond and Mangrove Lake to John Smith's Bay, which is an excellent spot for a swim. Nearby is Devil's Hole, a limestone hollow connected with Harrington Sound by an underground channel. There are turtles in it and all sorts of fish which seem to rise happily to the visitor's bait. You continue along the South Road to North's Point and Spittal Pond where there is a bird sanctuary run by the Bermuda Audubon Society. The waters under North Point's shelving cliffs are virtual fish sanctuaries. You have to get out of the car and walk, but it is worth it because the views are magnificent and

you can see the inscription on Spanish Rock which suggests
that a Portuguese called Ferdinando Carmelo, who had asked
the Spanish King's permission to colonise the Bermuda islands
as early as 1527, might have landed there more than half a
century before Somers and his men were shipwrecked. Equally
the inscription could have been made by any shipwrecked
sailors of the period whose name (presumably) began with the
letter F.

You continue westward for about a mile and three quarters
and should then turn right up Collector's Hill to Verdmont, a
late seventeenth-century house which is now under the care of
the Historical Society and contains some good period furniture
and *objets d'art*. There are, of course, in Bermuda several
privately owned period houses which have been just as well
restored as Verdmont and which contain first class contemporary furniture, pictures and china; but the custom does not
seem to have grown up there, as it has in England, of the
owners opening them to the public on two or three days a
week. The reason doubtless is that the rich owners of these
houses in Bermuda are not in need of the half-crown entrance
fee which contributes needfully to the upkeep of many of
England's ancestral "stately homes". So Verdmont has to fill
the gap; and it does so very satisfactorily.

You now rejoin the South Road and turn right at Point
Finger Road to re-enter Hamilton, pausing on the way, if
there is time, at the Botanical Gardens which are beautifully
maintained and contain hundreds of flowering trees, shrubs
and flowers, which are the result of some 300 years of collection. In fact there probably will not be time because, although
not long in geographical distance, this drive has included many
things which should be seen. There are those, indeed, who say
that you should spend a whole day in St. George; and they
may well be right. In fact, to do justice to Bermuda's eastern
section, several days are needed.

The western section of Bermuda is just as attractive and interesting as the eastern, and the best way to see it is probably
to begin by taking a trip across Great Sound on one of the
frequent diesel ferry services, having previously arranged for a

taxi to meet you at Watford Bridge. The first stop, Somerset Bridge, is reached (unfortunately) in less than half an hour. The boat threads its way through the two dozen or so islands in the sound (some curious Greek names : Alpha, Gamma and Lambda) and leaves the promontory on which the U.S. Naval Base is situated on its port side. People who live in Somerset commute daily across this Sound to their offices in Hamilton, and it is hard to imagine any pleasanter way of going to and from work, except, possibly, by the ferry boats which ply over the waters of Sydney Harbour in Australia. Somerset Bridge, which is the first stop (it actually links the island of Somerset to the rest of Sandys Parish) claims to be the smallest draw-bridge in the world; to me it looked like a minuscule copy of the canal drawbridges which you see in some French post-impressionist paintings. The ferry continues along Somerset's southeast coast on which you can see a number of attractive cottage colonies in the neighbourhood of the ruined fort on Scaur Hill. There is a stop at Cavello Bay, and you continue to Watford Bridge, where you disembark. This connects Somerset with Watford Island, Boaz Island and Ireland Island.

Those visitors more interested in scenery than history will be justified in getting into their taxi and telling the driver to take the route southwest through Somerset back to Hamilton; but the historically minded will ask him to drive eastward on Watford Island past the burial ground of convicts who were deported from Britain as late as the middle of the nineteenth century to build the naval dockyard on Ireland Island. Almost a quarter of the 9,000 men sent died of yellow fever and other tropical diseases while living in wooden hulks or in the bar-racks on Boaz Island. To visit the dockyard area of Ireland Island you should have a pass from the Crown Lands Cor-poration. It is a place full of naval nostalgia on a slightly more contemporary key than that of English Harbour in Antigua, the buildings being of a later, mostly early Victorian date; and some of its facilities are still used by frigates of the West Indies Squadron. Of particular interest from the naval historical point of view is the connection of the Ireland Island base with the famous engagement between H.M.S. *Shannon*

and U.S.S. *Chesapeake*, in 1813, off Boston. The ship's bell of
the *Shannon* used to hang (maybe still does) in the main twin-
towered dockyard building; but in general, despite the setting
up of a free-port area there, the Ireland Island Naval Base has
an aroma of past glory. Perhaps a group of benefactors equivalent to the Friends of English Harbour, which did wonders in
restoring Nelson's Dockyard in Antigua, will one day be
formed.

You have to retrace your steps now to Watford Bridge
where you can pause for a drink at the White Hart Bar; then
on to the main Somerset village community built on the shores
of Mangrove Bay and Long Bay. It contains many charming
period buildings centred round its single main street and on
the lanes which lead off it. A good example of an old Somerset
home is Belfield, now a restaurant, which has a beautifully laid
out garden. Indeed a feature of Somerset is the presumably
fertile soil which enables a great variety of plants and flowering shrubs to be grown in profusion. In the grounds of many
of the old homes—and the newer ones too—the traditional
style of English gardening, a mixture of the formal and the
informal, has been followed with great skill; and it is a matter
of debate whether the houses in Somerset, some with their
own little beaches on Mangrove Bay and Long Bay, have the
edge in attractiveness over those in Tucker's Town. My own
view is that, on the whole, they do.

It is a good idea to continue southward along West Side
Road and rejoin Somerset Road near St. James's Church on
Church Hill. You cross Somerset Bridge—in a matter of
seconds—and it is worth turning right shortly afterwards along
Wreck Road to get a view of yacht-filled Ely's Harbour, which
one of the guide books aptly describes as "one of the bonniest
bits of Bermuda". The road leads up to a ruined fort on Wreck
Hill, which got its name from the wreckage of a Dutch ship
there in 1618. Returning to the main road, you drive south
through Southampton Parish along Middle Road for a couple
of miles and then turn right on to the South Road to Church
Bay. This is the first of the famous bays of the south coast, and
for the next four or more miles you drive along a ridge from

which you look down to the right on a series of long and mostly unspoilt coral sand beaches. The one at Warwick Long Bay has a length of almost a mile. Most of these beaches and the land above them are government property, though here and there hotels and cottage colonies have been built; the most startling of them is the new Carlton Beach, which is plush American—not particularly attractive American—personified, and which you will see about three quarters of a mile beyond Church Bay.

At this point it is perhaps worthwhile making a short detour to the left to Gibb's Hill Lighthouse from whose 105 ft.-high gallery you get a superb view of almost all Bermuda. The lighthouse was built (of steel) on top of the 245 ft.-high Gibbs's Hill between 1844 and 1845, and it must therefore be among the oldest in the world still in use. You return to the South Road and continue along this remarkable four-mile stretch of coast, pausing, probably, at a suitable vantage point to survey the scenic and recreational expanse. Just beyond Coral Beach you turn left off the coast to return to Hamilton via Foot of the Lane, skirting the inner reaches of the harbour.

You have not yet seen the south shore of Hamilton Harbour nor the western section of Pembroke Parish in which Hamilton is situated. A good way to see the south shore is to drive to Waterlot Inn, near Gibb's Hill Lighthouse, for lunch. This is a charming old hostelry which offers excellent food and a delightful garden to sit in after lunch. On the way to the inn you will have passed, along Harbour Road, many little bays and inlets bordered by beautifully kept houses of early nineteenth- or late eighteenth-century vintage. Some of the larger ones, Inverurie for example, have been converted into hotels or guest houses—some also into "smart" shops—and one cannot help feeling that, after all, this coast may be the pleasantest spot in Bermuda to spend a week or two. Before arriving at Waterlot you pass the foot of Riddell's Bay, with its golf course overlooking a complicated plethora of small islands. On the return journey I suggest you abandon the taxi at the delightfully named Salt Kettle Jetty (salt was panned there in the

seventeenth and eighteenth centuries) and go back to Hamilton
by ferry.

If possible, the short trip should be made to Spanish Point,
the northwestern tip of Pembroke Parish. The drive there, past
the Yacht Club and the reconstructed Princess Hotel (the
original one was built in 1884 and named after Princess Louise,
a daughter of Queen Victoria), takes you mostly through a residential district. Pitts Bay, however is a pleasant little hamlet on
Great Sound, and just beyond is Norwood, one of Bermuda's
finest early eighteenth-century houses built by a member of the
Saltus family, after whom the island offshore was presumably
named. You continue along Pitts Bay Road and up Cox Hill,
from which you get an excellent view of Hamilton Harbour
and Great Sound. Spanish Point, about half a mile further on,
is one of the promontories of a small bay from which you look
northward to Ireland Island and the somnolent Royal Naval
dockyard. It is argued that Spanish Point could have been the
place where the ship of the Spaniard, Fernandez de Cordova,
was driven ashore in 1603, six years before Sir George Somers
made his famous enforced landing, but there is no direct
evidence of this. You return southeast along the North Shore
Road, turning right at the Ducking Stool and so back to
Hamilton.

*   *   *

I have specified the use of the taxis in these sightseeing trips,
but Bermuda is ideally suited for cruising around on motor-
assisted cycles, or "putt-putts", to use the horrible local name.
The "puff-puff", an even worse name, is the ordinary bicycle,
and this, too, because Bermuda is mostly flat, is a good and
cheap way of getting around. Both can be rented. There is also
a good regular bus service.

But, whatever form of transport you use, you should take
note of the fact that Bermudian houses are generally built in a
unique architectural style. With the exception, possibly, of
Barbados and Curaçao, no island in the Western Atlantic or
the Caribbean has such an evidently indigenous style. The
origin of the style is basically seventeenth- and eighteenth-

century England, but features have been added to cope with climatic needs; for instance, the outside lavatory with a steep pyramidal roof and a ball top; the buttery for storing food and keeping it cool; the rain-water tank with domed roof; the roof of the house itself with "tiles" of stone, always painted white, to catch the rain-water and lead it through pipes and gutters to the tank. All these features have been harmoniously blended (the early builders were mostly skilled shipwrights) into a whole which is most attractive. Some of these early small houses have been skilfully modernised; the buttery, for example, has been converted into a summer-house, or the roof of the tank has been made into a patio with a pergola. Bermuda has many attractions for the visitor, but perhaps the houses with their well-kept and beautifully laid out gardens, constitute the main one.

HOTELS, RESTAURANTS AND ENTERTAINMENT

Bermuda has at least six hotels in the A-plus bracket. In Hamilton there is the Princess, situated on the shore of the harbour and only three or four minutes away from the main shopping district. It has recently been completely reconstructed and offers its guests all the amenities of a top quality modern American resort hotel. It has its own private beach and golf club on the island's south coast. Nearby is the Bermudiana, even closer to the town's centre than the Princess. It is near the water's edge and has a swimming pool and terrace set in a semi-tropical garden. It also has its own beach club on the south shore, and a point of distinction is that it has Turkish baths.

On the south coast there is the ultra-modern Carlton Beach Hotel—superb beaches, every room with a private balcony overlooking the sea, gaudy-luxurious decoration, a shopping arcade, a night club; in short, the sort of resort hotel which, unless you want to, you need not leave during your entire stay in Bermuda; ideal, of course, for conventions. The Elbow Beach Surf Club, closer to Hamilton on the south coast than the Carlton, seemed to me to be an extremely gay hotel, full of youthful guests and parked bicycles and mopeds. It also has a first-class beach and caters in other respects for the visitor's every want—shops, nightly floor shows, balconied rooms and cottage accommodation; again, ideal for conventions.

The Castle Harbour Hotel is a towering, not so modern structure perched on a hill overlooking the sound of the same name. It is situated in 180 acres of semi-tropical gardens and has one of the finest 18-hole golf courses in Bermuda—which is giving high praise. You go down to the bathing place in a lift; it is an excellent centre for sailing and water-skiing because the harbour water is always calm. This is a resort hotel of high quality offering all the facilities, including nightly entertainment, for visitors who want to stay put.

The St. George Hotel does not, strictly speaking, qualify for an A-plus rating, but I include it here because it is a very good hotel on the outskirts of the most attractive town, St. George, which was Bermuda's first capital. It has its own private beach club and a nine-hole golf course. It rightly claims to be in the heart of Bermuda's sightseeing area and for this reason, if for no other, it must be given a high rating.

The Mid-Ocean Club also overlooks Castle Harbour and it, too, has a first-class golf course; in fact the two courses seem to run alongside each other. It has a delightful private beach. But this is more a luxurious club than an hotel. I am not sure about the rules for staying there, but I suspect you have to get an introduction from a member. It is the centre of the wealthy British-American-Canadian group and was the site of several "parleys at the summit" between Winston Churchill and American Presidents; pictures on the walls record these events.

There are two dozen or more hotels in Bermuda in the A-minus bracket and among these must be included the many charming cottage colonies which seem to be a speciality of these islands. The first of these colonies was opened at Cambridge Beaches, in Somerset, Bermuda's most westerly island, as long ago as 1921. From there, presumably, the habit spread and now there are more than a dozen such colonies dotting the coast. The number of guests which they accommodate varies from about 20 to more than 90, and the principle is that you live in your own cottage and eat (except breakfast) in a central dining room. There is normally a lounge, a terrace and a bar. Some of the prices charged are as high as you would pay in an A-plus hotel—for example, Cambridge Beaches and the Reefs Beach Club, near the Carlton Beach—but they cannot be given this classification because they do not offer the specified facilities. In fact, many people prefer a cottage colony holiday to one spent in a big hotel. Short of shopping arcades and night clubs, there is pretty well everything you want— tennis courts, swimming pools, beaches, good food and service. The Pink Beach Cottage Colony is a good example of the de luxe —in the best sense—type; it is almost on the Mid-Ocean golf course and is beautifully designed to fit in with its natural surroundings; it has an atmosphere of pleasing sophistication. Ariel Sands, on Devonshire's south coast, is another of the same standard. At the delightful village of Flatts there is the Palmetto Bay Cottage Colony, and there are two excellent smaller ones nearer Hamilton in Warwick Parish, the Sapphire Bay and the Mizzen-Top. The Coral Beach and Tennis Club, on the south coast of Paget Parish, is, strictly speaking, a club —tennis, bowling, croquet—and you have (theoretically any-way) to be introduced by a member, but its cottage accommodation is among the best in Bermuda, and it might even be said to warrant an A-plus rating.

The A-minus class hotels—as distinct from cottage colonies —number more than a dozen, and among the most notable are: Deepdene Manor on Harrington Sound; the Belmont Hotel and Golf Club in Warwick; the Harmony Hall (despite the name), the Inverurie and the Fourways Inn, all close to Hamilton in Paget Parish; the Sherwood Manor, and Waterloo House in Pembroke. There are half a dozen others which warrant a good rating in the A-minus class. In fact, I would say that Bermuda provides outstanding facilities for those who seek good accommodation and recreational facilities without having to pay the top prices.

In the B category, almost all B-plus, there are some 20 guest houses, mostly in Paget and Pembroke Parishes. Why they call them guest houses I do not know; they are almost all good quality small hotels and many of them are converted period houses. Most of them are delightfully furnished (cretonne-covered easy chairs and either reproduction or genuine antique furniture), spotlessly clean, and provide excellent service and food. Some of them even have small swimming pools. Of their kind and for the prices they charge, these B category establishments are probably the best value anywhere in the vacation-land world. There may be some C category establishments in Bermuda, but I have not experienced any.

A feature of the Bermuda holiday scene is that there are many cottages and small private houses which you can rent by the week or month, doing your own housekeeping but with a servant provided. Some, not all, travel agents know about these facilities, but the best thing to do is to write to the Bermuda Trade Development Board, 50 Front Street, Hamilton. It is also possible to get accommodation in private houses in Bermuda, and the Development Board is the place to contact for this also.

Apart from the hotel restaurants, where the food naturally varies according to classification (though in most there is a definite slant towards North American dishes), there are several places both in Hamilton and outside where excellent meals are to be had. I have mentioned the Waterlot Inn, which is among the best; equally good is Tom Moore's Tavern where the speciality is Bermuda lobster. This is a converted house dating from 1653, delightfully situated on an inlet of Castle Harbour, and is a "must" for any discerning visitor to Bermuda. The Gunpowder Cavern, St. George's, has an aura of history about it which goes well with the good food. Belfield-in-Somerset, situated where the name implies, is an old Bermuda house charmingly converted into a lunch and tea establishment. There are plenty of other excellent places where you can stop on a drive round Bermuda, and all the bigger hotels have restaurants where non-residents are only too welcome.

In the town of Hamilton—again not taking hotel restaurants into account—there are more than half a dozen good places to eat and drink in the waterfront (Front Street—East Broadway) area. These include The Ace of Clubs, the Hog Penny, the

3. The fifth hole at Bermuda's Mid-Ocean Club is world-famous

Long Tail Bar, the Penthouse Club, the Twenty-One Club, and the Waterfront. I know from experience that you can have quite a good lunch for not much more than $2.

Night entertainment is well catered for in the big hotels where there seems to be a system of artistes' alternating their performances each day of the week; and some of them are of a pretty high standard. Things like evening barbecues on the beach, with steelbands, are continually going on all over the island. In Hamilton there are two or three night spots, the biggest being The 40 Thieves Club on East Broadway. The Jungle Room on Queen Street is a late spot which specialises in local entertainment. Quite often the Hog Penny has a pianist for evening entertainment. In short, the Pembroke-Paget area—that is, around Hamilton—with its big, medium and small hotels and other spots for dining, wining and dancing, is geared to keep you going every night if you want to; and all within a radius of a couple of miles.

SPORT AND RECREATION

Bermuda claims, with some justification, to be one of the most sports-minded places in the world. It's waters are, of course, ideal for sailing and fishing; in fact the average Bermudian, like his English ancestors, is thoroughly attuned to the sea. One of the greatest annual sailing events in the world is the ocean race from Newport, Rhode Island, to Hamilton for the Bermuda Trophy, which takes place in June. At least twice a week (Thursday is a half-day holiday) local sailing races are held, and it is fascinating to watch the 14 ft. dinghies careering around with a weight of sail which, so one would think, a much larger boat would have difficulty in carrying.

Boats of all sorts, both sail and motor, can be hired, either with skippers and crews or without; and there is no more delightful way of exploring Great Sound than by spending a day, or even more, in a yacht whose size can be made to fit your purse. There is a glass-bottom boat which makes daily trips to the sea gardens; or you can take an all-day sightseeing cruise in one of several large launches, with lunch and

D

cocktails served on board. The hotel people can make the arrangements. There are a half a dozen or more yacht clubs in Bermuda—the most famous is the Royal Bermuda Yacht Club, which was founded in 1844—and members of recognised American and British clubs are normally given honorary membership which enables them to crew in one of the races.

Bermuda's best fishing season extends from May to November. The Fishing Information Bureau, part of the Trade Development Board on Front Street, is a mine of information on this subject and only too eager to help. The long-time head man of this bureau, Mr. Pete Perinchief, has said that Bermuda got its reputation for being one of the world's most outstanding fishing centres through the use of light tackle. "We do not," he said, "appear to attract the type generally known as 'meat fishermen', and this is definitely a step in the right direction if sport fishing is to retain its meaning."

Specially equipped boats are available for deep-sea fishing on the banks off Hamilton and St. George, and the catch is usually tuna, white, blue and black marlin, dolphin, barracuda, wahoo or amberjack. For this it is best to get in touch with the Bermuda Game Fishing Guides Association which controls hiring rates and efficiently takes care of everything. If you prefer reef fishing, there are regular scheduled trips available, or private boats can be hired; mackerel, snapper and bonefish are among the catches to expect. Shore or beach fishing is available for everybody along the public beaches of the south shore, and tackle can be rented quite cheaply.

Bermuda, with its sheltered waters, is, of course, ideal for water-skiing, and there are two schools in Hamilton where beginners can get a good grounding. Aqualung and snorkelling enthusiasts are well catered for, particularly around the Flatts area; and scuba divers should contact the Bermuda Divers Company, which has a fully equipped boat. (There are restrictions on spear-fishing.) Finally, of course, there are Bermuda's superb beaches on which you can just lie in the sun during the intervals of lying on your back—or doing something more strenuous—in the water.

There are six (probably seven by the end of the sixties) golf courses in Bermuda, four of which have eighteen holes of the highest international standard; in addition their scenic attractions are exceptional. For my money, the Mid-Ocean Club course is hard to beat anywhere in the world, and so is the neighbouring Castle Harbour course. Theoretically you are supposed to get an introduction from a member to play on most of the Bermuda courses, though on one or two the payment of a green fee is enough.

The story goes that an American visitor to Bermuda, a Miss Mary Outerbridge, was the first to introduce tennis to the United States, having played in 1874 at a house in Paget Parish called Clermont which then had the only tennis court in the western hemisphere. Be that as it may, there are now plenty of tennis courts in Bermuda in the grounds of private houses, in clubs and in hotels. There is even a tennis stadium near Hamilton. All the big hotels and many smaller ones have their own courts. Tennis is one of Bermuda's most popular sports and there are several high-standard tournaments during the year which make it a worthwhile spectator sport.

In tune with their English traditions, Bermudians are keen on cricket, though to nothing like the extent that the inhabitants of the British Caribbean islands are. Football, both soccer and rugger, is played and there are horse-race meetings at the Shelley Bay track. I have seen a darts board at at least one of the drinking hostelries, and I believe there are still one or two croquet lawns. Short of gambling casinos, Bermuda has pretty well everything in the way of sport to offer.

THINGS TO BUY

Shopping is one of Bermuda's greatest attractions because a great variety of high quality goods, imported from Britain, Europe and the Americas, are on sale at extremely advantageous prices. Quality, let it be repeated, is the key word, and the emphasis is probably on goods imported from Britain. Articles of clothing of all sorts are particularly good buys—cashmere sweaters, tweeds, Irish linen, cottons, wools, ties and socks, gloves, and so on. Prices are sometimes half what you would pay in the United States or Canada. Spode, Worcester, Wedgwood and Copenhagen are some of the names of famous china firms who ship goods to the shops on Front Street. Watches from Switzerland, cameras from Germany, cosmetics from France, all with famous names—these are some of the articles which you can buy at prices which save you between 35 and 45% of home prices. The principal shops of the Front Street area are almost as smart as you find on Fifth Avenue or Bond Street and, in addition, you come across chic smaller places in various other parts of the island. Those interested in antiques should also keep an eye open as there are several places where good things can be picked up.

Liquor of all sorts can be bought at in-bond prices which are far lower than what you pay at home. The system is that you should place your order at least 24 hours before your departure time so that the goods can be delivered to the airport or ship. A bottle of Scotch whisky, for example, costs about half what it does in New York, though it is essential to check on the amount you are allowed to bring home without paying duty.

USEFUL FACTS FOR VISITORS

The Bermuda islands—there are actually about 300 of them, including uninhabited islets—have an area of 20·59 square miles. The ten principal islands are connected by bridges and form a chain about 22 miles long from northeast to southwest. The largest island is 14 miles long with an average width of one mile and its highest point is 259 ft. above sea level. They are the most northerly group of coral islands in the world and are situated 568 miles east of the North Carolina coast.

Bermuda has an irregular coast line, with many little bays and coral sand beaches. As there are four large areas of salt-water enclosed by land and no rivers or fresh-water lakes the inhabitants depend for their fresh-water on rain catchment and on sea-water conversion plants. Up till about the mid-forties Bermuda had a large growth of cedar trees, but these were almost exterminated by an insect plague. There are, however, many colourful flowering shrubs and trees such as oleanders, hibiscus, poinciana and bougainvillea.

The climate is perhaps best described as being warm and gentle, with an annual average temperature of just over 70° F. (21° C.). During the summer months, particularly August and September, the temperature gets as high as 80° F., (26·6° C.), and, despite the Atlantic breezes, it can be a bit humid. In the winter months the temperature is at least ten degrees lower, but at all times of the year Bermuda offers near-perfect conditions for all forms of outdoor living and sport. There is no rainy season and the skies usually clear quickly after a shower. The average annual rainfall is 58·1 inches.

Bermuda has a population of about 48,000, of whom about 30,500 are of African descent and 17,500 of European descent, including descendents of Portuguese agricultural labourers who were brought there in the early 1920's. The population density is one of the highest in the world—just over 2,600 persons per square mile. The language is English, though a certain amount of Portuguese is spoken.

Bermuda is easily accessible by air from North America, Canada or Europe, frequent jet services being operated by Pan American, Eastern Airlines, B.O.A.C. and Air Canada. Qantas calls regularly on its route from Australia and so does Iberia from Spain. These, or other, scheduled carriers connect Bermuda with the Bahamas, the Caribbean and Latin America. By sea there are weekly services from New York and during the season many cruise ships operate over the same route. Several companies operate regular passenger-freight services from Britain, and Hamilton is a regular port of call for cruise ships from both Britain and continental Europe.

Direct enquiries about Bermuda should be made to the Bermuda Trade Development Board, Front Street, Hamilton. The Board also has offices in New York, Toronto and London.

THE ISLANDS OF THE
ELEUTHERIAN ADVENTURERS

The Bahamas

"There will be a change in direction and emphasis on many fronts."—Mr. L. O. Pindling, first Negro Premier of the Bahamas.

The Royal Standard flew at the masthead of the Royal Yacht *Britannia* alongside Nassau's main wharf, and nearby was the White Ensign of the escorting frigate, H.M.S. *Ursa*. A prominent Bahamian citizen pointed to them and said : "For a territory like ours with a scattered population scarcely equal to that of a small city in Britain or America, these two flags are the things that count; the first ensures the continuation of ordered democratic government, and the second means that we don't have to spend vast sums on defence and maintaining embassies abroad."

These words, spoken during the visit to the Bahamas in 1966 of Queen Elizabeth II, are worth quoting because they give a very good picture of the Bahamian atmosphere which has been created by the tourist boom of the late fifties and sixties. This group of 700-odd islands of varying sizes, which has been under British rule since 1647, and which has had a democratically elected House of Assembly since 1792, has prospered for two main reasons : first, the inflow of the American dollar; second, the fact that it is entirely independent of the United States—politically, if not economically.

Less than a decade before the Queen's visit, it did not seem that things were going so smoothly—tourists having to make their own hotel beds due to a strike, the Mace (symbol of British democracy) being thrown out of a House of Assembly window by an irate Opposition leader, and speeches at political meetings with disturbingly racial and violent undertones. The cause of the unrest was, largely, a feeling that the Bahamas had been run for far too long by an oligarchic clique known as the "Bay Street Boys" (from the name of the Nassau main street where the big merchants operate). Then, in January, 1964, Britain granted the Bahamas full internal self-government, and the full effect of the tourist boom in bringing prosperity—per capita income in the Bahamas is estimated at about $1,000 a year—took away the impetus of the movement to stir up unrest.

It is no longer true—as it once undoubtedly was—to say that the Bahamas are ruled by an established few with vast vested interests. It is now a territory where careers are open to talents. For example, all branches of the public service are open to native Bahamians, whatever colour they may be (about 90% of the population is Negro), whereas formerly the top posts were reserved for men appointed by London—or, if not by London, then by the "Bay Street Boys." London is now responsible only for foreign affairs, defence and internal security.

A great deal of this liberalisation had already taken place before the elections of January, 1967, when the islands were ruled by the white United Bahamian Party under the leadership of Sir Roland Symonette. There was an atmosphere of stability based on the British system of democratic government. The Union Jack, fluttering on Rawson Square in Nassau, the capital city, and the British-uniformed Negro policemen competently directing traffic, gave proof of this to the tourists who streamed down the gangplanks of the liners which in busy periods were entering the harbour at the rate of eight or nine a day; and, despite the unexpected victory in the 1967 polls of the Progressive Liberal Party, there was no indication that these things would change.

The day after he became Premier, Mr. Pindling, a London-trained lawyer, quoted Sir Winston Churchill: "In defeat defiance, in victory magnanimity." It would be difficult in any case, despite the new Premier's talk about change in direction, suddenly to alter the economy of a territory 90% of whose revenue was derived from United States tourist money. Nor did Mr. Pindling have plans to haul down the

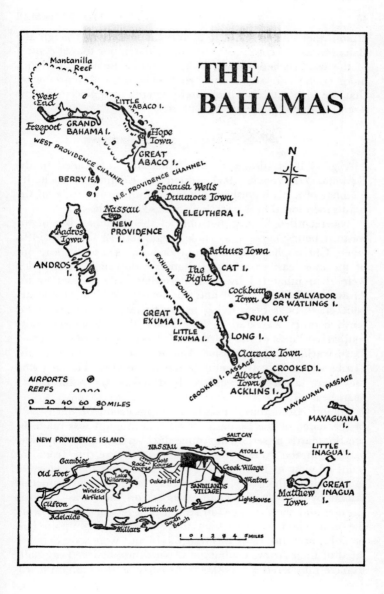

THE BAHAMAS

Mantanilla Reef

West End

LITTLE ABACO I.

Freeport   GRAND BAHAMA I.

Hope Town

WEST PROVIDENCE CHANNEL

GREAT ABACO I.

BERRY IS.

N.E. PROVIDENCE CHANNEL

Spanish Wells
Dunmore Town

Nassau
NEW PROVIDENCE I.

ELEUTHERA I.

Andros Town

ANDROS I.

EXHUMA SOUND

Arthurs Town

CAT I.

The Bight

Cockburn Town   SAN SALVADOR OR WATLINGS I.

GREAT EXUMA I.

RUM CAY

LITTLE EXUMA I.   LONG I.

Clarence Town

CROOKED I. PASSAGE   CROOKED I.

Albert Town
ACKLINS I.

MAYAGUANA PASSAGE

MAYAGUANA I.

AIRPORTS   ◉
REEFS   ∩∩∩∩

0 20 40 60 80 MILES

LITTLE INAGUA I.

GREAT INAGUA I.

Matthew Town

NEW PROVIDENCE ISLAND

SALT CAY

NASSAU

ATOLL I.

Gambier   Race Course   Golf Course

Creek Village

Old Fort

Lake Killarney   Oakes Field

SANDILANDS VILLAGE

Winton

Windsor Airfield

Lighthouse

Clifton

Carmichael

Adelaide

South Beach

Millars

1 0 1 2 3 4 5 MILES

Union Jack. As of 1967, therefore, it looked as though the Bahamas would continue to be one of the major tourist centres of the western hemisphere (with gambling facilities, perhaps, more controlled) and a tax-free haven, the difference being that the long established oligarchy would be replaced by new —and differently pigmented—faces.

HISTORY

A good brief history of the Bahamas is contained in the *Bahamas Handbook*, 1964, edited by Etienne Dupuch Jr., member of a distinguished Bahamian family, and some of the points mentioned in this section are based upon it.

The recorded history, not only of the Bahamas, but of the western hemisphere as a whole, began on 12 October 1492, when Christopher Columbus landed on San Salvador, one of the most easterly of the Bahamas group of islands, which were then inhabited by an Amerindian tribe known as the Arawaks. These peaceful and apparently amiable people are believed to have been living in the Bahamas since about the tenth century A.D. and to have come there from the more southerly islands of the Caribbean to get away from the other more warlike and aggressive Amerindian tribe known as the Caribs who sought to dominate the whole area. The fact that they were largely successful is illustrated by the name Caribbean Sea.

Though Columbus formally took possession of the islands in the name of the Spanish Crown, no attempt was made by the Spaniards to settle; the other discoveries which they were making in the New World were more interesting from the point of view of finding gold. Nevertheless, in the century or so after their discovery, the Bahamas islands were frequently visited by the Spanish conquistadores on their way between Europe and the Americas in search of a labour force to work the mines and estates which they were opening up in Hispaniola; and the result was that the islands were soon depopulated of their Arawak inhabitants which are believed orginally to have numbered some 40,000. As early as 1515, Spanish seafarers reported that there was hardly a trace of the Arawaks to be found in all the Bahamas.

The islands continued in the state of what might be called non-existence till almost the middle of the seventeenth century. In 1629, King Charles I of England made a grant to his Attorney General, Sir Ronald Heath, of "Bahama and all other Isles and Islands lying southerly to them and neare the forsayed Continent. . . ."; but Sir Ronald apparently made no effort to take up the offer. Then, in the 1640's, the English settlers in Bermuda, who had been having differences of opinion about religious matters—as was also the case in England—sent an expedition to survey the Bahamas as a possible place of refuge. In 1648, the Governor of Bermuda, William Sayle, sailed with about seventy people to the Bahamas. The island on which they landed, then called Cigateo, was renamed Eleuthera after the Company of Eleutherian Adventurers which had been formed in London the previous year for the purpose of developing the Bahamas.

The expedition does not seem to have been outstandingly successful, largely because one of its two ships was wrecked off the north coast of Eleuthera and most of the supplies were lost. Sayle set forth in the other ship to the mainland English colony of Virginia seeking to replenish his supplies; he even went as far north as Boston, Massachusetts, where he got further help from the English Puritans who had settled there. Despite this help, however, the first settlers in the Bahamas must have found life unduly hard because many of them returned to Bermuda. Though another group of settlers landed on what is now New Providence island in 1656, Sayle returned to Bermuda in 1658 and resumed the governorship.

In 1663 Charles II made a grant of the colony of South Carolina to a group of friends who were given the title of Lords Proprietors. They appointed Sayle governor and he must have talked to them about the possibilities which the Bahamas offered for settlement and development, because the Duke of Albermarle and five other Proprietors were given a grant of the islands by the King in 1670. These new owners made some attempt to govern and develop Eleuthera and

New Providence, but they seem to have had little co-operation from the settlers who had by then entered the profitable business of piracy. England and Spain were either openly at war or in a state of clandestine hostility. Spanish ships were continually being plundered by English buccaneers, and in 1684 the Spaniards retaliated by sacking New Providence, capturing Governor Robert Clark and reportedly roasting him to death on a spit. This was the start of the heyday of piracy in Bahamian waters. Soon the settlers were relying on the loot they got from these activities as their main form of sustenance. A new profession had sprung up—that of luring ships onto the rocks by shifting navigational lights, and the extent of the booty seized is illustrated by the taking of a treasure from a Spanish Galleon worth more than £90,000—probably some £500,000 in today's money values.

Obviously, however, this form of earning a livelihood could not go on forever, and in any case not all the settlers in the Bahamas were engaged in the piracy business. It is reported that by 1718 there were more than 1,000 pirates operating from New Providence but the rest of the population remained in a state almost of starvation. The law-abiding settlers had been petitioning the King to put the islands under the control of the Crown and to get rid of the Lords Proprietors, and in 1718 King George I appointed a Bristol sea captain, one Woodes Rogers, to the governorship. Rogers was himself a successful privateer, but on his appointment as the first Royal Governor, he devoted himself to stamping out piracy, granting a Royal Pardon to many hundreds of pirates who agreed to give up their illegal careers, and hanging those who refused to toe the line. Though piracy continued to be practised to a greater or lesser extent in Bahamian waters for many years afterwards, it was certainly Rogers who was responsible for introducing a more or less orderly form of government to the islands. He was a first-class administrator and he introduced many reforms, including the summoning of the Representative Assembly in 1729. He died in 1732 while still in office.

After Rogers' death, the Bahamas went through a generally peaceful period and were lucky to have two Governors of integrity and ability, John Tinker and Lord Dunmore, of whose terms of office there are many visible reminders—Fort Montagu, for example, which still stands at the entrance to Nassau harbour, and Dunmore Town on Harbour Island. But piracy again raised its ugly head with the outbreak shortly after the middle of the eighteenth century of another warring period between Britain on the one side and France and Spain on the other. New Providence once again became the centre for privateers prying on the supply ships sailing between Europe and the French and Spanish colonies. Things quietened down towards the end of the sixties decade and then the American revolution came along to make the Bahamas once again a main centre of activity in the western hemisphere.

A curious episode occurred in March, 1776, when Nassau was successfully attacked by a fleet of seven ships commanded by the American Commodore Ezekiel Hopkins, and the Stars and Stripes flew over the island for about twenty-four hours. The invaders only stayed long enough to capture what stores and ammunition they could but they took away with them Governor Montfort Browne as a hostage. He was later exchanged for an American prisoner held by the British. In 1782 Nassau flew the Spanish flag for several months having been forced to capitulate to a joint American-Spanish force headed by one Don Antonio Claraco; but in 1783 Britain, France and Spain signed a peace treaty under which the Bahamas were returned to British rule. They have remained under the Union Jack ever since.

The American revolutionary war had a lasting effect on the Bahamas because the islands became a place of refuge for the many thousands of people loyal to the British Crown who wanted to leave the newly formed United States of America. Between 1783 and 1790 it is estimated that about 8,000 such loyalists and their slaves arrived in the Bahamas, and it is largely due to them that the islands other than New Providence and Eleuthera were settled. By the end of the eighteenth century the population of the Bahamas had been more than doubled by these immigrants and the result was a certain amount of discord between the new arrivals and the old inhabitants. Even to this day Bahamians tend to be averse to other people "muscling in" on the affairs of their island; but things apparently got so bad in 1785 that the Governor gave up the struggle to restore order, and resigned. Things gradually simmered down, however, when it became evident that the newcomers, mostly skilled planters, were aiding the economy by introducing new crops (cotton among them) and helping to develop the colony as a whole. As they entered the nineteenth century, the Bahamas islands were reasonably prosperous.

There was a short interval in 1812 when privateering again became profitable during the brief war between Britain and the United States, but a new element had now entered into the affairs of the Bahamas—the Negro slaves brought in by the loyalists, who were estimated to number more than 10,000 in the first half of the nineteenth century. The slaves were essential to the islands' new agricultural economy and when emancipation took place in 1834 it was not surprising that the economy once again declined. Not for more than a hundred years was the presence of the freed negroes to be felt in the political sense, but the pattern of life on the islands as it is today was undoubtedly formed by the American revolution.

The Civil War, which broke out in America in 1861, also had its effect on the Bahamas economy. For four years a period of frantic trading went on in the Bahamas between the British, who needed cotton, and the Americans (both sides) who needed guns. Contemporary reports tell of Nassau Harbour being crowded with ships of all sorts and the city streets clogged with bales of cotton and barrels of gunpowder. Nassau, once more, was a boom town; but the defeat of the Confederacy in 1865 brought this prosperity to an end and the islands again entered a period of hard times. Some attempt was made to plant new crops such as pineapples and sisal, but without much success. There had, however, been a significant development in 1859 which might be said to have been the forerunner of the new type of prosperity which came to the Bahamas in the twentieth century. In that year the British ship owner, Samuel Cunard, set up a regular New York to Nassau steamship service. Though most of its first passengers were intriguers, blockade-runners and agents of one sort or another for both sides of the Civil War, they nevertheless brought in enough money to enable a profitable start in the hotel business to be made in Nassau. The Royal Victoria Hotel, still very much in evidence, was built at that time and so, like many other things in the Bahamas, can be said to owe its existence to a war.

The 1914-18 war, however, did not have much effect on the Bahamas; the age of piracy, which used to thrive on wars, was over. Once again, however, in 1919 an event took place abroad which was to have a considerable effect on the Bahamian economy and was to introduce a new type of buccaneer—the rum-runner. In that year the United States Congress passed the Volstead Act, the eighteenth amendment to the constitution (later repealed by the twenty-first amendment) which, anyway theoretically, deprived Americans of the pleasure of drinking and making alcohol in their own country. The Bahamas islands extend as near as fifty miles to the U.S. coast and it was natural that they should become one of the principle head-quarters for importing liquor. Once again, Nassau Harbour became filled with every sort of ship capable of carrying a cargo, and the town was filled with people of all sorts concerned with the business of bootlegging. Enormous profits were made from these transactions and they tell you with something approaching pride in Nassau that many of today's prominent local people made their original fortunes in the rum-running period.

With the repeal of prohibition it looked as though the Bahamas once again were heading for depression, but by this time the tourist industry was beginning to make itself felt. One of the people who helped to develop it was a Canadian-naturalised American who was probably just as important in the history of the Bahamas as was Captain Woodes Rogers. Harry Oakes, who was later made a baronet by King George VI, had made a fortune from gold mines in Canada and with this he bought a large tract of land in the Bahamas. He was one of the first people to see the attractions which Nassau had to offer visitors from colder climates. He built Nassau's first airport (Oakes Field), a golf course and several hotels, including the present Sheraton—British Colonial. He was reputed to be worth more than £3,500,000 when he was mysteriously murdered. The murderer was never found. Others followed in Sir Harry Oakes' footsteps and Nassau was on the way to becoming the popular tourist centre it now is.

In many ways, the Bahamas tourist industry, like that of Bermuda, was to benefit considerably from the second world war; the American servicemen who were sent there for training (mostly flying) and constructional work, and their British opposite numbers, brought a considerable amount of money into the islands, and the Bahamians profited by the demands for goods and services which their presence created. As was the case in Bermuda, the servicemen returned home full of enthusiasm for the attractions of the Bahamas; and during this period the Duke of Windsor (King Edward VIII of England, who gave up his throne for "the woman I love") was Governor, so yet another name was added to the long list of colourful personalities who presided over the affairs of a group of islands whose history, though it had its periods of doldrums, hardly ever lacked personalities to make it exciting in one way or another.

After the war there was an interlude of three of four years during which adjustments were made from a wartime economy and way of life to those of peace before the Bahamas were able to take full advantage of the fact that they had almost everything to offer that new group of peripatetic money-spenders and investors which was springing up first in North America, then in Europe, and later even in South America and other countries of the western hemisphere. Year-round tourism and the hotel building boom which followed were given the required boost in the Bahamas when a new and revitalised Development Board was appointed in 1950. In that year a record 45,300 visitors went to Nassau; now the number of annual visitors (including the Resort Islands) is on its way to the million mark, and the Bahamas have once again entered a period of prosperity as one of the world's leading tourist centres.

From the constitutional point of view things remained much

the same in the Bahamas for almost 250 years. It was the old British colonial system of government, similar to that which operated in the original thirteen North American mainland colonies, but it did progress broadly along the evolutionary lines of the British parliamentary system, though at a slower rate. Its forms were largely archaic and it relied very much on personalities. Then, in May, 1963, a conference was held in London, attended by Bahamians of all political views. In the previous year there had been a general election in which women had the vote for the first time. The constitution, which came into force in January, 1964, follows the normal pattern of political advance in British dependent territories. The Governor, who is the Queen's representative, has control only over defence, foreign affairs and security. There is a fully-elected House of Assembly and an Upper House, or Senate, whose purpose is mainly advisory. The Premier is the leader of the majority party in the House and the members of his cabinet are all members of this party. This is known as full internal self-government, and the next step in the British system of constitutional development is full sovereignty within the Commonwealth when the Governor—or Governor-General as he is then called—has no reserve powers and acts as Head of State on the advice of his Ministers on all matters.

The forebodings of disaster were numerous and vociferous after Mr. Pindling's accession to power but it soon became evident that tourists had no objection to spending a holiday in a territory run by a young (37) Negro Premier and Cabinet. They arrived in even greater numbers than the previous record year and it was clear that the Bahamas attraction of sun, sand and sea had in no way diminished. The construction of new hotels and the enlargement of older ones proceeded apace; the clatter of roulette wheels and dice was just as loud in the two large Grand Bahama casinos; the new "high-rise" bridge linking Nassau with Paradise Island was officially declared open in April 1967, and plans were announced to spend some $31 million that year on the already started mammoth resort hotel (plus casino) development on the island.

The main reason for the ousting of the "Bay Street Boys" establishment from power was connected with allegations about corruption in the gambling world and its dominance by undesirable Nevada-style operators. The Pindling government pledged itself to correct this and to ensure that the casinos were properly controlled; in addition, its policy was to ensure that the wealth brought in by the islands' natural attractions should not remain in the hands of a single minority group. All Bahamians should have a chance to get the top jobs in the tourist and banking industries and to this end it was intended that expenditure on education should be increased from about 12% of government revenue to 25%. By the end of 1967 it was already evident that the new Bahamas was taking shape; and its principal source of livelihood would still be the tourist dollar.

ECONOMY

There are two main reasons why the economy of the Bahamas has been remarkably bouyant in the sixties, and they are best given by two quotations. The first was made early in 1966 by the Ministry of Tourism : "All previous records were smashed by a mighty wave of tourism in 1965, carrying the Bahamas to a new crest of prosperity." The second was made in 1965 by the Nassau manager of the Canadian Imperial Bank of Commerce : "I keep telling everybody Nassau will be the biggest financial centre in the western hemisphere, but probably not in our time. We are relatively new as a major world financial capital, but we are already more important than Switzerland in world banking."

It is estimated that in the second half of the sixties decade tourists and foreign investors (the majority from North America) have been pumping something like a billion dollars each year into the colony's economy. Government revenue has been of the order of $30 million, which is remarkably high for a territory with some 135,000 inhabitants.

There is no income tax in the Bahamas; nor is there a business tax, a capital gains tax, a sales tax, a profits tax or a tax on the remission of dividends. This has made the islands

unusually attractive for private investors, international commercial banks and trust companies, and there are now more
than sixty financial houses of various sorts, including those
whose names are international household words, operating
in the Bahamas. Encouraged by the tax climate—as well as by
the climate in the more literal sense—a lot of money has been
coming into the Bahamas from people, both Europeans and
North Americans, who buy land either as an investment in
anticipation of capital gains, or with a view to building a house
and living there in retirement. Investors with both large and
small sums have been attracted; and not the least encourage-
ment to invest savings in the Bahamas has been the stability
of government. Referring to this recently, the former Minister
of Finance, Sir Stafford Sands, said : "I believe that when the
total value of all the assets of the government are brought to
account, the figure will amaze even the most optimistic."

Apart from the products of new industries in Grand Bahama,
the main exports of the Bahamas are pulpwood, salt, crayfish,
a few vegetables such as tomatoes and cucumbers, sponge, and
marine curios. Nearly all the islands' requirements are imported, apart from a few products such as locally grown vegetables, fruit, and fish. Main imports are liquor, machinery,
motor vehicles, petroleum oil and foodstuffs of all kinds. Easily
the most important trading partner of the Bahamas is the
United States.

Up till 1966 the official currency was the Bahamas pound,
on a par with sterling. This has now been changed to a decimal
dollar system, though this, like the dollar currency of the
Eastern Caribbean, is still based on sterling. U.S. and Canadian
dollars are acceptable in shops and hotels and are, of course,
freely interchangeable at banks. Other currencies are con-
vertible at current rates.

SIGHTSEEING

In the eyes of the North American or North European who
hankers after warmth and sun the name of Nassau has always
had a glamorous, if often remote, appeal. Up till the second

world war Nassau was generally considered to be the only place to go in the Bahamas; now it is only one of several places among the 700-odd islands of the group whose attractions are enjoyed each year by more and more people; it still maintains, however, its unique flavour and zest for enjoyment.

The town, which dates from 1729, is the seat of the government of the Bahamas, and Rawson Square, named after Governor Sir Rawson Rawson (1864-1869), is its focal point. Situated on the square are the Public Buildings, which include the House of Assembly, the Senate, the General Post Office and the Law Courts. These charming colonial-style buildings blend happily with the modern ones—the Treasury Building, banks, offices and shops—which have been erected on the seaward side of the square. Bay Street, leading off Rawson Square, is the attractively gay main shopping area and some of the shops are as smart as any to be found in London, Paris or New York; it is a mixture of modern, not-so-modern, and period architecture. In the streets and alleys leading off Bay Street you will find more smart shops and attractive old buildings, some of which still retain the original louvres and wrought-iron work which are such a pleasant feature of early tropical architecture.

The waterfront is one of Nassau's biggest sightseeing attractions. It is a short walk from Rawson Square. The harbour has one of the finest sheltered anchorages in the world and is normally packed with yachts of all sizes, cruise ships, fishing schooners and a variety of local boats which have brought fish, fruit and vegetables, pigs and chickens, palm and sisal fibres, to Nassau from the Resort Islands. These boats usually arrive at dawn. Some of the goods are taken to the Produce Exchange and sold, and the rest is stacked on the dock to be sold to the local caterers, middlemen and housewives who go there to buy their daily provisions. It is a colourful scene.

Government House, built in 1801, is situated on Mt. Fitzwilliam, at the top of George Street, and commands an excellent view of the island. In front—midway up a flight of forty-five steps—stands a statue of Christopher Columbus, which was modelled in London by an aide of Washington Irving for

Governor Sir James Carmichael Smythe. The Governor presented it to the colony in 1831. Ten acres of grounds surround Government House in which are planted hundreds of tropical plants. The colourful changing of the guard ceremony is usually held there on alternate Saturday mornings. It is patterned after the guard-changing at Buckingham Palace and the ceremony lasts about twenty-five minutes.

The eight-sided building near the Law Courts which now houses the Public Library once served as a gaol, workshop and house of correction. The little alcoves which now contain bookcases were at one time prison cells, and the gardener's shed underneath the building formerly was a dungeon. Construction of the building was authorised in 1797, and the decision to make it octagonal was made by the Governor, the Earl of Dunmore, who seems to have had a penchant for that sort of thing. Twenty-two years earlier, when he was Governor of the then British Colony of Virginia, he ordered an arsenal to be constructed of octagonal design. It can still be seen in Williamsburg.

In 1873, when a new prison was built in Nassau, the building was converted into a library. Besides books and magazines, it contains various historical items, the largest collection of Bahamian prints to be assembled in one place, and such intriguing things as 500-year-old skulls, an old Spanish bell, and a copy of the original charter granted to the Eleutherian Adventurers who were the first settlers of the Bahamas. There are also maps dating from the seventeenth century, ancient pistols, and paintings of the Bahamas' various Governors and their wives.

The Ardastra Gardens should be visited either at 11 a.m. or 4 p.m., because then the flock of resident flamingoes is put through a sort of drill routine. It is fascinating to watch them obeying the commands of their trainer. The birds are flown to Nassau from Inagua, the southernmost island in the Bahamas chain, where they flourish under protection of the Bahamas government. They average about 66 inches in height and are reddish-pink in colour. Though the flamingoes are the main attraction at Ardastra, the six acres of gardens, which contain more than 4,000 different tropical and sub-tropical plants and shrubs, are well worth exploring.

In the Nassau area are three interesting old forts. Fort Montagu was built in 1741 to guard the eastern entrance to Nassau Harbour. Fort Charlotte (1789) protects the western entrance and is particularly interesting because of its network of underground passages and dungeons. It also has an interesting display of wax figures. Fort Fincastle overlooks the city of Nassau and was built by Governor Lord Dunmore in 1793. The best way to get to this fort is to go up Queen's Staircase which ascends from a deep canyon at the top of Elizabeth Avenue. This was cut out of solid rock by slaves as a way of escape for troops stationed in the fort. The Water Tower, overlooking the Fort, is a famous Nassau landmark and is the highest point in New Providence island. From its top a magnificent view of the city and, indeed, the whole island, is obtainable.

New Providence island, on which Nassau is situated, is believed to have been named by Captain William Sayle, of the Eleutherian Adventurers, to express his gratitude for being saved from a shipwreck there. It is only 21 miles by 7 miles at its furthest points, and so it is easy to drive round it in a day.

Leaving Nassau in an easterly direction, you drive down Shirley Street and pass St. Matthew's Church, the oldest in the island. Follow the line of Bay Street along the eastern arm of Nassau Harbour past the yacht marinas to Fort Montagu, where the harbour becomes a bay and where the Nassau Yacht Club and Royal Nassau Sailing Club are situated. Further east is Blackbeard's Tower, said to be the remains of a watch tower used by "Blackbeard" (Edward Teach), the famous pirate who operated in Bahamian waters in the late seventeenth century. Beyond the Eastern Point the road leads to the beach of Yamacraw, where smugglers and illegal immigrants —from Haiti, for example—still sometimes sneak ashore. Next you come to the native village of Fox Hill, three miles from Nassau. Here freed slaves were settled after emancipation. Near Fox Hill Village is St. Augustine's Benedictine Monastery, where there is a school and a model farm.

Leaving Nassau to the west, you pass Fort Charlotte, which was built by Lord Dunmore to guard Nassau's western approaches but which never fired a shot in anger. All around is public recreation land, and on Haynes Oval during summer weekend afternoons you may see cricket being played. Passing the plush waterfront houses, in one of which (Westbourne) Sir Harry Oakes was murdered, you come to the Bahamas Country Club and golf course. Some miles farther on you arrive at Gambier, a cluster of wooden houses and a school, which was once the centre of an old plantation and is one of New Providence's four country villages (Fox Hill, Adelaide and Carmichael are the others).

Next you come to Lyford Cay, a 4,000-acre estate which has been developed by a Canadian millionaire financier as (theoretically, anyway) one of the most exclusive residential and resort areas in the Caribbean. You have to become a member of the club before you can buy land and build a house. The central club house is elegant and impressive. When Britain's Prime Minister, Mr. Harold Macmillan, met the President of the United States, Mr. John F. Kennedy, in Nassau in 1962, they and their entourages were put up in two houses in Lyford Cay. A mile further on is Clifton Pier where cruise ships anchor when a northerly gale makes the Nassau anchorage uncomfortable. There is a generating plant there which daily produces a million gallons of fresh-water distilled from the sea. Next you come to Coral Harbour which is another smaller (2,500-acre) and less exclusive resort area being developed on lines similar to those of Lyford Cay. There is a central restaurant-hotel building around which houses are grouped. Nearby is one of the world's largest rum distilleries on a 40-acre site owned by the Bacardi rum interests.

You now head back for Nassau along Carmichael Road which passes through the southern part of the island where there are some farms growing sisal and garden produce. Having passed Carmichael Village it is worth while stopping the car and walking through the scrub about half a mile to Mermaid's Pool. There are several of these so-called Ocean Holes on New

Providence island : they have subterranean connections with the sea, but this one is reputedly bottomless.

Paradise Island, which actually forms the northern shore of Nassau Harbour, should be visited because it is fast becoming one of the most highly developed playground areas in the Bahamas and its near-perfect beaches have been made more accessible by the elegant bridge connecting it with the town of Nassau which was opened early in 1967.

Let it be emphasised again, however, that Nassau and its environs form only part of the Bahamas' outstandingly attractive scenic complex. Almost all the other islands are now easily accessible by air and warrant descriptions in their own right; they are accordingly dealt with individually in a separate section of this chapter.

HOTELS, RESTAURANTS AND ENTERTAINMENT

In Nassau and on New Providence Island there are half a dozen hotels in the A-plus category; it would be wrong, however, to suppose that Nassau, despite the somewhat luxurious connotation which the name possesses, caters only for the well-heeled visitor; there are plenty of good B class hotels and some even in the C category.

In the A-plus category are the establishments with names which are frequently bandied about in one-upmanship contests between vacationland experts—the Sheraton British Colonial, the Nassau Beach, the Emerald Beach; and the newest, the Paradise Hotel, has now been opened on Paradise Island. In the same category must also be put such establishments as the Lyford Cay Club, the Coral Harbour Club (both some distance from the town) and the Nassau Harbour Club, though these do not, perhaps, offer within their walls the multiple recreational facilities of the bigger hotels and they are, to some extent anyway, run on a club basis. The Montagu Beach probably also warrants inclusion in this category and so does the new Anchorage.

There are a dozen or more hotels in the A-minus bracket, of

which the most prominent—certainly from the situation point of view; it overlooks Rawson Square—is the rather ancient Royal Victoria. Two others in the centre of the town are the Carlton House and the recently modernised Prince George. The Beachcomber, the Mayfair, the Dolphin, and the Gleneagles can be listed among other names to remember in this category and among the "clubs" are the New Moon, the Pilot House and the Blue Vista; on Paradise Island there is the new Paradise Beach Lodge. In this category must also be included at least a dozen "cottage colonies" and buildings with apartments to rent, either with or without maid service.

About ten hotels in Nassau offer accommodation in the B category, both plus and minus, and there are about twice as many so-called guest houses of the same standard. Among the hotels in this category are the Buena Vista, the Columbus, the Cumberland House and the Towne.

As in Bermuda, C class accommodation is not greatly in evidence, but there are at least three guest houses where you can get a room in the off-season period between April and mid-December for between $2·50 and $3·50 a day without food; so it does not by any means follow that, if you want to spend a few days in Nassau, you have to have a lot of money.

Restaurants and nightclubs in Nassau are plentiful and generally of high quality, unless one goes to the outskirts of the town where standards are lower. Good evening entertainment of one sort or another is provided at the A-plus category hotels and several of the lesser grade are to be recommended both for the quality of the food in their restaurants and the entertainment they offer. Among these are the Buena Vista, which has a varied cuisine (dinner only) and some excellent specialities of the day. Some form of entertainment is usually provided and you can either sit on the patio or in the dining room. The Pilot House Club is a delightful spot for evening eating and entertainment. The Royal Victoria's Cafe Royal, with its swimming pool and a famous tropical garden, serves lunch either indoors or outside round the pool, and there is music and dancing in the evening. The restaurant of the Carlton House Hotel (it also has an Angus Steak House) is a popular gathering place at lunch time and there is usually some form of entertainment in the evening. Montagu Beach Hotel, about two miles outside Nassau at Montagu Bay, is a good place for dining and dancing and it has a bar at which you can sit and watch through plate-glass windows the under-water activities of people swimming in the pool above.

Among the smaller, non-hotel eating and drinking places in downtown Nassau which I found to be good are Ben Warry's Green Shutter Inn, which is run by an English couple and serves draught beer; Charley Charley's La Fin, which is remin-iscent of Greenwich Village; and, if you want such dishes as baked Bahamian crab, snails, or cheese fondu, the oddly named "Sun and. . . ." is the place to go.

Paradise Island, just across the harbour, is perhaps the best place for all-round evening entertainment. It now has a large casino-cum-theatre, one or two popular-priced restaurants, and the luxurious Cafe Martinique where you can get some of the best food in the Bahamas. There are many other places to go both for lunch and dinner, including at least three on Bay Street where snacks and sandwiches can be had in reasonably pleasant surroundings and at very reasonable prices. There are half a dozen nightclubs in the "over-the-hill" area with floor shows varying from the somewhat lurid to the respectable.

SPORT AND RECREATION

Almost every sport, literally under the sun, is available in the Bahamas. Some of the world's finest facilities for sailing and fishing exist in the waters round New Providence and the Resort Islands; and yachts and boats of all types are available for rent or charter. Some firms, particularly the Nassau Charter Boat Association, specialise in offshore cruising and fishing and you may sail away to Abaco, Andros, the Berry Islands, the Exuma Cays or Eleuthera on trips lasting a week, ten days or a fortnight, depending on the charter. There is in fact no better way to see and get an understanding of the Bahamas than to charter an offshore craft and cruise along a chain of bays fishing by day and anchoring for the night in some charming small harbour or inlet. It is nothing for the party to catch eight or ten different species of fish in a day's trolling or still fishing. When the party wants a break from fishing, there are some of the world's finest beaches to explore for driftwood and other odd objects thrown up by the sea. There are settlements to be visited—often with most attractive architecture—where the residents, some of whom live much as they did fifty or more years ago, offer a cheerful welcome.

For example, a fine cruise is the one from Nassau to Harbour Island, Spanish Wells, Eleuthera and the Exuma Cays. It covers some of the more populated and historic ports of interest and the 235-mile voyage can be sailed leisurely in a fortnight. Spanish Wells, the first port of call, has some of the best skindiving reefs that can be found anywhere. The passage to Harbour Island can be made along a reef known as Devil's Backbone. Other small settlements to be passed or visited include The Current, Hatchet Bay, Governor's Harbour, and Rock Sound, where a fine anchorage provides a pleasant night's stop on the journey south. The sail across Exuma Sound to Norman's Cay is normally a lively, broad reach. Anchorages are good and plentiful throughout the Exumas. This trip contains a little bit of everything in the Bahamas.

For people who like quiet water and fishing for bonefish on the flats, for jacks, barracudas and snappers in the channels, there are skiffs with outboard motors which can be hired with or without a guide. The angler who likes to spend the early mornings or the late evening hours fishing without renting a boat will find that the docks and jetties which only have schools of tiny fish swimming about during the day are visited by several species of fish when the sun goes down. Among these are jacks, snappers, groupers, runners, small bonefish and, in several Resort Islands, tarpon.

April is a good month to be in Bahamas waters because every year during this month a regatta is held out of the harbour at George Town, Great Exuma, in which the contestants are the commercial sailing boats which carry goods and produce, from conch shells to cabbages, from the various islands to the Nassau market. This is a three-day affair which draws scores of spectator yachts from the United States, as well as visitors who come by air just to join in the social activities. Only sailboats, built and manned by Bahamians who earn their living by shipping goods, are eligible to compete in the regatta. Every year it attracts some 75 Bahamian sailing craft ranging from small dinghys to trading sloops with crews of a dozen or more.

The regatta was originated in 1954 by the Out Island Squadron and one of the highlights of the social activities connected with it is the traditional "meet the skipper" cocktail party which gives visitors and spectators an opportunity to chat with the Bahamian seamen. A distinguished visitor in 1959 was Prince Philip, husband of Britain's Queen Elizabeth II, who was himself a naval officer and is a fine yachtsman.

The Regatta's main purpose, as established by it founders, is to improve the quality of the already proficient Bahamian commercial sailing fleet. But the Regatta has accomplished more than that; it has brought the strikingly beautiful waters and beaches of Exuma and its surrounding cays to the attention of yachtsmen and visitors from all over the world.

The Bahamas offer a full schedule of ocean racing, both for sail and motor boats. The annual Miami-Nassau Power Boat Race is held in April. With the addition of the 50-mile Around New Providence Island Race in 1962, the event became known as Nassau Ocean Speed Week.

The Bahamas ocean racing schedule also includes two of the important contests of the Southern Ocean Racing Conference. In February's Miami-Nassau Ocean Race and the Nassau Cup Race sailing yachts come to the Bahamas to compete for points in the S.O.R.C. scoring. Small-yacht sailors congregate in Nassau during two winter weeks for Bahamas Regatta Weeks, an international series for 5·5 Metre, Star, and Spine class yachts. Another important race is held at Guana Harbour Club, Great Guana Cay, Abaco, on Guy Fawkes Day.

The Yachtsman's Guide to the Bahamas gives useful information, including tide tables, new charts, distance measurements and landfall markings. But here is a piece of advice : when sailing in Bahamas waters keep a weather-eye for a "norther." There may be several scattered over a winter season and their high winds should command respect. The gentle trade winds from May to August make the summer months the most favourable for Bahamas cruising.

For the more stay-at-home type of sailor many hotels provide boats of various types which can be hired by the hour, and facilities for water-skiing exist at hotel beaches. Trips can be made to nearby reefs with full aqualung equipment; and instruction is available for all types of water sport, both for the beginner and the more advanced pupil.

First-class facilities exist at several hotels and clubs for golf and tennis. Race meetings with pari-mutuel betting are held regularly from January to April at Hobby Horse Hall. Sports car racing, with an array of internationally-known drivers, takes place in Nassau in November and December. Boxing and wrestling matches between Bahamian athletes and Americans and Canadians are staged several times a year. Bahamians play baseball, softball, basketball, cricket and soccer on an organised basis. Say what you will, however, about other sports, the Bahamas, to my mind, even more than Bermuda, offer some of the world's best facilities for sailing and fishing.

THINGS TO BUY

Many items are available in Nassau at well below U.S. or European prices. These include liquor, perfume, English golf balls, Irish linen, china, silverware, British woollens, Scottish plaids and German and Japanese cameras. Native straw-work is one of the most important of the Bahamian craft industries; Resort Island inhabitants bring strips of palm fronds plaited into bands of varied widths to Nassau where the bands are sewn into hats, slippers, mats, pocketbooks, baskets and other articles. These straw goods are sold in the colourful straw markets along Bay Street and in Rawson Square.

In several shops along Bay Street sea-shell jewelry and decorative pieces are made and sold by local craftsmen. The shells, gathered in the Resort Islands, are pierced with thin wires and arranged into floral patterns for ear-rings, necklaces,

and bracelets. Ash trays and lamps are also produced locally
from materials indigenous to the Bahamas. Carved wooden
bowls, letter-openers and figures depicting typical island
themes are offered at a number of shops.

Shorts, shirts, dresses and blouses made locally and hand-
printed with exclusive designs created by Bahamian residents
are available to visitors in numerous shops along Bay Street
and other downtown shopping area side streets. A large selec-
tion of clothing, blouses, jackets, etc., printed with typical local
scenes of the Bahamas, is on sale in many shops.

USEFUL FACTS FOR VISITORS

The Bahamas are an archipelago of about 3,000 islands and
rocks (taking the very smallest into account) extending for
some 500 miles from a point about 60 miles east of the Florida
coast to within 50 miles of Cuba and Haiti. The islands are
generally long, narrow and low-lying, with shallow soil and
overlying rock. All the islands were probably once thickly
wooded, and extensive pine forests remain on Andros, Abaco
and Grand Bahama. The combination of white coral sands,
lagoons, reefs, sub-tropical vegetation and brilliant sea colours
has made them one of the world's most inviting holiday areas.
The total land area is 4,375 square miles.

The average winter temperature is 70° F. (21° C.). Summer
temperatures vary between 80° and 90° F., (26·6° and 32·2°
C.), but sea breezes always ensure that the climate is not sultry.
Annual rainfall averages 46 inches, and the rainy months are
May, June, September and October.

Of the Bahamas population of some 135,000 (1966 estimate)
a little more than 90% are of African descent and the rest,
with a few hundred classified as "others", are of European
stock. The language is English.

Half a dozen international airlines provide frequent and
regular services to and from Nassau : B.O.A.C., Pan American,
Qantas, Bahamas Airways Limited, Air Canada and Mackey
Airlines. Places served include New York, Miami and other
parts of Florida, London, Montreal, Toronto, Mexico City,

5. The Queen's Staircase, Nassau, was cut out of solid rock and bricked by slaves in the late 1770's

6. Most of the Bahamas' hotels cater for both pool and sea bathing

South America and Australia. There are frequent connections with Jamaica and other Caribbean islands. B.A.L. also has an inter-island network and operates an extensive charter service.

Cruise ships provide regular services between Miami, Freeport, and Nassau and there is also a weekly service to and from New York. Many of the world's finest liners—British, French, German, Scandinavian and American—make calls at Nassau on cruises, and there are regular services operating between the Bahamas and the United States, Europe, Canada, the Caribbean, South America, Australia and New Zealand.

Information can be obtained from The Bahamas Development Board, Bay Street, Nassau. There are also offices in New York, Chicago, Los Angeles, Dallas, Toronto and London.

THE RESORT ISLANDS

Round about the middle fifties, those concerned with tourism in the Bahamas woke up to the fact that, though Nassau had already become one of the world's leading tourist centres, the Out Islands, as they were then called, had almost as much—in some cases more—to offer. Up until 1957, in fact, no figures were kept of the number of foreign visitors to these islands, but in that year it was recorded that, while 194,618 visitors went to Nassau, 15,095 went to the other islands; but this fifteen thousand returned home and spread the word about the attractions of the vast new holiday area which they had discovered. The name of the islands was changed to The Resort Islands, and their sudden popularity can be judged from the fact that in 1961 only some 54,000 went there; but the following year the number doubled to 108,000. Today, well over 200,000 tourists each year sample the delights of these islands.

The islands have a dozen or so hotels in the A category, but mostly the tourist is catered for in smaller but charming hostelries geared to informal relaxation in beautiful surroundings. The exception to this rule is Grand Bahama, a descrip-

F

tion of which follows. The other islands are described, beginning with those nearest to Nassau and then proceeding in a southeasterly direction. There are more than seventy hotels and places to stay of good quality in these islands but it has only been possible to mention a few of them. It is a good thing to keep an eye on the map when reading about these islands.

Grand Bahama

The official brochures describe Grand Bahama as "an island on the move", and this seems to be an apt description of the mammoth tourist-residential-industrial complex which is springing up at an astonishing rate over a 234-square mile area, known as Freeport-Lucaya, in the southwestern part of the most northerly of the main Bahamas group of islands. It is not so much a picture of hotels, shops, offices and private houses going up all over the place as of buildings going up in various selected positions; and throughout the greater part of the area are canals, lakes and marinas with sleek motor cruisers, ketches and yawls tied up alongside or riding at anchor.

A ten-minute drive from the airport (frequent flights from Nassau by Bahamas Airways Limited), takes you, via the burgeoning city centre at Freeport, to the deep-water harbour which claims to have the largest single bunkering installation in the western hemisphere. Only a few years ago this whole area was scrub, bush, sand and open sea. Another ten-minute drive over part of the newly constructed network of highways takes you to the residential area, Lucaya (named after the aboriginal Lucayan Arawaks), and on the way two large buildings are pointed out to you. One is a $50,000,000 cement factory put up by a subsidiary of United States Steel, the other a large chemical plant. There are, you are told, several banks of international standing and more than half a dozen private merchant banks. There are more than a dozen restaurants, including an English "pub". There are six large beach hotels and more than a dozen smaller ones. There are two gambling casinos; there are four 18-hole golf courses. And all this has happened in the space of a few years when a group of enterprising businessmen decided, with the help of the Bahamas government, to transform a more or less barren tract of land into something which might almost be described as a twentieth-century semitropical city-state.

The money (it will probably end up by being not far short of $1,000 million) which has been responsible for this rapid growth of a piece of real estate which is only 76 miles from West Palm Beach on the booming Florida coast comes from United States, British and Canadian interests, and, as a result, there is a chain of command reminiscent of General Eisenhower's allied headquarters in the last war—an American head of a department with a Canadian second-in-command, or a British head with an American in charge, say, of public relations. And there is a resident liaison officer whose duty it is to see that the interests of the Bahamas government are protected.

But perhaps the most remarkable facet of this development area is that it is controlled by the Grand Bahama Port Authority on the lines almost of an independent state. Under the agreement (known as the Hawksbill Creek Act), signed in August 1955, with the Bahamas government, the Port Authority is responsible for virtually all aspects of the area's life with the exception of internal security. It is a twentieth-century version of Britain's East India Company, or the Hudson's Bay Company. And the result is that the visitor gets the impression that the British-uniformed policemen who are seen walking around are there more as a colourful attraction for the tourists than as enforcers of law and order. And the American tourists who pour in by the thousands on the 15 or 25 minutes flights from Florida are doubtless equally fascinated by the fact that they can arrive so quickly in a foreign country.

Curiously enough, this whole project started in the mid-fifties with the idea of building an international transhipment harbour on the western shores of Grand Bahama island, which then had nothing to offer except fishing and magnificent beaches (though there was on the northwestern tip of the island, known as West End, a British-sponsored Billy Butlin resort project which has now been transformed by an American group into a $3 million hotel, marina, golf-course and general tourist pleasure dome). Combined with the harbour, a complex of large and small industries was to be built, and, because of the duty and tax concessions granted by government, the name Freeport was chosen for the new city.

It soon became evident, however, that people were not keen to go and work in a place where the living and recreational facilities (except sun, sand and sea) were minimal. So the parallel tourist and residential project began to take shape, and the result today is a planned piece of development which for its size, imaginative scope and speed of construction must be unique in the world—particularly as it is being done entirely with private capital.

The impression one gets is that Freeport-Lucaya is designed to be a complete city in every way, providing its own educational facilities, shops, churches, clinics, a drive-in cinema, and even an amateur dramatic society. One of the first moves was to build two schools in the area—one, the Freeport School, whose facilities include a gymnasium, an auditorium and classrooms accommodating 375 students; the other, a denominational school, Mary Star of the Sea, with similar facilities for pupils. Churches include Anglican, Roman Catholic, Jewish, Methodist and an interdenominational chapel.

Attention has even been paid to more academic matters, and one of the most noticeable and attractive buildings in Freeport is the new Colonial Research Institute for the advanced study of a wide variety of subjects including growing vegetables hydroponically, nutrition, and many other related fields. Directly across from the Colonial Research Institute is the Grand Bahama Clinic which has a complete staff of medical specialists, trained nurses, and nurses' aids. Facilities include a fully-stocked dispensary, an operating room, X-ray equipment, a laboratory, wards, private rooms, and a nursery. Adjacent to the hospital is the Dental Clinic, staffed by qualified dental surgeons and furnished with the most modern equipment. There is also a Diagnostic Clinic and a Medical Library. The Bahamas Oceanographic Institute, sponsored and financed by the Colonial Research Institute, is, among other research programmes, studying the exploitation of the island's underwater world, and one important project being considered is a natural marina preserve. It is an astonishing picture of planning ahead, literally from scratch, to meet the needs of a large twentieth-century community.

The Lucayan Beach, which was the first of the large, luxurious hotels to open, has everything to offer the visitor, including a gambling casino on the premises. For this reason it must be put in category A-plus. Nevertheless, I think it is best described by the following words of a tourist brochure : "So beautiful you'll think it's a Hollywood movie set." There are at least four other hotels of this category in Freeport-Lucaya and one of them, the Holiday Inn, claimed to be not only the largest hotel in the Bahamas but also "the talk of the entire world". It has now been outclassed by the even larger King's Inn. There is also a wide variety—and by the seventies it will be even greater—of hotels, apartments to let, and houses to rent, which range from the A-minus to the C categories. "You name it," as they say, "we have it."

Night life and restaurant eating are well provided for. It is fun to go to the English Pub-on-the-Mall where you can get draught beer in tankards. Marcella's has good Italian food which goes down well with a bottle of Chianti. The Caravel Club specialises in Polynesian and oriental dishes; and there are plenty of places where you can go for steaks, hamburgers or local sea food. Most of the evening entertainment is done in the big hotels, but there are one or two places, such as the Cat and Fiddle, which provide dancing and floor-shows.

Freeport now has an international airport with scheduled jet services to and from North America, London, the Caribbean and South America. There are also several flights a day from places in Florida.

The Abacos

Great and Little Abaco, to the east of Grand Bahama, consist of about 776 square miles in the most northerly section of the Bahamas. Many of the early settlers were loyalists from New York, New England and Florida who arrived about 1783.

Timber and pulpwood operations are carried on in the vicinity of Marsh Harbour, where a large American company has its headquarters. There is commercial farming of tomatoes, cucumbers and chrysanthemums, and experiments have been made in planting tobacco, strawberries and avocados. The island has a flourishing shipbuilding industry, and Abaco dinghys are among the best small boats obtainable anywhere. Hope Town has an excellent deep harbour, and the quietly pleasant settlement round it is popular with Bahamians on holiday as well as with overseas visitors. A variety of charter boats is available for fishing and cruising, and provisions and supplies are stocked for cruising yachtsmen. Accommodation at Hope Town includes the Elbow Cay Club, the Hope Town Harbour Lodge, the White Sound Club (all of moderate size), and the four-room Coral Cottage.

On the eastern shore of Great Abaco about five miles from Hope Town, Marsh Harbour is emerging as an agricultural, shipbuilding and ship-repairing centre. There is a resident doctor, a dentist and a nurse. At Snake Cay, a few miles south, an American firm has leased land for a large pulpwood operation, and several farms produce tomatoes and other vegetables. Test plantings of tobacco have proved promising. A new dock and packing plant, improved harbour facilities, electric power, a fuelling station and ship-repair facilities make Marsh Harbour an important port for commercial shipping and visiting yachtsmen. An airstrip nearby is served by scheduled B.A.L. flights, and the offshore communities of Hope Town and Man of War Cay are served by regularly operated water taxis.

Man of War Cay is a picturesque island a few miles north and east of Marsh Harbour with good harbour and dock facilities. There are no facilities for overnight visitors, but a group of American, British and Canadian residents have homes on the island. There is a clinic and a nurse and several small stores where groceries and other supplies may be bought.

Green Turtle Cay, because of its fine beaches and first-class fishing, is increasingly popular with visitors. Comfortable accommodation may be found at the settlement of New Plymouth, and there is good anchorage for yachts in adjacent Settlement Creek, in Black Sound, and in White Sound. Lobster and other fishing are the principal occupations of residents. Bluff House, New Plymouth Inn, and some beach cottages provide accommodation. The new Treasure Cay Inn offers a marina, swimming-pool, and good beaches. The main airstrip, on the mainland at Great Abaco, is a couple of miles away, and a water taxi transports passengers and cargo on a regular schedule.

Great Guana Cay is a long, narrow island with broad beaches washed by Atlantic waves. The settlement on the west coast has a good harbour and stores where modest requirements in supplies may be obtained. The Guana Harbour Club has some guest rooms and a bar. Skin-diving equipment and fishing boats can be hired.

Walker's Cay is the northernmost of the inhabited islands and is marked by the tall radio and radar towers of a U.S. tracking station. It has a good harbour and it can be reached by boat or chartered amphibian plane. Guests rooms are available at the Walker Cay Club.

Spanish Wells

Lying between Great Abaco and Eleuthera on the island of St. George's Cay, Spanish Wells is perhaps the best example in the Bahamas of a settlement by loyalist English people who fled the United States after the War of Independence, bringing with them the early New England style of architecture. It is rather like what one imagines Nantucket or Martha's Vineyard to have been in the early days. The 900 or so inhabitants share perhaps a dozen surnames, most of which are English—Pinder, Sawyer, Curry, Albury.

The harbour got its name because Spanish ships used to get fresh water supplies from the wells on the island. Its residents are good sailors and fishermen and transport much of the produce from Eleuthera to the Nassau market. Shops, excellent water, electricity and the latest in marine shipway facilities make this a popular port with yachtsmen.

The harbour at Spanish Wells is one of the most picturesque in the Bahamas and it has a first-class marina which can handle yachts up to 80 feet. There are good facilities for visiting yachtsmen and their crews. There are two places to stay on the island. "The Lloyds", as the name implies, is owned and managed by a young couple of that name and they cater most efficiently for every sort of diver, both amateur and experienced. In fact they maintain one of the most complete inventories of diving equipment in the entire Bahamas; they even have, or had, two submarines, one self-propelled and the other power-driven.

Roberts Harbour Club combines docks for visiting yachtsmen with attractive modern accommodation to stay in. The club maintains a small fleet of outboards for the excellent fishing which is found everywhere around the island. There is a "nautical" bar and a seafood restaurant.

To get to Spanish Wells you go by B.A.L. to the Northern point of Eleuthera island and then on by launch.

Harbour Island

Obviously any visitor to the Bahamas who has even the faintest bent for inquiry must go to Grand Bahama to see what is going on there. Equally, but for different reasons, a visit to Harbour Island should be made. The point about this $3\frac{1}{2}$-mile-long island off the northeast coast of Eleuthera is that it has an old-world atmosphere which is remarkable even in the Bahamas group where you get glimpses of the past in many isolated spots. A 30-minute flight by B.A.L. from Nassau takes you to a landing strip in the rather desolate northern section of Eleuthera island, and a five-minute taxi-drive brings you to a little jetty from which a launch takes you in about 15 minutes across a channel to Dunmore Town, which is Harbour Island's "capital".

Like some other places in the Bahamas, Dunmore Town, named after Governor the Earl of Dunmore (1786 to 1797), was first populated by loyalists fleeing from the American Revolution, and as the launch comes alongside the jetty, you can see a small house with green shuttered windows and white trellis work surrounded by bright tropical shrubs and flowers. It's name is Loyalist Cottage. It dates from 1797 and it is a fine unspoilt example of one of the earliest houses built by loyalist settlers in the Bahamas.

The trouble—or perhaps the advantage—of Harbour Island is that accommodation is limited and people who know it persist in going back there year after year. This is not surprising because, apart from its old-world charm, the island has a three-mile-long beach with glorious pinkish sand; and the experts tell you that, second possibly to Bimini, the waters round Harbour Island are the finest in the Bahamas for fishing.

Among the two or three charming hotels there, Runaway Hill combines quality of food and service with comfortable, but totally informal, living. It is right on the pink sand beach, and the nearest land which faces you as you lie in the sun looking at the distant Atlantic breakers is the coast of west Africa. Coral Sands Club, also on the beach, is one of the most popular places to stay, and not far away is the Picaroon Cove Club which consists of two graceful old houses cleverly connected by a tunnel through rock.

Half a mile south of Dunmore Town is the more modern Briland Yacht Club and Marina. Other places to stay include Sunset Inn and Mrythies Cottage. But wherever you stay on Harbour Island, you can hardly fail to be delighted by its charm. Talk to one of the fifty or so Americans who have built houses there and you will be told that the last thing they want is that more tourists accommodation should be built. It looks as though their wish will not be granted.

Eleuthera

A lot of good things can be said about this long (a little more than 100 miles), slim island which is less than an hour's flying time to the east of Nassau and could almost be regarded as Harbour Island's big brother. It is attractive from the historical point of view because it is almost certain that the Company of Eleutherian Adventurers, formed in 1647 in London under Captain William Sayle, former Governor of Bermuda, set up at Governor's Harbour (still the principal town on Eleuthera) the first republic in the new world whose constitution, written with idealism and foresight, embodied the basic principles of democracy. Visually it is also attractive—perhaps more so than any other of the Bahamas group of islands—because it has rolling hills, cliffs, first-class beaches, intriguing lagoons and inlets, and a number of charming old-world settlements on its shores. It also has a dozen or more A category hotels.

Governor's Harbour, situated in about the middle of the island, is a 300-year-old settlement struggling up a hillside which overlooks a pleasant harbour. Several fine modern houses have been built there and one or two good small hotels. Just outside the town on the Atlantic coast is one of the island's best hotels, known as French Leave, which has a mile-and-a-half pink sand beach. Legend has it that it was at this point that the Eleutherian Adventurers first landed. Further south is Rock Sound which is referred to in old charts as Wreck Sound—meaning, presumably, that this was one of the many places in this part of the world whose inhabitants tended to earn their living by misdirecting ships at night.

At Rock Sound Estate (30,000 acres) there is a 600-head herd of Aberdeen Angus cattle. Good docks, stores, banks and medical facilities are available, and the nearby airstrip has scheduled flights from Nassau and American airports. At the Cotton Cay Club, also on the estate, is a first-class golf course with an attractive clubhouse, pool and cottage and motel-type accommodation for guests. The Rock Sound Club is a plush establishment with a private airstrip. One mile east of Rock Sound is the remarkable Ocean Hole, a land-locked tidal lake of great depth which fish enter through subterranean tunnels from the sea.

Eleuthera now has a multi-million dollar industry in the shape of a poultry and dairy farm. Hatchet Bay Plantation, half-way between Governor's Harbour and the island's north point, is run by an enterprising American banker turned farmer. It yields 600 gallons of milk, packages 2,000 chickens, and processes 12,000 eggs daily. The poultry farm produces some 400,000 broilers per year and has 40,000 hens in five laying houses. More than 200 cattle graze on the plantation's 900 acres. The plantation is particularly noteworthy because it is virtually a self-sustaining community on which one can live quite comfortably without ever leaving the settlement. There are restaurants, stores, a power plant, schools, a water system, even a yacht club.

Andros

Andros Island (1,600 square miles) a brief flight westward from Nassau, is the largest of the Bahamas group, with a population of about 8,000 mostly scattered in settlements along the east coast. Criss-crossed by several mangrove-bordered creeks and inlets, Andros is actually composed of several islands. The reef which borders the east coast is second in size only to Australia's Great Barrier Reef. Pine and mahogany forests cover much of the island.

One of the most interesting aspects of Andros is the strange folk-lore supposedly evolved by the Seminole Indians who fled Spanish domination and slavery in Florida and formed the earliest settlements in the island in 1790. According to this the island is infested by tiny, red-eyed, tree-dwelling elves known as Chickcharnies who have potent powers for good or evil. Other such spirits are called the Bosee-Amasee and the Yahoo. And the story goes that Neville Chamberlain, Britain's

Prime Minister at the outbreak of the second world war, who managed a sisal plantation in his youth on the family property in Andros, incurred the Chickcharnies' anger and was forced to leave the island. It is an historical fact, anyway, that the plantation was a failure.

Today's fisherman, disappointed in his luck, can always blame it on the Bosee-Amasee, a water spirit who removes fish from hooks, fouls lines and occasionally tips over a boat, but normally an excuse will not be needed, because inside the reef and in the waters beyond blue marlin, amberjack, mackerel, bonito, bluefin, tuna and dolphins abound. In the rivers and lakes the angler casts for bonefish, snapper and tarpon.

Guides, charts, equipment and charter boats services are available at the island's modern resorts, and so are facilities for underwater exploration of the reefs by snorkel. Long stretches of solitary beach on the east coast are ideal for visitors who just want to lounge around and do nothing. Andros produces excellent sailors, and sailing boats of high quality are built at Mangrove Cay, Lisbon Creek, and some other settlements.

Among the places to visit on the island, Fresh Creek is popular with yachtsmen and anglers and has a deep, easily-entered harbour, good docks, and a wide range of supplies and facilities. Andros Town on the south shore is a growing planned community of the Andros Bahamas Development Company and is served by scheduled B.A.L. flights from Nassau. The Lighthouse Club has ample accommodation and offers high-class facilities. The Andros Yacht Club has berthing facilities for 30 or more boats.

Pot Cay is on the Northern Bight and may be reached by amphibian plane or yachts drawing up to five feet of water. Headquarters for bonefishing are on the shallow flats nearby. Mastic Point is the centre of timber and commercial farming operations. The Andros Island Company is developing 8,500 acres which will include a resort area. An airstrip nearby has scheduled services.

At Nicolls Town the Andros Island Fishing Club has cottages for rent. There is a small settlement of about 350 local people, with two or three small stores where groceries, fresh vegetables and fruit may be obtained.

Berry Islands

These islands consist of about 30 large cays and a number of smaller islets, many of them privately owned. They begin north of Nassau across the Tongue of the Ocean. At Whale Cay, British heiress Marion Carstairs established a successful agricultural colony, earning herself wide publicity as an "island queen". American financier Wallace Groves, who is connected with the mammoth Grand Bahama development project, has a house on Berry Island.

An airstrip for private planes has been built near Frazers Cay Yacht Club at Frazers Hog Cay, which has supplies, fuel and overnight accommodation for a few guests. The Rhoda Cay Club also has facilities for visitors. The Colony Club has a large marina, cottages and a clubhouse on Chub Cay. There is an airstrip for private planes.

The Biminis

North and South Bimini, about 50 miles east of Miami, have been famous among fishermen for generations because the surrounding waters have produced world-record catches of blue and white marlin, sailfish, dolphin and bonefish. During the era of prohibition in America, Bimini's docks and barges in the harbour were piled high with bottled goods waiting to be shipped to the Florida coast by rum-runners under cover of darkness. Today, the harbours are filled with the boats of sportsmen who go there every year for fishing competitions.

On South Bimini there is a yacht marina and a housing development, and there are half a dozen B class hotels, North Bimini has a good harbour for yachts, and ashore there is reasonable accommodation for visitors. B.A.L. connects with Nassau and with Miami.

Cat Island

This boot-shaped island, 42 miles long and four miles wide, was thought at one time to have been the place where Columbus made his landfall. It even used to be called San Salvador until the neighbouring island was officially given that name, and all the honours which go with it, in 1925. Legend persists, anyway, that early Spanish settlers did go to Cat Island, though there is no conclusive evidence of their having been there. It was, however, definitely settled by loyalists from America in 1783, and remains of their extensive plantations are visible today.

Cat Island has some of the most impressive scenery in the Bahamas with ranges of hills that rise almost to 400 feet, some of which are covered by forest. There is good farm and pasture land, fine beaches and excellent fishing. A large part of the island is privately owned and this may be the reason why there is no tourist accommodation in the normal sense of the word, though it is possible to get rooms in private houses in Arthur's Town. Two yacht harbours have been developed, and there is an airstrip five miles north of the New Bight settlement which is served by B.A.L.

Cat Island was once the second most populous of the Bahama islands (it is the sixth largest), but it now has a population of not much more than 3,000 people who live mostly from farming and fishing.

Great Exuma

One of the most delightful flights on B.A.L. is that from Nassau to George Town on Great Exuma Island. It is a trip of an hour or so and it is well worth getting a good window seat, as the view of the various cays, or small islands, to the west of Exuma Sound is quite enchanting; but my reason for first visiting Great Exuma was that I had been told there

was an excellent example to be seen there of a type of property development which is now popular in the Bahamas. Advertisements had been appearing in both British and American newspapers and magazines offering land for sale in Bahamas Sound, on Great Exuma, at prices ranging from $1,095 (or the equivalent in sterling) for a 10,000 sq. ft. lot. A lot would be bought by depositing $15 and paying the same amount each month till the full $1,095 had been paid. There are indeed, a number of such land purchase schemes in operation in the Bahamas, but this project operated by Bahamas Acres Ltd., with offices in Miami and London, seemed the most interesting.

Great Exuma is narrow and long—about 40 miles by from one to seven miles. George Town, its "capital", follows the pattern of most other Resort Island townships—quaintness and old world charm, with a magnificent sheltered roadstead in which the Out Island Regatta is held (see p. 63). It has two churches, a shop, a village school, a dance hall, and what amounts to a village green in the traditional English sense. There are three hotels there catering for tourists. I noticed that Queen's Highway was the somewhat grandiose name of the main street. It seems that this was changed from King's Highway on the accession of Queen Elizabeth and will revert to its original title when the Queen's eldest son, Prince Charles, becomes King. The villagers seem to think that this is the natural thing to do.

Until the tourists began to come there, the inhabitants of Great Exuma, of whom there are about 4,000, supported themselves largely by farming and fishing, though in the last war there was an active U.S. naval base on the island, and in the days of piracy much use was made of George Town's harbour. The newest of the three hotels there is the Pieces of Eight, which has a swimming pool and bathing facilities on five different beaches. The Two Turtles Inn, near the village green, is small—but of a high standard, and the Club Peace and Plenty (with 32 rooms), right on the sea, is perhaps architecturally the most attractive of the three because of its period charm; part of it was once a market place for slaves, and the bar is in the original kitchen where meals were cooked for them. Apart from their other charms, these good B category hotels have unusually attractive names.

The Bahama Sound project is about ten miles north of George Town and stretches from the west to the east coast, where there is an excellent bathing beach. I was told by the English people who showed me round that there had been an enormous response to their advertisements and, oddly enough, many people from Sweden had contracted to buy land. Being shown round with me were an American couple from Florida who had bought land "on spec" and had come to see what they had bought. They seemed satisfied, but chiefly, one felt, because, first, they had always wanted to be able to say that they owned land in the Bahamas and, secondly, they had paid so little for it.

Great Exuma is an attractive island, with all the recreational facilities—bathing, boating, fishing, etc.—which one would expect. There is a daily air service from Nassau. Bahamas Acres offer good terms for refunding money to unsatisfied buyers. There is no time limit for improving or building on a property. But my advice to potential buyers of land in the Bahamas would be to go and have a look first.

San Salvador

In the opinion of most historians and geographers, it was on this island that Christopher Columbus stepped ashore on 12 October 1492. The island is about 14 miles long and six miles wide, and much of the interior is composed of lakes. It has a U.S. base and landing strip where radar and other electronic devices are used to track missiles launched from Cape Kennedy. The strip handles commercial flights from Nassau, but private aircraft owners are advised to get permission before landing. Cockburn (pronounced Coeburn) Town is the main settlement where there are some cottages and apartments for rent; but many of these are occupied by personnel from the base.

7. Some of the most beautiful beaches in the world, on Paradise Island are now connected to Nassau by an impressive 'high rise' bridge

8. Colton House at Williamstown, Little Exuma, is a good example of an early Bahamian farm house. At the right are the old slave quarters.

Three widely separated monuments supposedly mark the beach site where Columbus and his men landed. Possibly none of them is in the exact location. Oldest of them is a weathered one erected by the old *Chicaco Herald* as a promotion stunt in 1891 on a rocky point on the lonely northeast coast overlooking the Atlantic. The other two monuments, a cement cross and a stone obelisk, are placed at different points on Landing Beach, just south of the main settlement of Cockburn Town. (Columbus Day, known as Discovery Day, is a public holiday throughout the Bahamas.)

Most San Salvadorans, of whom there are about 800, continue to lead uncomplicated lives. They grow some vegetables and fruit and raise sheep and goats for meat. Tourism has yet to catch on, but fishing could bring prosperity to this island. The records of the International Game Fish Association lists more than 55 world-record catches made in Bahamian waters, and those around San Salvador are still almost virgin territory for the sportsmen.

Rum Cay

About 20 miles east of the northern tip of Long Island and accessible by boat from there, Rum Cay was originally called Santa Maria de la Conception by Columbus. It is about 10 miles long and averages four miles wide. Near the eastern end of the island is a cave containing Indian figures engraved in rock. Port Nelson is the principal settlement. The island received considerable attention in 1961-62 as a possible site for resettlement of refugees from Tristan da Cunha.

Long Island

Columbus is said to have landed on this island on 16 October 1492, and to have found the natives growing cotton, which later became well known as the Sea Island (long fibre) type.

G

The natives lived in tent-shaped dwellings with high chimneys and slept in nets stretched between posts which they called hamacs. These swinging beds were promptly adopted by Columbus's crew and have been used by sailors ever since.

Long Island is 57 miles long and 34 miles wide, measuring from a long peninsula jutting out from the west coast; but it is mostly narrow and has an area of about 130 square miles. In the eighteenth century cotton plantations brought prosperity, but became uneconomical with the abolition of slavery. Pineapples were once exported, but now farming, fishing and stock raising are the main income-producers. Caves with walls of white limestone, some 600 feet deep, are a feature of the island. A government airstrip near Deadman's Cay handles scheduled B.A.L. flights.

Near Cape Santa Maria, on the northern tip of the island, an American industrialist has developed the first resort area, the Cape Santa Maria Club, on a 2,000-acre tract of land which includes thousands of yards of beach front. A landing strip near the club is available for small planes.

Ragged Islands

The Ragged Islands range of islands, with its principal settlement of Duncan Town, is near the southeast fringe of the Great Bahama Bank. This chain of cays stretches about 110 miles from southern Long Island and can be reached only by boat. The islands are barren and windswept and the few residents are primarily seafarers. Straw work is exported to the Nassau market and some salt is produced.

Crooked Island Group

Including Crooked Island, Acklins and Fortune Island, the Crooked Island group was visited by Columbus in 1492 in the hope of finding gold. He found no gold, but apparently he thought Crooked Island was the most beautiful he had seen, and the group for some time was known as the "Fragrant Islands." Fortune Island got its name from ship wreckers who operated there. Cotton plantations prospered briefly but were abandoned in the early 1800's.

The largest of the group is Acklins Island, about 275 miles southeast of Nassau. There are no facilities for overnight visitors, but stores in the settlement have supplies and fuel for boats. The population of about 1,500 supports itself mainly by farming and fishing. These lovely islands may be reached by mail boat, private yacht or chartered amphibian plane. Shallow draft boats may cruise the waters of the Bight of Acklins where such tempting place names exist as Delectable Bay, True Blue and Lovely Bay.

Mayaguana

This is one of the few islands which has retained its original Amerindian name. It is 24 miles long and six miles at its widest, and its inhabitants farm, fish or are employed at the U.S. missile station near Abraham's Bay. The airstrip handles B.A.L. flights from Nassau, but private planes must get U.S. Air Force permission to land.

Great Inagua

Lying just off the eastern tip of Cuba and not far from Haiti's north coast, Great Inagua is the southernmost of the Bahamas and the third largest (560 square miles). It is about 34 miles long and 25 miles wide but has only about 1,200 residents. Most of the island is low and flat with a shallow lake about 12 miles long in its centre, but there are hills over 100 feet high on the north and south coasts. On the flatlands and prairies there are wild cattle, horses and donkeys, descendants of animals brought to the island many generations ago. A large flock of flamingoes, the national bird of the Bahamas, flourishes in the island under government protection.

Inagua's principle settlement, Matthew Town, has wide, well laid-out streets largely due to the fact that before the first world war it was a prosperous place where freighters, mostly German, bound for ports in the Caribbean and South America, recruited crews for the journey south and back. On their return to Matthew Town, the seamen went ashore with good money in their pockets; but the war put an end to this boom and today most Inaguans are engaged in producing salt from sea water. An American concern took over the Inagua salt production in 1934 when the Inaguans were producing only about 500 tons of salt a year. Now nearly 250,000 tons are shipped each year from Matthew Town. The firm employs about 300 men and operates a fleet of a dozen vessels. It has brought electricity, machine shops, ice-making equipment, fuel depots and supplies to the island.

Because a large part of the island is still uncharted, inaccessible by road, and virtually unexplored, there are tales of buried wealth in Great Inagua. One story has it that Henry Christophe, the famous ruler of Haiti, buried somewhere on the northeast coast of the island a massive fortune in gold and silver. Christophe Lagoon is named after him.

There are no tourist facilities in the regular sense but Matthew Town has reasonable facilities for yachtsmen. B.A.L. operates scheduled flights from Nassau and the mail boat calls regularly.

Little Inagua

About five miles northeast of Great Inagua, this low, reef-fringed island has an area of about 30 square miles. It is un-inhabited, seldom visited, but has herds of wild donkeys, goats and a wide variety of bird life.

Turks and Caicos Islands

These islands, with an estimated land area of about 166 square miles situated at the southeasterly tip of the Bahamas group had been under the administration of Jamaica since 1874, but when the Kingston government became independent from Britain in 1962 they reverted to Crown Colony status. In November, 1965, the Governor of the Bahamas became also the Governor of the Turks and Caicos, though the islands retained their own Administrator and, surprisingly enough in view of the small population (not much over 6,000), a bi-cameral legislature. Here we have an example of an eccentricity typical of the British colonial system. Theoretically, the Governor of the Bahamas should put on a different uniform when he visits these islands, but when I saw Sir Ralph Grey there in 1966 he was wearing plain clothes—a good way of avoiding the issue.

The salt industry used to be the mainstay of the Turks and Caicos Islands, but this has declined and efforts are now being directed towards developing the fishing industry and tourism. Some farming and stock raising is carried on. Yacht supplies and ice may be obtained at the capital, Cockburn Harbour, where there are also radio and cable stations and a hospital. Limited accommodation is available at the Admiral's Arms Inn. The Americans have an important tracking station there which provides some regular employment. Scheduled air services are operated by B.A.L. to and from Nassau.

THE ISLAND WHICH COLUMBUS
LOVED BEST

Hispaniola

"There in that high and mountainous country is the land of God."—Christopher Columbus

When Columbus set sail to return to Spain in January 1493, having made his first land discoveries in the western hemisphere, he is reported to have pointed to the coast of Hispaniola and to have spoken the words quoted above. He was presumably referring to the beauty of the scenery and the fertility of the soil in this northerly Caribbean island which is now divided between the Republic of Haiti and the Dominican Republic; in most other respects it could be more aptly described as the land of the devil.

Almost since its discovery Hispaniola has had a history of unhappiness and disorders, and the present-day visitor to both parts of the island has the feeling of watching a cauldron which has boiled over several times and will certainly do so again. This feeling is just as pronounced in Haiti as it is in the Dominican Republic. In Haiti the people are generally miserable, poverty-stricken and oppressed by ruthless dictatorship. In the Dominican Republic they have only recently emerged from 31 years of similar ruthlessness, and the main trouble is that they are totally lacking in experience of how to run a responsible democratic system of government.

Haiti's President, Francois Duvalier, celebrated his tenth anniversary of achieving power in September 1967, and in the preceding decade atrocities were committed by his regime which would have shocked even the most stalwart members of Hitler's Gestapo. The police-state atmosphere immediately becomes apparent when one enters the Port-au-Prince airport terminal building. First, there is the medical check for the normally required certificates of vaccination. Then, at the next counter, passports, visas, etc., are methodically examined. You

think it is all over; on the contrary, there is another group of
officials waiting further along the counter to repeat the whole
process. Next you come to what you assume is the customs
counter where the luggage from the aircraft has been waiting
for some time. Everything is opened. All literature is scrupu-
lously and tediously examined. Everything OK? Not at all;
this group was the security police. The customs are the next
group along the counter. . . .

It should be said in all fairness that this was the treatment
I got as a visiting journalist on my first visit to Haiti in 1965;
the bona fide tourist gets a warmer welcome, and conditions
at the airport have now (1967) been improved. Nevertheless,
this was a somewhat discouraging initiation into the ways of
Duvalier's Haiti, a nation of roughly four million Negro inhabitants which managed to free itself from domination by
Paris as early as 1804. Nor was it encouraging to be plunged
into total darkness that evening at the hotel when all the lights
went out; but from this I learnt one of the basic characteristics
of present-day Haiti : that it is in a state of almost complete
"run-downness". Apparently the generating plant was so old
and decrepit that it could not provide enough current to give a
continuous supply even to that small percentage of the 200,000-
odd capital city dwellers who could afford to pay for it.

This background of darkness fits well into a country which
is largely run by a 10,000-strong gang of terrorists known as
the Ton Ton Macoutes (creole for bogeyman) who bear a
relation to Duvalier similar to that which the S.S. bore to
Hitler. A difference, however is that there is not enough money
to pay the Ton Ton Macoutes, so they get what they want by
pillage. One of them, for example, decided that he wanted a
car, so he simply shot the owner of a Mercedes-Benz in broad
daylight on a Port-au-Prince street and drove away with his
prize. "This man had one of the best dental surgery practices
in town before he disappeared. . . ." "Two years ago the Ton
Ton Macoutes came to the house and took away her husband;
she has never heard of him since. . . ." "The body of their dead
child was found one night on their doorstep. . . ." One continually hears sentences of this type; or : "The Ton Ton

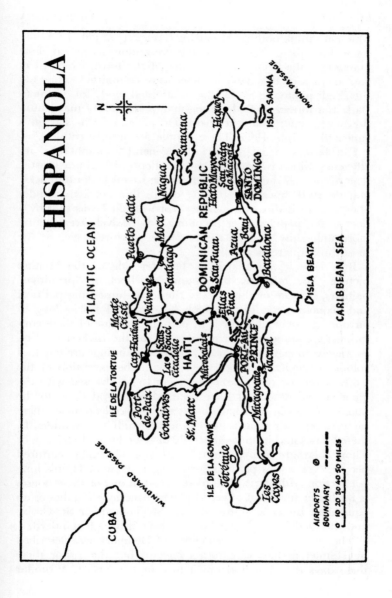

Macoutes think nothing of putting foreigners in jail. There are some fine pictures, too, in the 'reception room' at Fort Dimanche, the prison in the centre of the town, which gives you an idea of the atrocities which are committed. They are life-sized photographs of the multilated body of Clement Barbot, a former T.T.M. strong-man and killer of many hundreds who later quarrelled with Duvalier and was shot in a canefield in July 1963. These people are utterly ruthless."

Ruthlessness apart, it is Haiti's general atmosphere of inefficiency which is, perhaps, its most depressing characteristic. The telephones rarely work, cars in the streets look ramshackle and decayed, houses are falling down, thin chickens wander about, there is dirt everywhere. Worst of all, I was told by a doctor, the population is becoming progressively weaker and more unhealthy because the majority of citizens gets at the most three square meals a week.

But there is, fortunately, a brighter side of the Haitian picture. For instance, the country's school of "primitive" painters, in spite of the—to say the least—unsettling political and economic conditions which have existed for as long as anyone can remember (or is it, perhaps, because of these conditions?), continues to turn out work of the highest quality. Strangely enough, the majority of these paintings are gay and colourful, depicting happy scenes, with the exception of the work of one or two artists who seem to be obsessed with the gloom of voodooism. I have been taken several times to the houses of people who had some excellent collections of these pictures on their walls as well as to the studios of painters. In these houses and in those generally of the educated Haitian, of whom there are many, you meet the most charming, cultured people. Nor is this perhaps surprising in view of Haiti's long connection with Paris. The food served in one of these houses is far better than that offered by most American families of an equivalent financial status in, say, St. Thomas or St. Croix; and the food in the better hotels is also of a high standard.

The state—that is government—of Denmark was described by Hamlet as having a rotten flavour, but the visitor there these days does not find much to complain about. A similar change will, one feels, take place in Haiti; but it may take some time for the "wind of change" to have its effect on a country which has lived for more than a century and a half under a primitive and totally outmoded system of government.

I remember returning to my hotel one night, after having had dinner in the charming house in Petionville of a knowledgeable collector of paintings, to find the night watchman wandering about with an oil lamp; the electricity was off again and most of the town seemed to be in total darkness. I asked him how long this would last. "On ne sais jamais," he replied, shrugging his shoulders in a way which looked, for a Negro, remarkably gallic.

It is an interesting coincidence that Duvalier's counterpart in the neighbouring Dominican Republic, Rafael Leonidas Trujillo, was murdered just outside Santo Domingo (then called Ciudad Trujillo) in May 1961, at about the same time as the Haitian ruler was staging a bogus election to maintain himself in the presidency; and Haitian refugees in the Dominican Republic are at pains to emphasis the similarities in the overlapping lives of the two men, pointing out that, while it is claimed by his opponents that Trujillo killed 10% of the population of his country, Duvalier's record in this sphere (as of 1967) is not yet complete. The following description of Trujillo and his activities is taken in part from a booklet, *Things You Should Know*, by Luis Augusto Caminero (1962), because it gives a good picture of how Trujillo was regarded by citizens of the Dominican Republic who opposed —as far as they could—his ruthless authoritarian rule :

"Rafael Leonidas Trujillo Molina (1891-1961) seized power in 1930 by means of elections that were held under the terror he had imposed by his position as army commander. To remain in power he formed an army of 100,000 men whose activities were limited to the defence and protection of himself and family. While 35% of the national budget was reserved for the maintenance of the army, only seven% was assigned to the Ministry of Education. He was ambitious and conceited. He claimed that, as a leader, all titles befitted him, but that, as a man, he needed none.

"His first collective slaughter was carried out a few days after

he became President for the first time when he took advantage
of the devastating results of a hurricane on September 18, 1930,
in order to incinerate political prisoners together with the bodies
of the hurricane victims. He set up a strict watch over the whole
of the country by dividing it into 25 provinces, which were
divided into 72 communes, and these in turn into sections and
districts, so that the civilian and military authorities should have
under their charge only small areas and could effectively prevent
the outbreak of uprisings. The most important authorities were
transferred from one city to another every two or three months
to prevent any one leader from getting a foothold.

"It has not been possible yet to establish the exact number of
Dominicans who were killed under Trujillo but, according to
public opinion, 10% of the total population was involved. [In
other words, it is believed that Trujillo killed something like
300,000 people, which by any standards other than those of Hitler
or Stalin, is a fantastically high figure. In addition, Caminero
states that Trujillo ordered the killing of 20,000 Haitian residents
in the Dominican Republic in October, 1937.] Lord and master
of the 48,734 square kilometres covered by the Dominican
Republic and of the three million slaves who worked for him, he
became one of the most powerful and the wealthiest men in the
Americas. He collected for his own personal profit 10% of all
public works contracts and of public employees' salaries.

"It is said that Trujillo was responsible for the country's
progress during the 31 years of his dictatorship. To those who
make such claims I would reply that, whenever Trujillo did something, he always thought of himself first and last. Through his
fabulous fortune, estimated at more than one thousand million
U.S. dollars, not counting those of his children and other relatives,
Trujillo learnt to know the price of every man who visited him.
Not content with the internal power he possessed, or concerned
with the protests of international organisations—he had, for example, to get a henchman to pose as President as early as the
1938-42 term because of the slaughter of Haitians—the tyrant
did not cease to pry beyond the boundaries that divide humanity
and, following a series of international crimes, on August 16,
1959, the Organisation of American States (O.A.S.), at its meeting in San Jose, Costa Rica, found Trujillo guilty of attempts to
assassinate President Romulo Betancourt of Venezuala. The member nations severed diplomatic relations and imposed economic
sanctions.

"At about the same time the Catholic Church refused to bestow
on Trujillo the title of Benefactor of the Church [he had already
bestowed upon himself the titles of Benefactor of pretty well
everything else] to which the tyrant aspired as a means of offset-

ting his guilt. Highly indignant at this turn of events, he started anti-American and anti-religious campaigns which led him to the very edge of destruction. He tried to ally himself with Russia in his despair, but Russia refused to be tempted. Placed as he was in such a desperate position, he died, as his people had foretold, with his boots on. . . ."

So much for a (possibly biased) description of the man who made the Dominican Republic what it is today. Trujillo certainly did die with his boots on, but the trouble since his death has been that the mental stultification which these boots signified and symbolically created is still very much present. An incident which occurred when the republic, under the moderately able leadership of President Donald Reid Cabral, was going through a period of comparative peace and harmony four years after the tyrant's assassination, illustrates this point. I noticed that police contingents carrying fierce-looking pistols were to be seen dashing about more than was usual—even in the post-Trujillo era there seemed to be just as many armed police parading the town as during the dictator's heyday—and a local newspaperman telephoned me suggesting that we should go and have a look at what was happening. The sound of firing and explosions drew us to a street just off the main Calle El Conde and for the next twenty minutes or so we witnessed an astonishing scene.

In the street there was a large building housing one of the city's biggest secondary schools. Clouds of smoke were coming from the windows. The street in the school's immediate vicinity was deserted, but large crowds were watching at a safe distance. Suddenly three trucks full of armed, steel-helmeted police tore up to the school. As they passed the building two or three bomb-like objects were thrown through the windows and doors. There were explosions and more smoke began pouring from the building.

A little later more trucks rushed up; policemen jumped out and began running up and down the street with pistols at the ready. Some seemed to be making an attempt to enter the school; but nobody seemed to be in command or to have the slightest idea what he was supposed to be doing. Then they all

got into their trucks and rushed off again. Soon another contingent of trucks arrived and the whole process was repeated.
A few teenagers emerged from the school and were carted off
by the police (themselves little more than teenagers), but at
this moment my companion, who had been taking pictures
from rather close at hand, said : "Come on, let's go. They've
got a new sort of tear-gas which makes you vomit as well. It's
good stuff to keep away from."

But what was it all about? The answer was that the pupils
of this school were considered to be a disorderly lot. They had
staged a demonstration against the police, who, it seemed, just
felt they had to get their own back. And so resort was had to
trucks, bombs, tear-gas, pistols and all the paraphernalia normally required to quell a major revolution—all to bully and
terrorise a few school kids.

My companion and I repaired to an adjacent bar to get the
taste of the gas out of our mouths, and, from the conversation
which developed there, as well as from a later one which I had
with the well-known Dominican writer and opponent-in-exile of
Trujillo, German Ornes (then the editor of the leading daily
newspaper in Santo Domingo, *El Caribe*), it became clear
that such goings-on as we had witnessed were caused by almost
total political and administrative immaturity.

How, it was suggested to us, could this be otherwise? How
could anyone expect that things would run smoothly in the
Dominican Republic after 31 years of Trujillo rule? This period
amounts to something like an adult generation and few citizens
had any experience of a system of government other than
that imposed upon them by the dictator. If ever it was true to
say of any country that a vacuum had been created, this was—
and is—true of the Dominican Republic in the sixties decade.
The events of 1965-66 were, of course, far more tragically
serious than those of 1964, but both had the same pattern of
brutal imbecility; and the vacuum is still there.

So the present picture of Hispaniola, "the island which
Columbus loved", is of one republic (Negro and formerly
French) where ruthless dictatorship still exists, and of another
republic (of mixed stock and formerly Spanish) where right-

wing dictatorship was ousted in 1961 but where there is still every possibility that it, or its opposite, communist dictatorship, will return; in other words, the political climate is not inviting for the normal tourist. The island's generally unhappy past throws some light on its almost equally disturbed present.

HISTORY

On 5 December 1492, Columbus, sailing from Cuba, brought the *Santa Maria* to anchor in the harbour of what is now Mole St. Nicholas on the northwest coast of Haiti. He liked what he saw and christened the place Espagnola, or Little Spain; "the rivers", he wrote, "are many and big and most of them boast gold nuggets and other precious metals." Sailing along the north coast a few days later the *Santa Maria* grounded on a reef near Cap Haitien and became a total wreck. Having transferred his flag to the *Nina*, Columbus sailed on in company with the *Pinta* and, anchoring for a while in what is now Samana Bay on the northeast coast of the Dominican Republic, arrived back in Spain on 15 March 1493, having left a small party on the island to establish a colony. The troubled history of Hispaniola had begun.

When Columbus first arrived the island was inhabited by some two million Arawaks; 25 years later all but about 5,000 had been exterminated. When Columbus returned to Hispaniola on his second voyage later in 1493 he ordered the construction of the township of La Isabela (near the present Puerto Plata) and it was there that, on 6 January 1494, the first Mass was celebrated in the New World; in April the first Town Council in the New World was set up; and so, among the many "firsts" which Hispaniola can claim, are the massacre of natives by Europeans and the introduction of European religious beliefs and civic customs. (More than four and a half centuries later another "first" could be claimed from the fact that a dictator had managed to keep himself in power for as long as 31 years.) In 1496, following reports that the southern part of the island was richer in gold than the northern, the Spaniards moved to the western bank of the Ozama River

H

and founded the city of Santo Domingo de Guzman. The ruins of La Isabela are still to be seen, but the citizens of Santo Domingo have every right to claim that they live in the first permanent European settlement in the western hemisphere. Because the Arawaks were becoming fewer and fewer and because they were disinclined anyway to work for the Spaniards, Negro slaves were imported to the New World from Africa for the first time in 1505 and the original settlers in Hispaniola can thus claim to be the originators of the racial troubles which beset the United States in the sixties.

Seeds of decay, or rather stagnation, were already visible, however, in Hispaniola in the first half of the sixteenth century; it became more than anything else—Columbus's "gold nuggets" were not so plentiful after all—a jumping-off place from which the Spaniards went to colonise and exploit the rest of the New World. It remained for many years the official headquarters of Spanish rule in the western hemisphere, and it was during the sixteenth century that most of the best buildings and churches were constructed in Santo Domingo; but it was all little more than a "shopwindow". A series of incompetent Governors let the colony decay; in 1564 there was a devastating earthquake; in 1586 Santo Domingo was sacked by Sir Francis Drake; and in 1655 it was attacked by a force sent out from England by Oliver Cromwell. It became something of a ghost town.

Meanwhile, adventurers from France and England had been settling in the western part of the island, and in 1697, following several fierce engagements, Spain ceded that part to France. In the course of the next hundred years, while the Spanish section of Hispaniola fell more and more into oblivion (there were only 6,000 people living there in 1730) the French developed their section, which they called Saint-Domingue, into the most prosperous and lucrative European colony in the hemisphere. Shiploads of slaves were poured in to develop the new sugar, coffee, cacao and indigo estates, and by the second half of the eighteenth century the 500,000 Negro slaves outnumbered the French by about twenty to one; the seeds of further trouble in Hispaniola had been sown and the harvest was to be reaped as a result of the French Revolution of 1789.

The situation in Saint-Domingue was made even more explosive by the presence of a third racial factor : the mulattoes, or *affranchis*—that is people of mixed French and Negro blood, many of whom had become wealthy landowners—were resentful of the scornful way in which they were treated by the whites and which they considered to be wholly out of tune with the new principles of liberty, equality and fraternity. In 1791, therefore, when the Negro slaves revolted, the mulattoes joined them, intending to use the uprising as a means of getting control of the territory; and, in their turn, the whites tried to play the Negroes off against the mulattoes. Neither the whites nor the mulattoes were successful and the upshot was a mass butchering of landowners and burning of their estates. Hispaniola—the whole island was ceded by the Spanish to the French by the Treaty of Basle in 1795—now entered into its most fantastic period of history dominated by three remarkable Negro men : Toussaint l'Ouverture, Jean Jacques Dessalines and Henry (not Henri) Christophe.

Toussaint had established himself as leader of the successfully rebellious slaves and he soon became absolute ruler of the whole island, even driving out a British force which had arrived to protect "national interests". He was appointed military commander-in-chief by the Paris government and, in 1801, he set up a constitutional form of government under which he was to be President for life. Saint-Domingue prospered under his leadership and even the former slaves worked contentedly on the plantations in the interests of the territory as a whole. Toussaint showed tolerance and skill in ruling over the former Spanish part of the island. He became a figure with a worldwide reputation, but this did not please the First Consul, Napoleon Bonaparte, in Paris, who, in 1802 sent a large expeditionary force to Hispaniola commanded by his brother-in-law, General Leclerc. Toussaint was beguiled into accepting an "honourable" capitulation but at a subsequent parley with Leclerc he was seized and sent to imprisonment in France, where he died the following year.

The Negroes, infuriated at this treachery, went on fighting under the leadership of Dessalines who, together with Christophe, had been one of Toussaint's commanders. The French forces were defeated and evacuated the island; in 1804 Dessalines declared Saint-Domingue to be an independent state, having slaughtered every white French man, woman and child he could lay his hands on. He had himself crowned Emperor of the rechristened country of Haiti and ruled tyrannically, but efficiently, for two years. He was murdered, probably by a group of mulattoes, in 1806. Henry Christophe was the logical successor to Dessalines but the mulattoes were determined not to fall once again under the domination of a Negro ex-slave, so they grouped themselves under an educated *affranchi*, Alexandre Petion, with the result that the country was split in half, the Petion faction dominating the Port-au-Prince area and the south while Christophe ruled the north as King Henry the First. Apart from the megalomania which caused him to build a palace, Sans Souci, to create titles of nobility, and to construct the fantastic—and costly in human lives—Citadelle La Ferrière, Christophe was evidently a man of astonishingly commanding personality who could inspire loyalty and get people to work hard. His main ambition was to make Haiti rich and its people prosperous and educated. Towards the end of his 14-year rule, however, his supporters began deserting him to serve under Petion in the south—a less exacting way of life, no doubt—and in 1820 he shot himself. So ended a remarkable chapter in the history of Hispaniola.

In the meantime, in 1809, the French—or rather the Haitians—in Santo Domingo were defeated by the British and the eastern part of the island once again became Spanish; inevitably, for the next thirteen years it went through a period of misrule and almost total neglect. For a few months in 1821 and 1822 it actually became affiliated, for no apparent reason, with the Republic of Gran Columbia. Then, in 1822, the mulatto who had succeeded Christophe and Petion, Jean-Pierre Boyer, sent an army to occupy Santo Domingo, and for the next twenty-two years the whole of Hispaniola was once again unified under the name of Haiti; it was a period of anarchy

and chaos as far as the eastern part was concerned; the
Spanish planters mostly left and agriculture virtually ceased;
there was no police force to maintain order; the Negro army
of occupation did more or less what it pleased; morality,
according to one contemporary report, was in a "low stage . . .
marriage is scarcely thought of. . . ."

In 1843 Boyer was driven out by a revolution (shortly afterwards Santo Domingo broke away) and for the next three-
quarters of a century chaos reigned in the western part of
Hispaniola, or Haiti, until it was occupied by United States
Marines in 1915. One President after another was assassinated;
anarchy and bankruptcy were the country's lot; slaughter and
blood baths were the tools of politics. There was, however, one
comic opera period—perhaps tragic opera would be a better
description—when a Negro called Faustin Soulouque got himself elected President in 1847 and declared himself to be the
Emperor Faustin the First. He reigned for ten nightmare years,
creating, like his predecessor on the "throne", Henry Christophe, a noble hierarchy of princes, dukes and barons. Corruption, fanatical voodooism and gestapoism were the order
of the day; and they have largely persisted ever since in Haiti.

Despite the efforts of a remarkable man of Spanish descent,
Juan Pablo Duarte, the eastern part of Hispaniola also followed the path of misrule and disorder. This young man—he
was born in 1813—had the qualities of asceticism and, almost,
of sainthood. In 1838, he and some associates founded a society
called "La Trinitaria", the purpose of which was to free Santo
Domingo of Haitian rule. He was forced to flee to Venezuela
in 1842; and the revolutionary movement was left in the hands
of his two principal associates, Francisco Sanchez and Ramon
Mella. On 27 February 1844, these two leaders staged a *coup
d'etat*, ousting the Haitian rulers and setting up an independent Dominican Republic. Duarte, who had spear-headed the
independence movement, returned in triumph from Venezuela
the following month and a governing triumvirate was formed.
It was agreed that free elections to the presidency should be
held, in which Duarte would inevitably be successful; but
already there were signs that the young Dominican Republic

was not destined to enjoy constitutional democratic rule. The commander of the army in the south, Pedro Santana, marched on the capital (shades of 1965!) and proclaimed himself ruler. Duarte, Sanchez and Mella were arrested and expelled from the country. The Dominican Republic, like its neighbour, Haiti, had embarked on the road of dictatorial rule, crime and disorder.

From 1845 to 1860, during most of which time the lunatic "Emperor" Faustin was ruling in the western part of Hispaniola, the government in Santo Domingo alternated between Santana and a man of similar ambition to rule, Buenaventura Baez. The territory became poorer and poorer and the people more and more miserable. By 1861—Santana was then at the helm—a move necessitated by total bankruptcy was made which was contrary to all the contemporary trends in New World Spanish possessions to free themselves from rule by Madrid : the Dominican Republic handed itself over to the autocratic rule of Queen Isabela the Second of Spain. The "wind of change", such a feature of colonial affairs in the second part of the twentieth century, had in this case started in the nineteenth century by blowing in the opposite direction. Spanish rule in Santo Domingo, however, proved to be nothing more than a fiasco and, following an insurrection, the Madrid government decided to withdraw its troops and get out in 1864. Santana, who was responsible for it all, died the same year, but Baez was still very much on the scene and a further decade of misrule followed, including an attempt, in 1869, to hand the country over to the United States. (Congress in Washington would have nothing to do with it.) Insurrection followed insurrection, Baez was finally disposed of in 1878, and from 1879 to 1899 the country was ruled by a Negro who rejoiced in the name of Ulises Heureux and who had the same ruthless gestapo tendencies as his later successor, the dictator Trujillo. Heureux met the common death of Dominican dictators when he was shot in 1899.

Further disorders followed until, in 1916, the United States Marines stepped in, having taken over in the equally chaotic Haiti a few months previously. Apart altogether from the issue

of safeguarding financial interests, President Wilson was about
to lead the U.S. into the first world war as an ally of the British
and French and he could not afford to leave Hispaniola in a
disturbed state subject, possibly, to exploitation by the Ger-
mans. (One or two U-boats did actually arrive at Port-au-
Prince.) There is an analogy here with the purchase by the
United States of the Danish Virgin Islands in 1917 (see
page 185) and there is a further analogy between the official
communique describing the purposes of United States intervention in Santo Domingo in 1916 with statements made by
Washington at the time of the 1965 intervention : "It is not
the intention of the United States Government," announced
the U.S. Admiral commanding in 1916, "to acquire by con-
quest any territory in the Dominican Republic nor to attack
its sovereignty, but our troops will remain here until all revolutionary movements have been stamped out and until such
reforms as are deemed necessary to insure the future welfare
of the country have been initiated and are in effective operation."

United States forces remained in Haiti from 1915 to 1934
and in the Dominican Republic from 1916 to 1924. Order and
solvency—with financial aid—were restored to both countries.
In the Dominican Republic elections for the presidency were
held in March 1924, and General Horatio Vasquez, a man,
like Duarte, of sound and honest democratic convictions, was
elected. The last contingent of U.S. Marines left the following
September. Once again, however, democratic principles were
not to survive long in the Dominican Republic, and in August
1930, General Rafael Leonidas Trujillo Molina, then army
Chief of Staff, and, ironically enough, trained to some extent
under U.S. military supervision, got himself elected to the
Presidency by a rigged ballot and ruled, whether as President
or as the power behind the scenes, for the next 31 years. In
Haiti, after the Marines left in 1934 (the U.S. continued to
administer the customs till 1941), there was a series of more or
less violent revolutions up to the time Duvalier took charge in
1957.

It used to be said of Benito Mussolini that he was a good

ruler because he made the trains of the Italian State Railways run on time. In a similar sense Trujillo can be described as a good ruler of the Dominican Republic. He made the country solvent; he gave it a modern road network, water supply and electricity; he enormously improved dock facilities and built a modern international airport; he built several million-dollar hotels; he made the sugar industry so efficient that it brought in some $50 million annually, or nearly 50% of the country's exports; he revitalised the coffee, cocoa and tobacco industry; he built schools and hospitals; if there had been a railway in the Dominican Republic, one can be certain that it would have been efficient and punctual. But money for development was for the most part obtained by high indirect taxation which hit the poor far more than the rich. Far more even than Jamaica, the Dominican Republic was a country of "Haves" and "Have-nots", and Trujillo himself, plus his large family, got their cuts of pretty well all businesses, including prostitution. The regime relied on at least half a dozen security and spying agencies and several of the prisons had torture cells. It was a police state par excellence. It is, nevertheless, a fact of history that several prominent United States citizens lauded Trujillo during his heyday.

The dictator met his end on the night of 30 May 1961, when he was driving from Santo Domingo to his estate near San Cristobal. Not far from the city his chauffeur-driven car was intercepted by two carloads of armed men, and Trujillo died with twenty-seven bullets in his body. A bloodbath inevitably followed. Though President Joaquin Belaguer, then a comparatively moderate supporter of Trujillo, was nominally in charge, the dictator's two brothers, Hector and Arismendi, and his son, Ramfis, who was in command of the armed forces, did everything they could to preserve the family heritage. Crisis followed crisis. The people, making use of their new-found opportunity to air their views, made it quite clear that they did not consider that either Belaguer or his successor, Rafael Bonnelly, were making a serious effort to liberalise the political and economic life of the country or to get rid of "Trujilloism". This expression of feeling gathered momentum, emergent political parties gained strength, the constitution was redrafted, the remaining members of the Trujillo family were forced to leave the country, and finally, free presidential elections were held in December 1962, which resulted in a victory for Juan Bosch, a scholarly writer and professor with left-of-centre views who had long been living in exile. He was a failure almost from the start.

In September 1963, the seemingly inevitable pattern of Dominican politics took charge and Bosch was ousted because, in the view of the right-wingers and even of some responsible moderates, he was, whether he knew it not, handing over the country to communism. "If only," a prominent Santo Domingo businessman told me at this time, "Bosch had had the talent and persistent ability of Venezuela's Betancourt, who faced similar problems in his country when it was suddenly pitchforked into democracy after years of dictatorship, things would have been very different. The truth is Bosch just had to be got rid of if his country was to avoid chaos. He left the door wide open for every type of exile to come back—communists, Castroites, subversive elements of all types. Communist cells were being established everywhere, even in the schools. He was also hopelessly inefficient as an administrator."

In Bosch's place a triumvirate of generally worthy administrators, by no means unduly right-wing, was put in power with the backing of the military. One of their tasks was to rewrite the constitution once again and prepare the country for another election, which was to have been held in 1965. The three original triumvirate members soon resigned, largely through a feeling of frustration at not being able to get anything done because of the persistent rivalry and bickering of the politicians and the military—and pretty well everybody else. This left Donald Reid Cabral, whose father was a Scot and who joined the triumvirate in December 1963, in sole charge. He showed himself to be, possibly, the ablest of all the men who have sought to run the Dominican Republic's affairs since Trujillo's extinction, but the task he faced of educating the people politically was too much even for him, and he was not helped by the fact that strong left-wing forces were at work which sought to thwart any move towards political education. At this time there were no less than three open and official Communist parties in the Dominican Republic—the Fourteenth of July Movement, the Partido Socialista Popular, and the Movimento Popular Dominicana. In addition there was a "fellow-travelling" group, the Agrupacion Politica 20 de Octobre.

A good picture of the immediate background to the 1965 uprising is given in a booklet called "Dominican Action—1965" published by the Center For Strategic Studies, Georgetown University, Washington, D.C. Here is a brief quotation :

"The unrest had roots that were economic, political and personal. From the Trujillo era the nation had inherited deep-seated personal hatreds that will persist for years. From the short régime of Juan Bosch there stemmed labor problems that grew in magnitude as the world price of sugar dropped far below the cost of production in the Dominican Republic. And, finally, Reid's attempts at austerity offended many Dominicans as he struggled to solve economic problems that were beyond his control. Reid had been particularly hard on the armed forces, closing their post exchanges and shutting off the lucrative smuggling rackets that had been a prerogative of the military officers. By these actions he split his own support. And there was a growing suspicion, though unsubstantiated, that Reid had no intention of allowing the Dominican people to go to the polls in September, 1965, to elect a constitutional President.

"In the period of increasing unrest among the groups to the right and left, the Moscow, Peking and Havana leaders found a situation ripe for action. They had watched for opportunities in the Caribbean. They were training potential agitators and discontented Dominicans in Moscow, Havana and elsewhere. Two important articles in the 'World Marxist Review' (December 1965, and January 1966) recounted the earlier planning and showed the direction of Communist thinking. These articles contain a manifesto of 16 March 1965, which describes the 'Eve of Explosion' :

'Bosch should be returned to power through popular action, and not through compromise with the enemies of the people. The return of Bosch on the basis of mass actions signifies not only the restoration of the national dignity and sovereignty of the people. It will signify above all an extremely important step towards uniting the forces which will lead the Dominican people to complete liberation. At present the struggle for the fulfilment of this task must be headed by the Dominican working class—

the only class capable of leading the people as a whole and heading the struggle for their supreme objectives.

Therefore the Popular Socialist Party calls on the working class and the people as a whole to launch a struggle for the return of President Bosch to the post of head of the legitimate government of the Republic on the basis of the democratic gains recorded in the 1963 constitution. Fight in the streets, squares, factories and in the countryside for the return of President Bosch as head of the constitutional government!'

"Earlier, in November 1964, a secret meeting of Latin American Communist parties was held in Havana. The only indication at that time of the proceedings of that conference was in a vague communique released by Tass [the Soviet news agency] in January, 1965. This statement reaffirmed the duty of Communists everywhere to support 'the national liberation struggle', including the struggle in the Dominican Republic. Subsequently, the radio propaganda attacks against Reid emanating from Communist countries, notably from Cuba, became increasingly inflammatory. The stirring of a Communist-style 'people's revolution' became increasingly evident. . . . On 24 April 1965, the violence of the revolt engulfed Reid, and Santo Domingo's ordeal began."

What followed is still more in the realm of current events than history. On 25 April Reid was forced to resign the presidency when it became clear that the army would not support him against an assorted group of revolutionaries, including communists, who had initiated street riots demanding Bosch's return. (Bosch was then in neighbouring Puerto Rico.) In the next two or three days some 2,500 people lost their lives as a result of the total collapse of law and order and the wild street fighting which ensued. The trouble was that the senior army officers, while generally agreeing that Bosch must go, were not agreed about who his successor should be, and this left the door wide open for the various communist groups to take charge of the revolutionary movement; Santo Domingo and its environs became the scene of almost total anarchy. The upshot was that, on 28 April, President Johnson announced over national television in Washington that a force of 400 Marines (later considerably increased) had landed in the Dominican Republic to protect the lives of Americans and other non-Dominicans. More than 5,000 people, including British and French, were evacuated. The Organisation of

American States, prodded by Washington, got into the act two days later and an International American Peace Force was formed which began arriving in the Dominican Republic towards the end of the first week in May to restore order and supervise a cease-fire. There were more than 1,000 Brazilian troops and smaller units from Paraguay, Costa Rica, Nicaragua and Honduras, and the whole force, including United States troops, by then numbering about 14,000, was under the command of a Brazilian general. This was undoubtedly one of the most significant developments in Caribbean affairs which has taken place this century, and the Brazilian Ambassador to the O.A.S. is on record as having stated that the U.S. intervention had saved the Dominican Republic from chaos and communist domination.

On 3 September—it took as long as this to restore any semblance of order—a provisional government was set up headed by Hector Garcia-Godoy, a more or less neutral diplomat and businessman, and in January the following year rebel and other controversial military officers were despatched overseas to various posts in order to ease tension and prepare for free elections which were to be held under O.A.S. supervision on 1 June 1966. Bosch, Belaguer and other political leaders returned to the country and started campaigning furiously. The upshot was that Belaguer, as leader of the Reformist Party, defeated Bosch and his Dominican Revolutionary Party by 769,265 votes to 525,230. It seemed to be a victory for the moderates and an indication that the citizens of the Dominican Republic wanted peace and quiet. Belaguer was installed in July and the last of the U.S. troops left on 20 September; ever since there have been rumours of impending coups.

At the end of 1966, nevertheless, the Dominican Republic was being governed by constitutionally elected authority. How near it came, however, to being engulfed in communist dictatorship is made clear in a book published in November of that year by the U.S. Ambassador in Santo Domingo, Mr. John Martin, who was very close to these historic events. He says Castro had schemed ever since Trujillo's demise "to seize control of the capital's streets, the first step in the classic Marxist revolutionary pattern". Francisco Caamano Reno, the damagogue colonel who led the revolt, "had few political advisers in Santo Domingo at that time but Communists." General Elias Wessyn y Wessin, says Martin, was the man who helped U.S. troops to beat the Reds, despite his failings.

As of late 1967 it is not possible to forecast a peaceful future for the historically disturbed and embattled Dominican Republic, one reason for this being that the vast quantity of arms distributed by the Communists to the people in the early days of the 1965 revolt has not been recovered; the country is still explosive in both the literal and symbolic sense. Nor does the immediate future look much surer for the island of Hispaniola as a whole. Haiti, under Duvalier, has been virtually at daggers drawn with the Dominican Republic since 1963 when an incident occurred which is worth recording because it illustrates graphically how totally the two nations are out of tune with late twentieth century political thought—how, indeed, they are anachronisms in the Caribbean area where the other territories, whether still occupying some sort of colonial status or having become independent nations, are making rapid progress in peaceful economic and political development. In April that year there was a shooting affair in Port-au-Prince—one of several directed at unseating Duvalier—after which members of the Haitian army and the Ton Ton Macoutes tried to storm the Dominican Republic's embassy in order to capture people taking refuge there who were believed to be responsible. This led to threats and counter-threats, to some abortive fighting on the frontier and to the breaking off of diplomatic relations; but the significant thing is that President Bosch, then in the midst of his brief rule in Santo Domingo, said he would send the Dominican air force to bomb Duvalier's palace. It is hard to imagine anything savouring more of a totally outmoded nineteenth-century "Balkan" attitude to foreign affairs.

Another factor militating against a peaceful future in Hispaniola is the presence in the Dominican Republic of almost all the active opposition to Duvalier; and I had the pleasure of meeting in Santo Domingo the leader (so he said) of an "army" of some 500 Haitian exiles who were ready to cross the border and attack. The crates of food to be seen stored in his house were supposedly sent to him by "friends in the States" to support his impoverished armada. This sort of thing, though it looks absurd in print, is both true and typical of the attitude and outlook of many of the inhabitants of Hispaniola. The Strategic Studies publication quoted above ends by saying of the situation in the Dominican Republic : "The future will require statesmanship in the United States, in the O.A.S., in the Dominican Republic. The legacy of a troubled past remains." So it does in Haiti.

*   *   *

Both from the historic point of view and because of its recent and present disturbed political condition the two countries which make up the island of Hispaniola essentially constitute a descriptive enity; but their economic patterns and their features of interest to the visitor are dissimilar, so the two countries are treated separately in the second section of this chapter.

Haiti
"I rise again from my ashes."—Henry Christophe

ECONOMY

For a country of its size Haiti has an astonishingly small budget of about $30 million annually, and its annual export-import pattern is of the order of $45 million. Hardly anybody earns more than $55 or $60 a month, though there is a small elite class with money abroad whose women get their clothes in Paris and whose children are educated in France.

The backbone of the economy is agriculture, and the livelihood of the country depends on the production of the main agricultural products which are exported. The principal crops are coffee, sugar-cane, sisal, bananas and cotton. Of these the most important is coffee, which normally accounts for some 50% by value of the whole of Haiti's exports, and provides, by virtue of an export tax, an appreciable proportion of total revenue receipts.

There are two textile mills, a pharmaceutical plant, a tannery, a cement factory, two shoe factories, a flour mill and a paint factory. There are also small plants for manufacturing nails, aluminium and enamel household ware, and a plastics plant which makes buttons, combs, toothbrushes and ceramic type tiles. The most important industrial plants in the country are the Haitian-American Sugar Corporation at Port-au-Prince, the five sisal decorticating plants, of which one is American-Haitian-Government owned and operated and the others American owned and operated, and the two compound lard and cotton-seed meal plants at Port-au-Prince. Haiti's principal imports are cotton goods, flour, petroleum products, iron and steel manufactures, motor vehicles, chemical and pharmaceutical products.

The currency is the gourde, though the U.S. dollar is universally used.

SIGHTSEEING

In the decade of the sixties Haiti has been going through, to put it mildly, a difficult time, and it could be that in the next decade it will present a much more attractive picture to the visitor than the one which I have had to present. With that proviso in mind, it is perhaps fair to begin by saying that Port-au-Prince is generally a depressing place from the sightseeing point of view. A good place to start is the Champs de Mars, which is roughly in the centre of the town. This is a square, or small park, dominated by the Palais National, a large white building of reasonably pleasant "modern classical" (it was built in 1918) architectural style, where the President is supposed to live and conduct state business. Armed soldiers stand on guard at all the gates in the iron railings which surround it and give it the air of being a grim fortress rather than the official residence of a Head of State. Nearby are various government buildings and the headquarters of the army, or Garde d'Haiti; and surveying it all are the statues of Haitian heroes —Dessalines, Christophe and Petion; that of Toussaint L'Ouverture is actually in the adjoining Place which bears his name. The National Museum on the Champs de Mars contains some mildly interesting exhibits mostly connected with Haitian history, and it could be that the anchor which, it is claimed, came from Columbus's flagship, the *Santa Maria*, is the genuine article—unlike the several others which are on show in various Caribbean territories—because the *Santa Maria* was, after all, wrecked on the Haitian coast.

Just off the Champs de Mars to the north is one of the most interesting sights in Port-au-Prince, the Anglican, or Episcopal, Cathedral of the Holy Trinity. It is perhaps significant, and a hopeful sign for Haiti's future, that this denomination, led by an American Bishop, has come to have an influence in Haiti out of all proportion to its numerical size both in the sphere of education and in that of trying, in general, to wean Haitians from their superstitiously ignorant outlook at the same time as encouraging the better aspects of their traditional way of life. As part of this policy they commissioned some years ago a group of talented local artists to paint a series of murals in the cathedral; and this is easily the most outstanding contemporary work of its type in the whole Caribbean. The four murals surrounding the apse prove that the Haitian primitive school is still one of the most striking movements in modern painting; and it is a good idea, having seen these murals, to go to the nearby Centre d'Art, the official headquarters of the movement, where there is a first-class collection of paintings and sculpture.

From there the Old Iron Market is within easy walking distance. This is a fantastic edifice, presumably built round the turn of the century when it was fashionable in Europe to use iron for construction and "oriental" decorative motifs—in this case two "minarets." Inside there are hundreds of stalls and more hundreds of vendors selling every conceivable product. It is fun to watch and listen to the bargaining and haggling which goes on. Walk back from the market through the grounds of the International Exposition which was opened in December, 1949, on a cleared slum area and where there are now some impressive modern buildings housing government departments, shops and offices, plus an attractive fountain in the main plaza. The words "cleared slum area" are important because in the walk from the Palais National to the Exposition Grounds you cannot fail to notice many uncleared sum areas; and you have been walking in the centre of the town. The truth is that a great part of Port-au-Prince is little more than a vast, dirty, shanty town. The area between the Old Iron Market and the airport is squalor and poverty personified. Even parts of the two or three main streets are little more than tropical slums. You enter a comparatively new air-conditioned café obviously built near the Exposition Grounds to accommodate tourists; nobody is there except a drab, disconsolate waiter sprawling asleep over the bar, and the crowd of beggars in the street outside reminds one of displaced persons thronging the streets of German towns after the war.

Anyway, you are now in the smartest area of the town and should continue your walk southward along the Boulevard President Truman past the casino and the Beau Rivage Hotel to the Theatre de Verdure, an open-air theatre where good local actors and dance groups perform, and the neighbouring Gaguere cockfighting arena. Adjacent also are two museums. Beyond this point the road continues along the coast to the new resort and residential area which, let it be emphasised again, contrasts starkly with the city's general run-down decrepitude and sluminess.

An easy and worthwhile drive to make from Port-au-Prince is that to Petionville, about six miles southeast and situated 1,500 feet up on the mountain slopes. For most of the way you drive on what is supposed to be a modern highway, but perhaps the less said about its modernity the better; its most prominent feature seems, anyway, to be entirely ancient—a stream of women walking into town to market with baskets on their heads. The Petionville neighbourhood is where many of the richer Haitians and foreigners, mostly Americans, have their villas and where there are two or three good hotels. The town has a pleasant enough little square and the general impression is that it is much cleaner than Port-au-Prince. I was told that there is quite an active night life, but it was particularly interesting to be shown round a former nightclub, the Bacalou, which had been converted by an architectural (and spiritual) tour de force into a church, St. James the Just. This again is an instance of the remarkable work being done by the Anglican community; the dance-floor became the sanctuary, the bar the sacristy, the cloak-room the baptistry, and the orchestra platform the pulpit. It is a church "in the round," with the altar in the middle. Four adjacent bedrooms (formerly used for you-can-guess-what type of business) were transformed into offices for the Church's diocesan headquarters. The priest who showed me round was justifiably proud of what had been accomplished in little more than a month. And I went away thinking that perhaps this sort of thing, even more than United States aid, was what is needed to lift Haiti from its state of abysmal ignorance, poverty and unhappiness.

From Petionville it is worthwhile going further up the road to the village of Kenscoff (how did it get this un-French name?), roughly 5,000 feet up in the mountains. This is a popular resort, but its main attraction to the tourist is the fact that it is the centre of the flower-growing industry, and it is a sight indeed to see the acres of radiant blooms, from sweet peas to poinsettias and bougainvilleas, which are grown there and shipped by air mostly to North America. The market gardeners of the area add to Kenscoff's attractions by obligingly displaying their wares in a "market" on the hillside slopes. Having got as far as this you might as well drive to the end of the road, 2,000 ft. higher up, at the village of Furcy where you get a magnificent view both of the Baie de Port-au-Prince to the northwest, and to the southeast the area dominated by Mont La Selle, which rises to nearly 9,000 ft. and is Haiti's highest peak. You have to return to Port-au-Prince the way you came.

It would be a pity, having got to Haiti, if you did not make the trip to Cap Haitien on the north coast, and easily the best way to do this is by one of the scheduled flights operated by

the local airline, the Compagnie Haitienne de Transports
Aeriens, or C.O.H.A.T.A. (It is, in fact, the army.) You can go
by road but it takes about five hours and, unless you are a
dedicated tourist determined to see all aspects of Haitian
country life, it is simplest to settle for the 45 minutes air
journey. Cap Haitien is full of history, dating back even to
Columbus who was wrecked nearby in the *Santa Maria*. It
was the leading city (then called Cap Francois) and one of
the most prosperous and elegant cities in the Caribbean during
the days of French rule. Toussaint L'Ouverture, Dessalines
and Henry Christophe walked its streets; Napoleon's sister,
Pauline Bonaparte, built a palace there. Most of the old colonial
buildings, however, were demolished by an earthquake in 1842,
though the cathedral still stands, and there is an interesting
array of nineteenth-century "gingerbread" houses. In the early
fifties the government spent some money on bringing the city
to life again; and it now has paved streets, sewerage, a pleasing modern waterfront and other facilities, including reasonable hotel accommodation which could be described as modern
in antique Haiti.

To get from Cap Haitien to what are probably the two most
astonishing man-made sights in the Caribbean you drive about
20 miles to the village of Milot where Henry Christophe, feeling, doubtless, like Frederick the Great of Prussia, that he
needed a residence to rival the French Bourbons' Versailles,
built himself the palace of Sans Souci. With the exception
of the restored chapel, with its interesting, almost Muscovite,
conical dome, the building, which was four stories high and
covered an area of about 20 acres, is now magnificently ruined.
This is how one writer on Haiti, Blair Niles, described it:

"To reach the palace we pass between the huge columns of
the gateway. There are sentry-boxes to guard the entrance,
but in the boxes there stand no soldiers, and the gate itself is
gone. We cross a dirty unkempt courtyard to the foot of a
great stairway, and there two more empty sentry-boxes permit
us to pass on unchallenged. We climb to the landing where
in front of the basin of a fountain the grand staircase divides,
with again two sentry-boxes to protect the long flights. Above

the fountain on the landing the great façade of the front rises
in a beauty of arched panels and arched entrances and columns
in half-relief; with, stepped back from the centre section, the
main body of the building, whose arched doorways multiply
themselves in seductive repetition. The staircase mounts to the
palace and to the terrace, and lovely is the line and the delicate
moulding of the balustrade. Under the graceful stairway are
dungeons with iron gratings, but the dungeons are empty and
grass grows on the steps of the staircase."

Another Haitian expert, Selden Rodman, wrote : "We pray
that it will remain untouched in its crumbling golden glory."
It almost certainly will if only because the Haitian government has not got the money to spend on its reconstruction; and
so the visitor can give free rein to his imagination in picturing
the Emperor Christophe receiving in the palace's richly decorated rooms the quaintly named members of his court—His
serene Highness the Prince du Limbe, His Excellency the
Count de la Tasse, the Duke de Limonade, the Duke de Mar-
malade. One is free to wonder also whether Christophe did
not have a highly developed sense of humour, though the
thousands of enslaved labourers who built the palace doubtless
did not think so.

Having pondered over this truly remarkable ruin you should
proceed on muleback or horseback—you can walk but it is a
very steep climb—for about two hours to an even more fabulous memorial to Christophe, the Citadelle La Ferrière which
was built between 1804 and 1817 (also by enforced labour)
on the highest peak, known as the Bishop's Bonnet, of the
mountain range overlooking Cap Haitien. The story goes
that 200,000 Haitians, men, women and children, were con-
scripted by Christophe to build this colossal and, as it turned
out, utterly useless chunk of masonry; 20,000 or more are
believed to have lost their lives in doing so. Enough stone
had to be brought up some 3,000 feet to build walls 12 feet
thick and, in places, 140 feet high; cannons, mortars, gunpowder and every requirement for 15,000 men to withstand
a siege of a year or more had to be man-handled up the
mountain side. The only thing in the Caribbean remotely

approaching the Citadelle in scale—arsenals, stores, barracks, cisterns, forges, elaborate quarters for the Emperor, and so on—is the fort on Brimstone Hill in St. Kitts, but even this is not nearly such a compactly massive structure.

You go up a stone staircase to the topmost battlements and a vast parade ground from which, so the story goes, Christophe, in order to impress a foreign visitor, ordered a detachment of his soldiers to "quick march" over the side to their death many hundreds of feet below. Unlike Brimstone Hill, not a shot was ever fired in anger from the Citadelle which was built by Christophe to make sure that the French would never again rule Haiti. They never did; instead, the tragic and useless madness of this mammoth stone bastion came to an end when, in 1820, Christophe shot himself in his equally mad palace of Sans Souci and his body was carried up the mountain to be buried in quick lime (to save it from angry mobs) in the upper court of the Citadelle. The inscription on the tomb reads (translated from the French): "Here lies Henry Christophe born 6 October 1767, died 20 October 1820, whose motto was : 'I rise again from my ashes'." In the meantime Duvalier and his Ton Ton Macoutes have provided a reasonable substitute in the realm of authoritarian ruthlessness.

There are several other places in Haiti which the dauntless tourist can visit. The town of Gonaives, for instance, nearly 100 miles along the coast northward from Port-au-Prince, is historically noteworthy because it was from there that Dessalines proclaimed Haiti's independence from France in 1804. Les Cayes, about the same distance on the south coast of the southern peninsular, has the distinction of being the place where President Abraham Lincoln had the idea in 1862 of starting a colony of freed slaves. (The people he had in mind can perhaps consider themselves lucky that nothing ever came of this project.) Another distinction it can claim is that the great Latin American liberator, Simon Bolivar, stayed there for a while in 1815 when he was forced to flee from what is now Venezuela. Jacmel, once a prosperous coffee port on the south coast, has a nostalgic past but a decrepit present; and the beach nearby is nothing like as good as it is made out to be by the tourist people. From the scenic rather than the historical point of view a trip to the Bassin Zim waterfall, about 30 miles beyond the town of Hinche in the central plain, is worthwhile. The water cascades in a wild setting a hundred feet or more into a supposedly bottomless pool; and there are caves nearby with pre-Columbian carvings. But the hotel and tourist people are the best sources for information on these places and how to get to them. My own view is that the best way to travel in Haiti, except the trip up to Petionville, Kenscoff and Furcy, is by air; unlike the telephones and the electricity, the service seems to be efficiently run.

HOTELS, RESTAURANTS AND ENTERTAINMENT

One of the purposes of the International Exposition which was opened in Port-au-Prince in December 1949 was to encourage tourism and develop the hotel business; and the result is that Haiti can boast of having one or two hotels in the A-minus category. Probably the best of these in the city area is the Riviera d'Haiti; a bit further out on the southern shore of the Baie de Port-au-Prince is the International Club Thorland, which also has cottage accommodation; El Rancho is up in the hills near Petionville in which neighbourhood there are, or were—one can never be sure of continuity in Haiti— two or three other A-minus hotels. All of these hotels have swimming pools and the food and service is of a reasonably high standard.

A good B-plus hotel in town, with a swimming pool, is the Sans Souci, where the manager and his charming wife do everything to make you comfortable. There are a couple of B-minus hotels in town and several C-category guest houses. In my view, the Sans Souci, an impressive and dignified old building, gives the best value for money to those who want to sample the atmosphere and flavour of life in Port-au-Prince. At Cap Haitien there is one hotel, the Roi Christophe, which might warrant a B-plus rating and a couple of others in the C class. At other towns—townships would be a better word—

the accommodation can be most politely described as limited; only the venturous tourist who does not mind "roughing it" for the sake of getting local colour should stay anywhere outside the Port-au-Prince area or, possibly, Cap Haitien.

I may have visited Haiti at the wrong time, but, outside of the hotels, I cannot recall a single restaurant worth visiting. Perhaps the best bet is the international casino on the Exposition Grounds. Theoretically there is gambling and dancing there, but it is impossible to be dogmatic about what goes on in Haiti. Several of the hotels offer weekly dancing (the merengue bands are excellent) and floorshows. Obviously, however, most visitors to Haiti will want to see a voodoo ceremony and this can be arranged through the hotel people; or any taxi driver will take you to a *hounfor*, or temple, on a Saturday night, when most of the ceremonies are held. Voodoo-ism is a religion and it is absurd to suppose that a genuine ceremony would ever be staged for the benefit of a few gaping tourists. Nevertheless, excellent "phony" shows are put on; after all the tourist's dollar is even more welcome in Haiti than in other Caribbean territories. You will be regaled with first-class drumming, singing and dancing and you may even witness a (phony) act of possession. It all makes an excellent story to tell the folks at home.

SPORT AND RECREATION

By no stretch of the imagination can Haiti be said to have good beaches for swimming, and the visitor to Port-au-Prince must be content for the most part with hotel pool facilities. At Kyona, about 45 minutes drive away, there is a reasonable beach and they tell you that near Jacmel on the south coast—if you can survive the atrocious road—there is a beautiful small beach called Carrefour Raymond. Some quite good spear-fishing and snorkelling can be done on the reefs in the Baie de Port-au-Prince for which boats can be hired at the casino pier. There is (or was) a glass bottom boat which will also take you out to see the marine life on the reefs.

Haiti is one of the best places in the Caribbean for hunting

—quail, guinea fowl, pigeon, duck, wild boar, wild goat, and even crocodiles. The hotel people say they can arrange trips, but I suspect that anyone who attempts to bring a gun into Haiti would run into enormous difficulties—to say the least—at the customs. One or two of the hotels have tennis courts and there are others at the Petionville Club and the Port-au-Prince Tennis Club. There is a nine-hole golf course at the Petionville Club, which seems to be largely an American-run concern.

Cockfighting might almost be described as Haiti's national sport. There is a "stadium" in the Exposition Grounds and there are hundreds of other smaller pits all over the country. Addicts of this type of entertainment describe the fights as being better even than those staged in the French islands of Martinique and Guadeloupe. The betting is frantic and quite incomprehensible to the uninitiated. Carnival, or Mardi Gras, is a highly colourful spectator sport in Haiti during the three days before lent and it has an even more African flavour than in the other Caribbean islands where it takes place. The mulatto girls who contest for the prize of Carnival Queen have remarkable beauty.

SHOPPING

Port-au-Prince offers a variety of goods at virtually free-port prices, but, to my mind, the best buys are the paintings of the country's famous primitive school and the mahogany sculpture. There is a "shopwindow" of these works for the tourist in the Exposition Grounds and there are three or four other places, including the Gallerie du Centre d'Art near the centre of town where paintings are on view. These are mostly enchantingly gay and colourful works, stylised according to tradition, depicting scenes of local life and scenery; but some, as I have said, have the sinister, off-beat gloom of voodooism. Paintings of this school have been and still are exhibited in galleries in New York, London and Paris; and the returning visitor to Haiti can acquire a definite cachet if he can bring back with him a picture painted by one of the dozen or so top local artists. The prices you pay are far below those asked abroad. And the same applies to the mahogany carvings, which is another art field in which Haitians have managed to build up an enviable reputation. Even the cheap statuettes offered to you in the streets by pedlars have considerable charm.

Other good local things to buy include embroidered skirts and blouses; hand-worked cottons and hand-woven rugs; bags and sandals made of sisal; baskets, hats and mats made of palm fibre; and jewellery with the voodoo motif. In the field of local liquor the Rhum Barbancourt is excellent. Among imported goods the best offerings include china, glassware, silver, Irish linens, gloves, sweaters, watches, cameras, perfumes and, of course, wines and liquors of all sorts.

USEFUL FACTS FOR VISITORS

Haiti has an area of 10,714 square miles and occupies the western third of the island of Hispaniola. It is covered to a great extent by mountain ranges from which short but swiftly flowing—after heavy rain—rivers run down to the Atlantic in the north and the Caribbean Sea in the south. The frontier between it and the Dominican Republic to the east extends for about 190 miles.

The climate varies considerably from one part of the country to another. In the coastal areas there is a temperature range between 75° F. and 95° F. (24° C. and 35° C.); in the mountain town of Kenscoff, 4,800 feet up but only about ten miles from Port-au-Prince, the thermometer is often in the sixties. December, January and February are the driest and coolest months. Temperatures are normally high in the capital, Port-au-Prince, because it is at sea level and is sheltered by hills from the prevailing winds.

The population of Haiti is now about four million, almost all of whom are of pure Negro or mixed Negro-European stock. French is the official language, though the vast (uneducated) majority speak only Creole; most of the educated Haitians speak English.

Pan American operate daily scheduled jet flights connecting Haiti with North America westward via Jamaica and eastward

via the Dominican Republic and Puerto Rico. Cruise ships
call not infrequently at Port-au-Prince from North America
and there is a regular passenger-freighter service to and from
New York. Two or three European lines operate freighter-
passenger services to and from Haiti.

The tourist people in Haiti are keen to do business and you
should get intelligent answers from the Departement du
Tourisme, Port-au-Prince, Haiti. Embassies or consulates
should be contacted elsewhere.

The Dominican Republic

"Politics and nightlife don't mix."—Hotel porter

ECONOMY

The Dominican Republic has been largely dependent this
century on the sugar industry both for earning money abroad
and for local employment. It is not easy to get reliable figures
these days about anything in the country, but in the early
sixties total Dominican Republic exports amounted to something like $141 million, 60% of which went to the United
States. At this time the national revenue was of the order
of $130 million annually, and per capita income was about
$190—far higher than neighbouring Haiti, but low in com-
parison with a number of other Caribbean territories. United
States aid amounting to $94 million in 1966 (plus other
undisclosed amounts in 1965), and the political disturbances
in the second half of the decade, make it almost impossible,
however, to give anything like a clear picture of the country's
economic position. In addition to sugar, other export crops
include coffee, cacao, bananas, and tobacco; some livestock
is also exported. Rice, corn, plantains, oranges and pineapples are produced primarily for domestic consumption. Experiments have been made with sisal, cotton and rubber. On
the whole, however, and despite the extremely fertile soil, the

agricultural resources of the country are still—disturbed political conditions do not help—relatively undeveloped.

Towards the end of the Trujillo era there were developments in the mining of iron ore, bauxite and gypsum, and substantial deposits of nickel have been discovered. A small amount of oil has been found, and the export of iron ore began in 1960. Manufacturing mostly consists of the processing of agricultural commodities such as the refining of sugar, the production of rum, chocolate, peanut oil and cigars. There are plants for the canning of food and the processing of meat. Other industrial enterprises include brewing and the production of cement, textiles, soft drinks and flour.

The currency is the peso oro symbolized by the sign RD$, implying that it is on a par with the U.S. dollar.

SIGHTSEEING

The old part of Santo Domingo occupies a comparatively small area on the west bank of the Ozama River and it is a good idea to start a walking tour of this part of the city at the Puerta del Conde (Count's Gate) on Independence Square. This is a well-preserved ruin of one of the gates in the old city wall and it is also the country's national shrine; beneath the gate are buried the three heroes who declared Dominican independence from Haiti in 1844—Duarte, Sanchez and Mella. The story goes that the gate got its name from a Count Penalva who is supposed to have repulsed single-handed a British attacking force in 1655. From there you should walk eastward down the Calle El Conde, which is the main shopping street, until you come to the Parque Colon, a small square on which is situated the Cathedral of Santo Domingo de Guzman, the oldest cathedral in the New World.

Most guide books say that construction began in 1521, but there is evidence that Diego Columbus, the Viceroy son of the explorer, laid the foundation stone in 1514. The Cathedral was completed in 1540—the splendid west façade dates from about that year—and in 1547 Pope Paul III gave it the status of a metropolitan cathedral. It is interesting that the Bishop who supervised its construction, one Alessandro Geraldini, was a contemporary and friend of Pope Leo X, the patron of Michelangelo whose work is to be seen in the most famous cathedral of the Old World, St. Peter's, Rome.

The columned nave has unfortunately been disfigured by an ornately ugly late nineteenth-century tomb which supposedly contains the bones of Christopher Columbus. These were discovered in a nearby crypt when some restoration work was going on in 1877, and it is certainly possible that they, rather than the ones which lie in the cathedral at Seville, are the true bones of the explorer. The known facts are that Columbus died in Spain (Valladolid) in 1506 and that in 1542 his remains were shipped to Santo Domingo and re-interred in a vault in the cathedral there. When records and memories must have been dim, 253 years later, an exhumation took place and remains believed to be those of Columbus were removed, first to Havana, and then, in 1899, to Seville. The discovery of 1877, however, is now believed by archivists to have taken place at the correct spot where the interment was made after the remains were shipped from Spain, and it is suggested that the remains in Seville may be those of another member of the Columbus family. The visitor to both Santo Domingo and Seville is at liberty to take his choice.

The cathedral's baroque high altar, which dates from 1684, contains jewels and relics presented by Pope Paul in 1547; other treasures include : a Madonna by Murillo and a Velasquez painting of the Twelve Apostles; a sixteenth-century mahogany episcopal throne; jewellery given by Queen Isabela to Columbus to take with him on his second voyage; and a silver cross in which is inset a piece of wood from the "True Cross."

A few yards east of the Parque Colon on the bank of the river is the Ozama Fortress behind whose walls is the Torre de Homanaje (Tower of Homage) which, dating from 1503, is the oldest fort in the Americas built by Europeans. They tell you that Columbus was imprisoned there but there is no evidence to support this claim; the fortress and the tower have, however, been continually in use as the "gestapo" headquarters of whatever tyrant might be at the helm in the Dominican Republic; and it figured prominently in the 1965 disorders. It is not normally open to visitors.

Walking north up the river you come to Columbus' Palace, sometimes called the Alcazar, which was built between 1510 and 1514 by Diego Columbus who was appointed Viceroy in Santo Domingo in 1509. Its basic design is Spanish gothic but parts also have a Moorish and renaissance flavour. It was restored between 1955 and 1957 and fitted out with contemporary furniture, pictures, tapestries and *objets d'art*, some of which were sent over from Spain. Among notable pieces are the four-poster bed used by the Viceroy and his wife, several excellent seventeenth-century tapestries, a cross probably dating from the fourteenth century, and a fifteenth-century wood carving depicting the birth of Christ; there are also many fine-quality contemporary chests, tables and chairs. The atmosphere of authenticity is heightened by the display of contemporary dinner plates, glass and silver such as might have been used at the viceregal table. Diego Columbus' wife, Maria Toledo, was the niece of one of Spain's foremost noblemen, the Duke of Alba, and the affairs of the palace were conducted in royal state.

While Diego Columbus and his wife were waiting for the palace to be built, they lived in an adjacent house called the Casa del Cordon which dates from 1502 and has a good claim to be the oldest existing non-Amerindian residence in the Americas. Also in this area north of the Calle El Conde is the magnificent church of Las Mercedes, the ruins of the hospital of St. Nicholas of Bari and those of the Franciscan convent, all of which date from the early years of the sixteenth century. It is possible to wander around this historic part of the town in a morning or an afternoon—politics permitting, of course—but it is difficult to get a clear picture of what it must have looked like four and a half centuries ago because many modern buildings—the post office, banks and so on—and some not so modern, slum-looking and ugly, now crowd the area. Nevertheless, this is the place where the foundations of present-day western hemisphere civilisation were laid and, having passed through earthquake, seige and turbulence, it warrants all respect from the visitor.

It is best to get a taxi to have a look at the modern, or Trujillo, part of Santo Domingo, which lies to the westward of the old town. It is impressive enough in its way. There is the Palacio Nacional, a vast, typical, modern-classical edifice built of pinkish stone standing in a small park north of the Avenida Bolivar. It was completed in 1947 and its pretentious grandiosity is reminiscent of its opposite number in Port-au-Prince. There is the Bellas Artes—again neo-classical—building which Trujillo put up to house every sort of art and artifact connected with the Dominican Republic's history. There is the 125-acre site of the 1956 International Peace and Progress Exhibition, which is now mostly government buildings; and on the Avenida George Washington, a clean-looking waterfront boulevard, you see a large, white obelisk erected in 1936 to commemorate the changing of the city's name from Santo Domingo to Ciudad Trujillo (it was a temporary arrangement as things turned out). On the east side of the Ozama River is the Columbus Memorial Lighthouse, a vast cruciform affair built under United Nations auspices, which is to be the site of a Columbus museum and to which, so it is planned, the explorer's remains will be transferred from the cathedral.

Briefly, therefore, in Santo Domingo you have a small section which is unsurpassed in the Caribbean for its historic associations; a modern section which contains typical examples of the sort of building—including many smart residences and villas—which a dictator likes to see going up around him; and in between a nondescript area in most of which it is only too evident that poverty is the dominant factor in the lives of the people who dwell there. It is impossible yet (1967) to say whether or not the plush hotels will ever be full again or whether the city will ever acquire an atmosphere of stability and happiness.

Scarcely anybody these days, except possibly the odd businessman, travels far outside the Dominican Republic's capital city other than to the airport or to the nearby resort of Boca Chica. In Haiti, because the all-powerful government needs the tourist dollar, it is easy to go sightseeing, but in the Dominican Republic, though the need there for the tourist dollar is almost equally great, stability has not been a factor in the country's political life since the demise of Trujillo, and the atmosphere is just not conducive to touring, though adequate hotels do exist. Even in Trujillo's day the security regulations made it difficult for anyone to make a trip from the capital. There are, nevertheless, one or two places of interest.

On the way to Punta Cauceda airport, for example, you might turn right shortly after crossing the bridge over the Ozama River to a place called Tres Ojos (Three Eyes) where there is a group of caves and three subterranean pools with vaulted roofs and some impressive stalactite and stalagmite formations. Returning to the main south coast road, you can pause at the beach resort hotel at Boca Chica and then continue for about 20 miles to the curiously interesting "ghost" town of San Pedro de Macoris which, at the beginning of this century, was the most prosperous city in the Dominican Republic and the centre also of its cultural life. It was the main port for the shipping of sugar which is now almost entirely centred on Santo Domingo. With its "Opera House", at which famous European singers, including Caruso, used to perform, it is reminiscent of that other Latin-American city-with-a-past (in this case based on the prosperity created by rubber), Manaos, on the upper reaches of the Amazon, which also attracted the elite of the grand opera circuit up till the turn of the century. Going back even further, it is interesting to speculate on the comparison between life at San Pedro and that at Cap Haitien when neighbouring Saint-Domingue, under French rule, was the most prosperous and, from all accounts, the most cultured place in the Caribbean.

Having got as far as this, it is worthwhile turning north to the provincial capital, Seibo, whose foundation dates from as far back as 1502, and then on to Higuey which was founded by one of the most famous conquistadores, Juan Ponce de Leon, who brought both Puerto Rico and Florida under the Spanish flag in the early years of the sixteenth century. Not much remains of the town's ancient buildings but it is interesting to contrast the early seventeenth-century church with the large, new modernistic, Trujillo-era concrete church. From Higuey you can turn south and go back to Santo Domingo by the south coast road via the largely United States-dominated sugar and cattle town of La Romana.

About twenty miles west of Santo Domingo is the town of San Cristobal where Dictator Trujillo was born and it is, needless to say, full of parks and pretentious public buildings; there is also a semi-luxurious hotel. But the most interesting place to have a look at is the mansion called El Cerro which was built for El Benefactor by his grateful serfs. It contains, or contained, no less than seventeen bathrooms; but apparently this was not enough; Trujillo never lived there.

Setting out from Santo Domingo to the north by the modern and scenic Duarte Highway, you head for Santiago, the second largest city in the country, about 135 miles away, which might be described as the industrial and agricultural marketing centre of the northern part of the country. It is historically interesting because its full name, Santiago de los Caballeros (St. James of the Gentlemen), given to it because it was founded in 1504 by thirty cavaliers, or gentlemen adventurers, who came inland from the north coast, is reminiscent of the English "companies of adventurers" who first established settlements in the Bahamas and Bermuda. Practically nothing remains of the early Spanish buildings, so one has to be content with the Trujillo Monument to Peace and a good modern hotel overlooking the town.

The drive northward to Puerto Plata, about 35 miles, takes you through countryside so lush and highly cultivated that it is easy to understand why Dominicans claim their country has the most fertile soil in the world. Puerto Plata is the main port of the Atlantic coast, but, apart from this fact, it has little from the tourist point of view to distinguish it. The site of the first Spanish settlement in the New World, La Isabela, is on the coast about 35 miles west of Puerto Plata. One has heard about plans to reconstruct the settlement, but at the moment there is nothing to see except a few stones. Only a dedicated historian would consider this long journey from Santo Domingo

9. Haitians love to gather round a waterfall on a hot day. This is the one at
Ville Bonheur

10. A splendid arch amongst the ruins of the sixteenth-century St. Francis monastery at Santo Domingo in the Dominican Republic

worthwhile. About 50 miles further along the coast at the end of the Duarte Highway is the port of Monte Cristi at the mouth of the Yaque del Norte River, and about 20 miles south from there is the frontier town of Dajabon from which it is theoretically possible to motor into Haiti, but at the present time I would say this is a very doubtful proposition.

HOTELS, RESTAURANTS AND ENTERTAINMENT

When it was opened in 1956, the Hotel Embajador (one of the Intercontinental Group) could claim to be among the top-notch establishments of the Caribbean and fully justified an A-plus rating. Its exterior is functionally modern and the interior is luxurious. It has an Olympic-size swimming pool, a golf course and a gambling casino; in short it has everything which the well-heeled tourist could possibly want and it is attractively situated on a hill overlooking the sea at the western end of Santo Domingo. Nearer the town and closer to the sea is another A-plus hotel, the Jaragua, which also has a large swimming pool, a casino, tennis courts and golf privileges; it also offers cottage accommodation. The Paz Hotel is really an offshoot of the Embajador whose recreational facilities it shares; an A-minus rating. These three hotels were all built towards the end of the Trujillo period when efforts were being made to put the Dominican Republic in the top rank of Caribbean tourist resorts. They are good examples of how the best-laid schemes of hoteliers can be made to go awry by politics because in early 1967 the Jaragua was shut and the Paz had only just returned to partial existence. There are two or three hotels in downtown Santo Domingo with B ratings and the best of these is probably the Commercial.

Outside Santo Domingo there are two hotels with A-minus ratings : the Hamaca, on the coast about 19 miles east of the capital at Boca Chica, which offers all the facilities of a water-side resort; and the Nueva Suiza, situated 4,000 feet up in the mountains near Constanza, about 50 miles northwest of Santo Domingo, which is a good centre for hunting, hiking and horse-

K

back riding. At Santiago, the republic's second largest city in the rich agricultural region known as the Cibao about three hours' drive northwest from the capital, there is a good B-plus hotel (it had—maybe still has—a gambling casino) called the Matum, and there are others in the same category at San Cristobal, Sosua (on the north coast) and at San Juan in the central-western part of the country. In other words, it is theoretically possible to find good accommodation when touring the Dominican Republic, but even in the Trujillo days the authorities did not like people to wander around too much, and in the post-Trujillo era the country has not been blessed with an atmosphere which is conducive to pleasant motoring.

There are two or three restaurants in Santo Domingo where you can get a good meal. Lina's, a small place on the Avenida Independencia, serves good Spanish food, and the Vesuvio, a larger establishment on the Avenida George Washington, tends to be more Italian. The restaurant at El Ambajador was trying, quite successfully, in 1967 to be an eating place of high quality. Night life used to be fairly hectic—floor-shows, gambling and entertainment in the big hotels and in the nightclub in the building of La Voz Dominicana, one of the main radio-television stations. You could also go to one of several small night spots in downtown Santo Domingo to dance in a gay atmosphere to the merengue rhythm. As of 1967, however, night entertainment in Santo Domingo was minimal; even the casino at El Ambajador, the only one open, was sparsely populated. "Politics and night life don't mix," as one of the porters at the Hotel Paz remarked to me somewhat lugubriously.

SPORT AND RECREATION

The main centre for beach activities in the Santo Domingo area is Boca Chica, where equipment can be rented for water-skiing, spear-fishing, snorkelling, and so on. It used also to be possible to rent deep-sea fishing cruisers from the Tourist Board. There are actually several good beaches in the Dominican Republic which, even in the Trujillo era, had not been opened up to tourists—notably at Sosua and Nagua on the north coast and in the Samana Bay area on the east coast. It may be that in the next decade these will be opened up for visitors; in the meantime one has to be content either with the hotel swimming pool or the Boca Chica facilities—which, in fact, as beaches go in the Caribbean, are not all that impressive.

The Santo Domingo Country Club, just outside the town to the west, has tennis courts, and a reasonably good 18-hole golf course; theoretically anyway, the three main hotels also have tennis courts. The Perla de las Antilles track, northwest of the city, used to have year-round horse-racing and polo; maybe one of these days it will again. Baseball and soccer are the most popular sports, and cockfighting has its enthusiastic devotees.

THINGS TO BUY

The Dominican Republic certainly cannot be called a particularly good place for shopping, the main goods on offer being take-home souvenirs such as carved mahogany figurines, amber beads, embroidery and straw goods of all kinds. There used to be a free-port shop in the Exposition grounds where you could buy watches, jewellery and liquor at low prices, but in the main shopping district of Santo Domingo there never seemed to be much to attract the foreign buyer; nor is there now.

USEFUL FACTS FOR VISITORS

The Dominican Republic occupies the eastern two-thirds of the 28,249-square-miles island of Hispaniola, and from its easternmost tip to the Haitian border the distance is 260 miles. It has a coastline of about 950 miles. The Cordillera Central range of mountains bisects the country from northwest to southeast and rises to a height of 10,300 ft. at Pico Duarte, the highest point in the country, which was once called Pico Trujillo. Fertile and well-watered lands are a feature of the central and eastern areas and there are desert stretches in the extreme west. There are three principle rivers (the longest is the Yaque del Norte, about 240 miles) which flow from the main mountain range. About 70% of the country is still wooded.

The average temperature is 74° F. (23° C.), in January and 81° F. (26° C.) in August. The driest period of the year is from early December to late April, and the rainy season corresponds with the hotter summer months. The northern part of the country is generally drier than the southern part.

The population was estimated to be 3,580,000 in 1965, with a 3·5% annual growth rate. About 25% are estimated to be of European stock and the remainder mixed. The language is Spanish, but English is widely understood, at any rate in Santo Domingo.

The Dominican Republic is connected with Puerto Rico to the east by several flights a day operated by Pan American, Caribair and the country's own airline, Dominicana. Pan American has daily flights westward via Haiti and Jamaica to North America. By sea there are fairly regular freighter services from North America and Europe in some of which passenger accommodation is available. It is hoped that tourist ships will once again make Santo Domingo a port of call, but there was no evidence of them in 1967. You can write to : Direccion General de Turismo, Santo Domingo, Dominican Republic. In New York and London the best, though limited, sources of information are the consulate and the embassy.

THE BOOTSTRAP ISLAND

Puerto Rico

"If ever there was a territory looking for an identity, this is it."
—Anon.

The words quoted were spoken to me by a New York business-man who has been in Puerto Rico—the "Bootstrap Island"—for many years, and they were given emphasis in the first week of December 1966, when a Bill was put before the Legislature by Governor Sanchez Vilella providing for a plebiscite to be held on 12 July 1967, to decide whether this 3,345-square miles Caribbean island of some 2,750,000 inhabitants (1967) which the United States took from Spain in 1898, should remain in its present state of being a Commonwealth in "free association" with the United States, should become the fifty-first State in the Union, or should become an independent nation.

The result of the plebiscite means that Puerto Rico will continue on the "free association" basis; nor was it surprising that the voters should have taken this decision, for it is only too apparent to anyone who goes there even for a short visit that they have benefitted economically to an enormous extent since their island was given Commonwealth (not to be confused with the British use of the word) status in 1952. Under this they enjoy virtually all the advantages of being United States citizens without the disadvantages of having to pay for them through federal taxation. Due to tax and other incentives designed to encourage investment from the United States mainland, the inhabitants of this Spanish-speaking and, on the whole, Latin-American-orientated island, saw their total net income increase in the 1955-1965 decade from $959 million to $2,322 million. There has been an annual growth rate of real net income of 9·3 % and annual per capita income is now well over $900.

I talked to a visitor from Texas in the intervals of losing a few dollars at the roulette tables in the softly-lit and softly-carpeted casino in one of the luxury hotels. "When I get home," he said, "I'm going to start a movement to get Commonwealth status for Texas." The point he wanted to make was that under such a constitutional arrangement you just could not go wrong in the sphere of making money and, in general, of having a pleasant life. Indeed, on the basis of the 1964 election figures there could have been little doubt how the plebiscite would go. The popular Democratic Party, which advocated a continuance of Commonwealth status, polled about 60% of the votes and the Statehood Republican Party about 34%, most of the remainder (about 3%) going to the Popular Independence Party, a highly vociferous minority group (including a few Communists) which wanted—and still wants— Puerto Rico to sever all ties with the United States.

Fundamentally, as most informed Puerto Ricans will tell you, the issue was that both the "statehooders", as they are called, and the "indepentistas" were tired of seeing their island continue in what they considered to be an essentially transitory relationship with the U.S. which had, so they maintained, a Big Brother-Little Brother, almost colonial, connotation. The plebiscite did not, of course, render the people who hold these views any the less vocal, nor did it in any way permanantly fix Puerto Rico's status; but it did clear the air and get a highly controversial issue out of the way at any rate for the time being; and in this connection the former Governor (now Senator) Luis Munoz Marin, who was the architect of the island's post-war prosperity in close association with Washington and is generally considered to be "Mr. Puerto Rico", is on record as having said before the plebiscite that the island could become neither a state nor an independent nation till a period of 20 years had elapsed. On the other hand, he said, if the Commonwealth formula were to continue, the status issue would be settled for the next 25 years and the people would be able to free their minds of this distracting argument and get on with the business of developing the territory both economically and socially.

That Puerto Rico's economic development in the fifties and

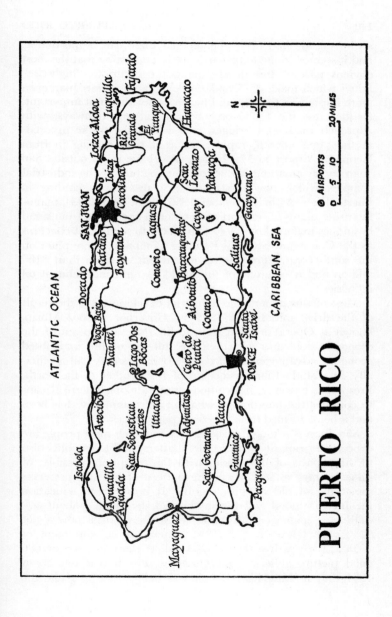

PUERTO RICO

sixties decade had been phenomenal there can be no doubt; and it seemed to me to be particularly interesting that the most obvious part of this development, the luxurious "high-rise" hotels which make the Condado Beach area of San Juan even more impressive than Miami Beach, is not the most important. Neither are the four-lane, or even larger, highways, with approach roads and bridges, over which the traffic proceeds at the same smooth, rapid pace as it does coming in from Kennedy Airport to Manhatten. You have to go outside San Juan to get anything like a complete picture of the industrial complex which now exists and is constantly expanding in Puerto Rico. As of November 1966, there were 2,431 manufacturing plants of one sort or another in operation, from small businesses making household appliances to such giant concerns as the Commonwealth Oil Refining Company whose plant on the south coast represents an investment of more than $160 million and is now one of the world's largest independent oil refineries.

Most of this remarkable industrial development is the result of the drive initiated in 1949 by Governor Munoz Marin, known as Operation Bootstrap, to lift Puerto Rico out of the economic doldrums and to make full use of the undoubted economic advantages entailed from being, as they call it officially, an Estado Libre Associado of Big Brother to the north. Prosperity, however, has caused many thinking Puerto Ricans to consider the question of what sort of community has been and is being formed from the social point of view.

San Juan is a tough, bustling city in which most people are concerned primarily with money matters; and this applies also to other parts of the island, with the exception, possibly, of some country estates where the pattern of life still preserves something of old Spanish dignity. It is true that education facilities are good and that a third of the budget, about $90 million, is spent on education. The literacy rate is now about 90%; the University of Puerto Rico has an enrolment of 20,000; there is live theatre and ballet; there are one or two good picture galleries and museums. But it was felt about 1964 that nothing like enough was being done to make the average Puerto Rican aware of the better type of life—there are still slum areas in San Juan—which was being more widely opened up to them each year.

Munoz had a bright idea : Operation Bootstrap was to be replaced by Operation Serenity, so that considered plans could be formulated by experts whereby Puerto Ricans should be enabled to make better use of recreational, cultural and educational facilities, and whereby existing facilities in these fields should be expanded. For example, why not channel the money which comes in from tourists indulging in such an essentially uncultural activity as playing Black Jack, not into building more Black Jack facilities, but rather into building a school or a concert hall? Operation Serenity is still supposed to be going on, but the visitors to Puerto Rico cannot help feeling that it is not having the rapid and dramatic success which Bootstrap had. Nevertheless, the fact that it was initiated is a tribute to the wisdom and far-sightedness of some of the island's leaders.

The Bootstrap apologists tell you that Puerto Rico's two decades of progress are a shining example of what can be done if the American free enterprise system is given full rein; and it is not easy to argue otherwise. But to somebody not brought up wholly in this tradition—as indeed a great percentage of the Spanish-speaking Puerto Rican population has not been —there could be something distasteful in the taxi-loads of rich Yankee tourists seen driving almost every minute of the day from Isla Verde airport to the plush San Juan hotels with their private beach rights. It was even suggested to me that what has been going on in Puerto Rico is not entirely unlike what went on in the tourist heyday of Batista's Cuba. (All the more need, one would think, for the success of Operation Serenity.) And an incident reported in the San Juan papers in 1965 is significant in this connection. At a party in San Juan celebrating Argentina's Independence Day on 25 May the president of the Puerto Rican Bar Association was reported to have said to a group of twenty-three lawyers from Argentina "with tears in his eyes" that he publicly lamented that Puerto Rico had no Independence Day to celebrate. "We have made tre-

mendous social and economic progress," he was quoted as saying, "but this one main problem remains to be solved". Despite
the 1967 plebiscite, the problem is still not solved.

Puerto Rico is less than one hour's flying time from the
neighbouring Dominican Republic whose citizens also have to
face, though from a different angle, the problem of their own
relations with the United States. And it is in general undeniably
true to say that the Puerto Rican feels more at home with a
kindred Latin American than he does with somebody, say,
from New York or Chicago, of whom there are several thousands in Puerto Rico dominating industry, commerce and the
pattern of life in general. There is the further point to be considered that Puerto Rico is now believed to be a military and
naval base far more important to Washington than Guan-
tanamo in Cuba. In November 1966, it was announced that
new facilities for the U.S. Navy costing more than $5 million
had been opened. Washington, it is to be presumed, would
not like to see Puerto Rico become independent—at any rate
in the foreseeable future—and it is questionable whether
Congress would welcome Representatives and Senators whose
basic language and outlook is Spanish. In twenty-five years
the picture may have altered, but, in the meantime, the Puerto
Rican rationalists argue, why not leave things as they are?
After all, the golden eggs are still pouring in from the United
States financial goose.

HISTORY

Columbus discovered the island which is now called Puerto
Rico on his second voyage in 1493. He sent a party ashore for
water and food and one of its members was Juan Ponce de
Leon, a young Spanish nobleman, who was later to be the
island's first Governor and whose name is commemorated in
today's Avenida Ponce de Leon which is one of the main
streets of modern San Juan. The Spaniards found the island
occupied by the Amerindian Arawaks, a peaceful people who
had achieved a limited form of culture—they had a knowledge
of writing as can be seen from cave inscriptions—and who

mostly fled to the hills of the interior when the strangers arrived. They do not appear to have been molested unduly and as time went on they became to some extent absorbed by the Spaniards. Estimates vary about the number of Arawaks, or Borinquen Indians as they were called, but it is generally put at between 20,000 and 50,000. Several communities exist today in the interior whose inhabitants have Amerindian features and names, but none of them has anything like pure Arawak blood.

No immediate attempt was made by the Spaniards to colonise the island which Columbus christened San Juan Bautista (St. John the Baptist) as they were much more interested in developing Hispaniola and Cuba, not to mention the new discoveries on the mainland of Central and South America. (The name Puerto Rico, incidently, originated from the name later given to the city, San Juan de Puerto Rico, or rich port, and the second part seems gradually to have come to denote the whole island.) Then, in 1508, Ponce de Leon sailed at the head of an expedition from Hispaniola, landed not far from San Juan, and built a settlement called Caparra, the ruins of which can still be seen. He remained there for four years as Governor and then took time off to sail at the head of an expedition to Florida. By this time there were about 400 Spaniards in Puerto Rico.

The early settlers went through the customary period of vicissitudes—plagues, hurricanes, droughts and floods—and in 1519 they moved the capital to the position which the old town of San Juan occupies. Ponce de Leon, who seems to have been obsessed with the desire to find the legendary Fountain of Eternal Youth, again went to Florida. This time his expedition was fiercely attacked by Indians and, being wounded, he was forced to retreat to Cuba, where he died shortly afterwards. The body of this man who is very much Puerto Rico's National Hero was later moved first to the church of San Jose in San Juan and then (1908) to the cathedral, where it now is.

Though sugar cane was introduced as early as 1515, the Spanish settlers were mostly concerned with gold-mining. They

did, indeed, extract a fair amount of gold, with the enforced
assistance of the Arawaks, but by about 1570 all the mines
were exhausted and the more adventurous Spaniards headed
for Mexico and Peru. Those who remained did manage to
build up a reasonably prosperous export trade in sugar, cotton,
ginger, cacao and indigo. Life, however, continued to be somewhat precarious; there were frequent raids by the bellicose
Caribs from neighbouring islands, sickness and disease were
persistent, and there were the increasing depredations of English, French and Dutch adventurers who had begun to show
an interest in the wealth which Spain had discovered on the
other side of the Atlantic.

Towards the end of the sixteenth century and during the
following hundred years the waters of the Caribbean and the
western North Atlantic became the hunting ground for corsairs who sought to get possession of the Spanish treasures
which were being shipped home. Madrid, which had previously not shown much interest in Puerto Rico, realised that
something would have to be done to fortify the island and so
the fortress of San Felipe de Morro was built at the entrance
to San Juan harbour. Shortly afterwards this fortress had the
distinction of repulsing an attack by the hitherto invincible
Sir Francis Drake. San Juan was captured and held for five
months in 1593 by another Englishman, the Earl of Cumberland, and in 1625 a Dutch force, under Bowdoin Hendrik,
managed to get possession of the town, but not the fortress,
and hold it for a short period.

The pattern of life in Puerto Rico during most of the seventeenth and eighteenth centuries seems to have been more or
less static, the people in the country concentrating on their
agriculture and trading happily but illegally with the corsairs
while the inhabitants of San Juan, including the officials sent
from Madrid, lived their own reasonably elegant and comfortable lives within the city walls. In 1702 the English attacked
Arecibo and in 1703 they landed at Loiza, but on both occa-
sions they were repulsed. The last such unsuccessful attempted
invasion took place in 1797 under Sir Ralph Abercromby.
For nearly a hundred years after this Puerto Rico remained

in peaceful isolation. The first recorded census, taken in 1765, revealed a population of 44,883, of whom 5,037 were slaves.

Towards the latter part of the eighteenth century, when Spain was ruled by Bourbon kings, several progressive economic and administrative changes were introduced in Puerto Rico. Non-Spanish immigrants were allowed to go and live there and they brought with them new ideas about making agriculture more efficient. Sugar, tobacco, cattle and the newly introduced coffee became profitable industries; the island entered something of a boom period, and by 1800 the population had increased to 155,426, of whom some 13,000 were slaves. Shortly after the turn of the century Puerto Rican ports were officially opened to foreign traders and among the more liberal constitutional measures introduced was one which entitled Puerto Ricans to send representatives to the Cortes (parliament) in Madrid. It is not, therefore, entirely true to say, as the Americans later did, that the Spanish government did little or nothing to develop Puerto Rico along progressive lines.

In the early decades of the nineteenth century many of the Spanish territories on the mainland of America were in revolt, demanding total independence from Madrid, and this led to the arrival in Puerto Rico of many thousands of loyalists who went there to settle; and this was doubtless one reason why there never was a concerted move in the island to gain independence from Spain by force. There was sporadic rioting in 1835, 1838 and 1867 but the truth seems to be that, during the second half of the nineteenth century, due to the presence in Madrid of a reasonably (for the period) enlightened government, Puerto Rico and Spain co-existed in considerable harmony. Moves in San Juan to get more liberal conditions were, in the main, based on constitutional means.

Nevertheless, in 1868 a minor rebellion did occur over the issue of the abolition of slavery. This had been taking place in the British and French Caribbean islands since before the middle of the nineteenth century, but in Puerto Rico the urgency of the matter does not seem to have been appreciated by the Spanish rulers. It was perhaps not surprising, therefore, that the Negro slaves decided to take things into their own hands. In 1868 a group of them banded together and marched on the small town of Lares, in the interior, with slogans such as : "Independence !", "Down with Spain !", and "Liberty or Death !" They took over the town and proclaimed the Republic of Borinquen. In a day or two, however, their revolutionary ardour cooled off—they had looted most of the rum shops— and the inevitable hangover resulted in dampened enthusiasm and the disintegration of the movement. The revolutionary "army" dispersed and its leaders were imprisoned.

By this time Puerto Rico and Cuba were the only remaining Spanish possessions in the western hemisphere and Madrid had plenty of time to devote to considering a more liberal constitution for San Juan; and so, in 1897, a new constitution was promulgated which included an elected legislature and virtual autonomy in internal affairs. It was a constitutional arrangement which corresponded to a considerable extent with the British system of giving full internal self-government to certain dependencies. But before this could come into operation the Spanish-American war had broken out and by the middle of 1898 Spain had no further say in anything that happened either in Cuba or Puerto Rico.

The origins of this brief war date from about 1895 when the United States government began to see itself as the champion of the Cubans' struggle against Spain for independence which had been going on then for about thirty years. On 15 February 1898, an event occurred which provided an excuse for direct intervention. The U.S.S. *Maine* sank in Havana harbour following an explosion which was said to have been caused by the Spaniards. No direct evidence has ever been produced that Spaniards were responsible, but the event served to inflame the war spirit of both the American nation and the Washington administration; and the result was that Congress authorised President McKinley to use force to compel Spain to recognise Cuban independence and to withdraw her forces from the island.

The Spaniards in Cuba soon capitulated and immediately afterwards United States troops landed in Puerto Rico. Most Puerto Ricans actually welcomed the Americans as a pleasant

11.   Puerto Rico's San Juan cathedral has many historical associations

Porta Coeli church overlooking the plaza in San Germán, one of Puerto Rico's earliest and most charming

change from the domination of the Madrid-orientated Spanish oligarchy of senior civil servants, businessmen and military officers. Anyway, the whole island was "captured" with only a handful of casualties on both sides, and the U.S. commander, General Nelson A. Miles, issued the following proclamation :

> "We have not come to make war upon the people of a country which has been for several centuries oppressed, but, on the contrary, to bring protection to you and to your properties, exalting and imposing on you the guarantees and blessings of the liberal institutions of our government. It is not our purpose to interfere with existing laws and customs which are good and beneficial to your people, provided they are in accordance with the principals of the military administration and with those of order and justice."

This, of course, was the accepted style of proclamations of that period announcing a country's acquisition of a colony, and there is an interesting comparison with the proclamation made by the Commander of United States troops which entered the Dominican Republic in 1965 (see page 105). The main difference, of course, is the implication of a permanent occupation in the 1898 document.

The Americans set about thoroughly reforming Puerto Rico's administration, abolishing such things as imprisonment for political offences and introducing trial by jury and freedom of speech, press and assembly. Military government was superseded by civil government in 1900 but, despite all the American efforts to give Puerto Ricans "the blessings" of liberal institutions, the economy of the island suffered a severe setback. A disastrous hurricane wrecked plantations in 1899; what business there was under the Spanish administration had virtually ceased to exist; thousands were almost starving. Washington became aware for the first time that, having got control of Puerto Rico, something would have to be done to make it a viable entity; and Congress voted $200,000—worth at least five times as much then as it is now—in the form of an economic rehabilitation grant. But the trouble had a deeper basis. The following paragraph from Ralph Hancock's book, *Puerto Rico, A Success Story*, makes a startling criticism of American colonial administration at this time :

"Whatever the advantages of American government in the island the cost from the beginning was terrific. When American civil authorities took over, according to one reliable eye-witness, the cost of administering the island trebled, with money extracted from the already impoverished native population augmented by the bottomless bags of the Federal Treasury. Many of the Yankee newcomers were carpetbaggers, political and commercial opportunists who perpetuated the worst features of the Spanish regime and colonial exploitation and they would not tolerate criticism of their own corruption. Governors who drew an $8,000 salary enjoyed the Fortaleza Palace [still the Governor's residence in old San Juan] as a residence, had a $12,000 a year appropriation for expenses and $75,000 more as a 'contingent fund', to be spent as they chose without accounting to anyone. The example was aped by the ranks when lesser American officials wangled rent-free homes at public expense and purchasing clerks in every department doubled as salesmen at substantial profit. One Yankee, appointed Commissioner of Education, distributed so many school books of his own authorship that school superintendents protested they had not sufficient space to stack them."

Despite this corruption, however, Puerto Rico had entered the era of political progress. The first important issue was that of citizenship; both major political parties, then called Republican and Unionist, insisted on Puerto Ricans becoming citizens of the United States, and Congress agreed to this in 1917. An Act was passed whereby Puerto Rico became a Territory of the United States "organized but not incorporated." (A curious sideline on history is the fact that, out of about a million people then living on the island, 288 opted, as was their right, not to become U.S. citizens.) Even after the passing of this act, however, Puerto Ricans were not allowed to take charge wholly of their own affairs; the Governor and all senior officials were still appointed by Washington, and here, again, there was a similarity with the contemporary British system of colonial administration.

Nevertheless, political development was getting under way and the present-day pattern was emerging. Even in the early twenties the Republican party was campaigning for statehood; the Unionists were demanding greater autonomy, while the new Nationalist Party sought immediate independence. All of these were paramount issues in the sixties.

Economically Puerto Rico was changing too, due mainly to the fact that the island was now within the tariff walls of the U.S. and had become part of the same currency system. Sugar cultivation was introduced on a large scale with new American big-business capital and know-how; and the result was that by the thirties no less than 75% of the labour force was employed in the sugar industry, the products of which were almost entirely exported to the mainland. This was all very well when the mainland was prosperous, but when the depression of the thirties arrived the Puerto Rican economy was hard hit. The population, partly due to more efficient health provisions, was expanding rapidly, but there were now few farmers producing foodstuffs. Puerto Ricans entered yet another period of hardship from which (apart from the war interval) they were not to recover till the advent of Luis Munoz Marin and his famous Operation Bootstrap in the fifties.

Munoz Marin, who was to play a role as important in Puerto Rica's modern history as Ponce de Leon played in its early days, first came to the fore in 1940 when the Popular Democratic Party was formed under his leadership. The party's slogan was "Bread, Land and Liberty!" and its aims, broadly, were to improve the lot of the masses. The new party managed to get various reform measures enacted by the legislature, including minimum wages and tax reform, and in the 1944 elections it got a sweeping mandate from the voters to go ahead with the introduction of further reforms within the framework of a comprehensive development programme. Three years later Congress passed an Act permitting Puerto Ricans to elect their own Governor, and in 1949 Munoz was the first man to be so elected.

The phenomenal effects of the Bootstrap campaign, conducted during Munoz's periods of governorship to get Puerto Rico out of the economic doldrums, are described in the section headed Economy; but Munoz also led his country to further political advances. In 1952 Congress authorised the Munoz administration to draw up a new autonomous constitution providing for the establishment of the Commonwealth of Puerto Rico, which means, in effect, a self-governing territory in voluntary association with the United States. Under the new constitution, a resident Commissioner is sent by the Puerto Rican electorate to the Washington Congress for a four-year term, but he cannot vote; nor do Puerto Ricans vote in U.S. presidential elections except—but subject to local electoral laws—when living on the mainland. This rather curious anomaly of being citizens of a country without the right to take part in choosing its administration has been one of the several issues dominant in Puerto Rican politics in the sixties.

Professor Gordon Lewis, one of today's leading authorities on Puerto Rico and the Caribbean area as a whole, has this to say in his book, *Puerto Rico—Freedom and Power in the Caribbean* : "Puerto Rico, all in all, is on the move. But no one, as yet, can be certain about her final destination."

ECONOMY

Any description of Puerto Rico's economy must begin with Operation Bootstrap, and a good succinct account of this was written by William C. Baggs for the 1962 Britannica Book of the Year. The author became editor of the *Miami News* in 1957 and was appointed in 1961 by President Kennedy to be United States observer at the newly established Caribbean Organisation. The following passages are based on excerpts from his account, brought up to date :

After the reformers, led by Munoz Marin, won control of the Legislature in 1940, they initiated the economic programmes that in time were to become known collectively as Operation Bootstrap. It was intended to promote all sectors of the economy, involving every agency of the Commonwealth Government and private interests as well. In 1942 the Economic Development Administration was established. Known in the island as Fomento, a Spanish word meaning development, the new public corporation was given the task of creating new jobs by building up Puerto Rican industry. To start off, it had an appropriation of $500,000 and was presented with a $2,000,000 cement plant which had been built by a federal government agency to provide employment. The appropriation was soon raised to $20,000,000 when the proportions of Fomento's task became apparent. With these funds, Fomento began by building a glass-container plant to provide bottles for the increased production of rum; and a plant to manufacture paper cartons for the filled bottles was the second Fomento enterprise. Within five years Fomento had five plants in operation : the original cement plant, the bottle factory, the carton plant, a shoe factory and a plant manufacturing structural clay products. Funds were committed for a $7,200,000 resort hotel and a $4,000,000 cotton textile plant. By that time almost all of the original $20,000,000 appropriation was gone. Only 2,000 jobs had been created by the Fomento industries and 100,000 were needed. Furthermore, the extent of government participation in the island's economy had aroused fears on the mainland, particularly in Washington, that Puerto Rico was becoming socialist.

Then, in 1947, Fomento sold the glass plant, the clay factory, the paper-container factory and the cement plant to a private firm for $10,500,000 following public bidding. The Fomento administration had come to realise that the island government could not possibly provide sufficient investment capital to create 100,000 new jobs, which was the goal of the programmes. At the rate Fomento spent its capital in proportion to jobs created, $2,000,000,000 would have been required to provide 100,000 new jobs. So Fomento changed itself into an agency for attracting industry rather than building it. It offered factory space to investors, assisted in financing new enterprises, answered enquiries, helped in selecting factory sites and, above all, tried to convince potential investors that Puerto Rico was a good place in which to set up a business. A ten-year exemption from corporate income taxes was given to new enterprises; as an incentive to disperse industries in the distressed areas of the island, the tax-free period was extended to thirteen years in 1961 on condition that Fomento select the site for the new factory. Another attraction was a wage scale lower than that on the mainland.

Asked to describe the philosophy of Operation Bootstrap, Senor Rafael Pico, President of the Government Development Bank, answered that its basic meaning was to increase the self-reliance of the islanders. "Puerto Ricans," he said, "relied too much in the past years on what came from Washington. We are trying to use the latent energy of the people on our island. Uncle Sam helped Puerto Rico for 40 years and nothing much happened. We believe that financial and other help is needed for a developing society, but we also believe that the greater part of the work must be done by the people who live in the developing society."

Pico acknowledged that many critics of the development scheme believed there was more socialism than capitalism in the programmes. "There are people who disagree with the way things have been done. But the Government has no desire to operate any factories. It is true that we have built and we have managed factories, but the difference is that we built and managed factories like socialists and then we sold the factories to private interests like capitalists. Every factory building owned by the government is for sale and we will finance the purchase from us. A 60% loan, based on appraised value, is available from the development bank and another 20% can be obtained from the Development Corporation."

The success of Fomento is in the main attributable to the Munoz administration and to the distinguished Puerto Rican, Senor Teodoro Moscoso, who was given the job of running it until his appointment as U.S. Ambassador to Venezuela in 1961. Senor Moscoso, who later became head of the Kennedy Administration Alliance For Progress, knows perhaps more than anybody else about Puerto Rico's "great leap forward"— to coin a phrase originated by a totally different type of economist—and in an address to the Board of the Commonwealth Oil Refinery Company, of which he became Chairman in 1965, he gave a clear summing up of Puerto Rico's present economic situation in the late sixties. The following excerpts from the address speak for themselves :

"I have participated in the struggles that have led Puerto Rico from terrible poverty to a much brighter place in the economic sun. I know how ripe the island is for still further development industrially. I know how badly the island still needs such development economically. By all acknowledged standards, Puerto Rico a quarter of a century ago was an undeveloped area. Its economic growth rate was extremely slow, its per capita G.N.P. [gross national product] was only $120 per year. Today per capita G.N.P. is $1,068 per year; industrial income has grown from $27 million to $540 million, far outstripping agricultural income; over the past five years the per capita net rate of economic growth at constant prices has averaged 9·3%—one of the highest rates in the world and matched only by Japan, West Germany and Israel.

"In 1964 we displaced Venezuela as the Latin American area with the highest per capita income; since then we have pulled farther ahead of Venezuela—no mean trick when you consider their oil and iron ore wealth, which we don't have in Puerto Rico. Aside from a conscious planned effort by Puerto Rico to raise the level of education, health and welfare of its people, the principal factor in this transformation is the politico-economic relationship of Puerto Rico with the United States. This has permitted a reciprocal free flow of goods and capital between the island and the mainland which has benefitted both partners. In addition, we have an abundant supply of skilled labour, capable of high productivity at lower costs than on the mainland. And there is the attractive incentive of local tax exemptions, ranging from ten to seventeen years.

"Today approximately 1,200 of our manufacturing plants operating on the island were established under the auspices of Operation Bootstrap. Among them are plants run by 24 of the one hundred largest U.S. corporations and by hundreds of smaller U.S. companies. About 130,000 people are now employed in manufacturing in Puerto Rico. This is substantially more than the average number working in agriculture, and the difference in employment betwen the two fields is certain to become much greater as our young and vigorous petrochemical industry expands. The weekly payroll of plants sponsored by Fomento today is about $3·4 million—or more than $160 million per year. The net income from manufacturing on the island which amounted to about $540 million in 1965 will almost triple by 1975, according to estimates by Rafael Durand, Administrator of Fomento, and his staff. 'Never before has an underdeveloped agricultural region achieved such remarkable results in such unpromising circumstances,' the Canadian economist Murray Bryce wrote a few years ago.

"Another highly significant statistic is this: In fiscal 1965,

Puerto Rico, with a population of only 2,650,000, exported merchandise valued at $943 million to the United States and imported goods worth approximately $1·3 billion from the United States. Only Holland has so much export-import business per capita. [Preliminary 1967 figures indicate exports of more than one billion dollars.] Under the economic stimulus of Operation Bootstrap, Puerto Rico has developed into the fifth largest market in the world for the U.S. Only Canada, Japan, West Germany and the United Kingdom buy more—and indications are that Puerto Rico will soon surpass both the United Kingdom and West Germany as a consumer of U.S. goods. On a per capita basis, Puerto Rico buys more from the United States than any other country in the world."

In addition to the development of industry, tourism was always regarded by Fomento and the Bootstrap people as being one of the best ways for Puerto Rico to make economic progress, and in 1949, when the Caribe Hilton was opened, an intensive campaign to promote it was started. Fomento had, in fact, invested $7,200,000 to build the hotel, which was then leased to the Hilton chain. Its immediate success encouraged further hotel construction by private interests, and the result today is that some 620,000 tourists visit the island and spend about $120,000,000 each year. The tourist industry now provides employment all over the year for some 7,250 people, and in the busy months—January, February and March— more than 8,000 are employed.

Agriculture is just about the only industry in Puerto Rico which did not expand in the late sixties, and the total annual value of agricultural products is now only about $273 million, which is not much more than twice the amount which the tourists spend. Sugar is still the largest agricultural industry, producing about $90 million in value; coffee and tobacco produce about $22 million and $15 million respectively; livestock, poultry and kindred industries produce together about $100 million. Puerto Rico's total net income is of the order of $2,322 million.

The main impetus behind the island's recent economic boom, and indeed the basis on which Bootstrap and Fomento have been operating, has undoubtedly been the tax incentives which the island provides. With no vote in Congress, Puerto Rico is legally protected from all federal income taxes, both corporate and personal. It is the old principle (shades of the Boston Tea Party!) of no taxation without representation. In addition, an exemption from Commonwealth taxes is granted for a period of years to eligible manufacturers of new products. Even after the tax-free period—up to thirteen years total exemption or twenty-six years 50% exemption—it is still advantageous for firms to operate in Puerto Rico because rates of corporate taxation there are only slightly more than half the mainland federal corporate rate. The Government Development Bank of Puerto Rico puts it this way : "At the end of the tax exemption period corporate taxes are applied gradually, reaching the full tax burden in steps spread over a three-year period. As an added incentive, Puerto Rico allows taxpayers to depreciate fixed assets at their own discretion. The importance of this is that at such time as a firm's income becomes taxable, depreciation accruals can be materially increased and taxable income reduced. Experience thus far indicates that termination of the tax exemption period will have only a limited impact, as to closing of plants, on the industrial program and the economy of Puerto Rico."

From the economic, if not perhaps entirely from the political, point of view, Puerto Rico claims to be the "Showcase of Development" in the Caribbean. There seems to be considerable justification for the claim.

SIGHTSEEING

From the visitor's point of view the city of San Juan is divided into two parts, the modern larger section known as Santurce, with its Condado and Miramar areas, and the old section, San Juan Antiguo, which is actually an island connected with the main city by two bridges. Old San Juan is easily the most rewarding of the two sections from the sightseeing point of view and, assuming that you are staying in or near the Condado Beach area, where most of the hotels are, the best thing to do is to walk to the Puente dos Hermanos and get in a bus. By doing this you will be able to savour—if that is the correct word—the astonishing architectural phalanx which has sprung up since the war on both sides of the Avenida Ashford in the form of luxurious hotels constructed in the —sometimes quite pleasing—modern concrete idiom. There is no need to pause during the walk to the bridge but no visitor to Puerto Rico should leave without having glimpsed in passing this glittering monument to the twentieth-century tourist age.

The bus ride, costing a dime, takes you to the Plaza de Colon (this is at the end of the route, so there are no complications about not knowing where to get out) and you find yourself at the entrance to the town of old San Juan proper. Unlike Santo Domingo, which was founded at about the same time, but now has a decayed and disintegrated appearance, Old San Juan has the look of a composite whole which has not changed much, except for the traffic in the narrow streets, since the days of Spanish rule. Almost all the streets, if they do not contain buildings of the sixteenth and seventeenth centuries, provide excellent examples of Spanish colonial architecture of the two subsequent centuries.

It does not much matter what route you take to stroll through the town. Proceed westward along one of the three main streets, crowded now with shoppers, sightseers and "natives" scurrying about their businesses, and you will arrive at the Plaza de Armas, which was Old San Juan's central square in Spanish times. Part of it is now, unfortunately, the site of modern offices, but its essentially Spanish flavour remains. To the north of it is the Alcaldia, an eighteenth-century building which is now the City Hall. To the west of the square is the Intendencia building which was reconstructed in 1851 on the site of a much earlier edifice and now houses the Treasury. Continue westward and, turning right on the Calle Cristo, you come to the Cathedral of San Juan Bautista, parts of which, including a fine Spanish gothic roof, date from about 1540. It is not, however, such an impressive piece of architecture as its contemporary counterpart in Santo Domingo because it was altered and added to through the years and was largely rebuilt in the eighteen-nineties. The remains of Puerto Rico's national hero, Ponce de Leon, were transferred to the cathedral from the church of San Jose in 1908 and are enshrined in marble. Adjacent to the cathedral, on the Plazuela de las Monjas, is the El Convento hotel which is well worth looking at because it is an excellent example of how a seventeenth-century building can be converted into a first-class hotel. Notice the two stepped streets in this part of San Juan which climb from south to north.

It is perhaps a good idea now to stroll southward towards the Bahia de San Juan down the Calle Cristo and note the eighteenth-century La Casa del Libro, which contains a good collection of rare fifteenth-century books, and the Capella del Cristo, which dates from the seventeen-fifties. You should then turn right along part of the old city wall and arrive at La Fortaleza, which has been what the Americans call an executive mansion—or at least the site of one—for more than 400 years. The first building, or fort, on the site was put up in 1533, but rebuilding took place several times in the seventeenth and eighteenth centuries and the present elegantly dignified main building is a mid-nineteenth-century construction. Two of the original fortified towers are among the sixteenth-century remnants of this historic building which is still the centre of Puerto Rico's executive branch of government.

Proceeding northward from La Fortaleza, you see on your left the San Juan Gate, which dates from 1640 and which was the principal entrance to the city from the seaward side. A little further on is the Casa Blanca, one of the most historically interesting buildings in Old San Juan. It was on this site that Governor Juan Ponce de Leon built his first house in San Juan two years after the capital was transferred from Caparra in 1519. It was rebuilt in 1523 after being damaged by a storm and remained in the possession of the Ponce family till 1773 when the Spanish Government bought it and made it the residence of the local army commander. It is now the residence of the United States military commander.

Turning eastward back to the Calle Cristo, you come to three interesting religious buildings : the Bishop's Palace, the convent of Santo Domingo, and the San Jose church. The first is an eighteenth-century building; the second dates from the first half of the sixteenth-century and was the headquarters of the Dominican Order in Puerto Rico but is now occupied by the U.S. military; the third, parts of which date from about 1530, is one of the oldest still existing churches in the western hemisphere. It has a variety of architectural styles, having been added to during the seventeeth, eighteenth and nineteenth centuries; it could also be described as having been the Ponce family church. It was there that the first Governor's body was interred after his death in Cuba from wounds received during his last expedition to Florida; there is a plaque near the high altar of the family coat of arms and the sixteenth-century Spanish crucifix is believed to have been presented to the church by the Ponce family.

You are now adjacent to the main entrance to the El Morro fortress, or rather the fortress of San Felipe de Morro, as it was originally called. Work started on it about 1540 and it was enlarged and strengthened during the next two centuries. This is one of the earliest and best preserved strongpoints set up in the western hemisphere by Europeans and it is still on active service in that it forms part of the United States Fort Brooke military enclave. Those with a nostalgic historical bent will want to wander round its extensive grounds and loiter on the walls and battlements which have a history of more than 400 years. There are guided tours three or four times a day; or you can just wander round by yourself.

Having had your fill of embattled history, you should stroll eastward along the Boulvard del Valle, just inside the northern city wall, till you come to the entrance to Fort San Cristobal, which was the major strongpoint erected to protect the town of Old San Juan from attacks by land from the east. (El Morro was mainly designed to repel invasion from the sea and to protect the harbour entrance.) Here again you can wander round the battlements and fortifications before returning to the nearby Plaza de Colon and the bus terminal. On the way back to Santurce you should notice the grandiose El Capitolio (Capitol) building on the north side of the Avenida Ponce de Leon, which was built in the nineteen-twenties in the somewhat pretentious semi-classical style which is peculiar to buildings of this type and period. Just before arriving at the Puente dos Hermanos you might stop and have a look at the partially restored ruins of Fort San Geronimo, the most easterly of the Old San Juan island fortresses, which now contains a military museum. It is near the Caribe Hilton hotel, which is one of the plushest of the plush residences of today's North American tourist conquistadors. It is interesting, if not profitable, to sip a rum punch there and consider what the Spanish conquistadors who founded San Juan four and a half centuries ago would think of the present goings-on; in many ways, I suspect, they would approve.

There is little of architectural or historical interest, apart from one or two good new buildings, in the sprawling Santurce section of San Juan, or New San Juan, as it might be called. It is essentially a bustling commercial centre and the fact that it is in the tropics makes it only minimally more attractive than its North American equivalents. It is interesting, however, to take a trip to the southern Rio Pedras area of the city along the Avenida Luis Munoz Rivera (named after Munoz Marin's distinguished writer-politician father) on either side of which you can see an impressive array of modern, efficient-looking factories, many of which owe their origin to Operation Bootstrap. In this area there is also the main campus of the University of Puerto Rico, which was founded in 1903 and which is now, with its 20,000 or more students, one of the biggest centres of advanced study in the Americas. There is a museum, an art gallery and a theatre where an annual music festival, known as the Festival Casals, is held in honour of the famous cellist who has lived for many years in Puerto Rico.

You would be well advised to round off this trip by turning right off the Avenida at the University Agricultural Experimental Station and driving along Routes 21 and 20 till you come to the Villa Caparro on Route 2. This is the site of the first Spanish settlement in Puerto Rico and the foundations can be seen of the house which Ponce de Leon built there in 1508. You can return to the centre of the city along Route 2.

One of the most interesting drives in the vicinity of San Juan is that which takes you along Route 3 to the townships of Carolina Luiza and Rio Grande and then southward to the famous rain forest in the Sierra de Luquillo. You drive up the slopes of Mount El Yunque (The Anvil) to an altitude of nearly 3,500 ft. through one of the most luxuriant forest growths in the Caribbean where the annual rainfall is as high as 184 inches. This northeast corner of Puerto Rico has been sensibly "developed" as a sort of national park, on similar lines to those which have enhanced the natural beauty of the National Park in the island of St. John in the American Virgin Islands. You can swim in fresh-water pools and walk along trails between giant ferns and lush tropical vegetation on which wild orchids grow.

Before you go back on Route 3 to Rio Grande it is worthwhile turning eastward for about four miles to the coastal village of Luquillo where there is one of the best white sand beaches in Puerto Rico. (It can be a bit crowded on weekends and holidays but it is a beautiful spot for a swim.) On the way back you should turn right just beyond Rio Grande along Route 187 and pay a visit to the charming coastal village of Loiza Aldea, which was first settled in about 1511 and which is full of early Spanish colonial charm. You then cross the the Loiza river by a little ferry and drive back to San Juan along the coast road (still Route 187), pausing, if you feel like it, for another swim on the Boca de Cangrejos beach near the Isla Verde airport. This is a very pleasant drive which can be done in a day, or even half a day, if you are pressed for time.

Another pleasant trip from San Juan which takes a day is that along Route 2 westward to the town of Arecibo which was first settled by the Spaniards in about 1555 and which is named after an Arawak chief. You can have lunch at a good restaurant on the plaza and savour the historic atmosphere of a coastal town which repulsed an attack by the English in 1702. There is a good beach presided over by an old Spanish lighthouse where you can lie in the sun and consider the fact that Sir Francis Drake is supposed to have attempted a landing here almost four centuries ago. You should return to San Juan along the coastal road (Route 681) and stop, about four miles east of Arecibo, at La Cueva de Indio (Indian Cave) where there are some interesting pre-Columbian carvings and inscriptions. You cannot do this trip in less than a full day, particularly if you feel like visiting one of Puerto Rico's major rum factories just outside Arecibo which hospitably offers you a taste of "the wine of the country."

Puerto Rico claims to have more than 3,000 miles of good roads and it is easy enough—pleasant enough, too—to spend a whole week, or more, touring the island. Perhaps the best way to do this is to travel by the method of transport known as the *publico*. There are scheduled bus services which take you almost anywhere you want to go in Puerto Rico, but the *publico*, which is actually a large taxi in which each passenger pays his own fare, is perhaps more comfortable and it will stop anywhere on its route—sometimes even off the route—to pick you up or let you get off. The fact that Puerto Rico has quite a high population density (about 750 people to the square mile) might suggest that it is not easy to get away from the crowds; but this is not the case. Outside the San Juan area and the areas of the two other major towns, Ponce and Mayaguez, there are literally hundreds of places whose seclusion and rural remoteness makes you forget all about Fomento and the wonders of industrialisation; and there are dozens of lovely beaches where you can picnic and bathe in splendid isolation.

There is no point in suggesting lots of specific places and routes to visit. There are so many that it would be impossible to be anything like comprehensive; but you should see the mountainous countryside and some of the small towns of the interior, and you should go to both the south and the west coasts—that is, if you have time to spend two or three nights at any of the wide choice of hotels en route. Puerto Rico is about 95 miles long and 35 miles wide, so there is no question of seeing it all in a day, or even in two.

A good way to go south, either in a *publico* or a rented car, and at the same time see the interior, is via Comerio and the hill towns of Barranquitas, Aibonito and Cayey. On this route you pass through some beautiful mountain scenery which makes you think that the story they tell you about how Aibonito got its name is probably true. It seems that the early Spaniards kept on exclaiming "Ai, bonito!" ("Oh, how beautiful!") when they first came to this part of the island; and from Cayey on to Guayama, on the foothills of the south coast, the steeply spiralling road keeps up the scenic standard.

At Guayama you should turn right along the coast (Routes 3 and 1), via Salinas and Santa Isabel, and head for Puerto Rico's second biggest city, Ponce, named, of course, after the first Governor. Ponce, which was first settled in 1692, is very much a city in its own right; it has a university, a museum and a cathedral. Despite the fact that it is now the centre of a major industrial complex—cement plants, iron foundries, canneries, textile factories and a huge petro-chemical complex —the city itself still has something of the flavour of an important Spanish colonial town and it is well worth spending an hour or so wandering round the central plaza—or rather two plazas, with the Cathedral of Our Lady of Guadelupe in the middle—and the adjoining streets which contain a number of attractive Spanish colonial balconied houses. Ponce now has at least one first-class hotel, so it is quite a good place to spend the night.

From Ponce you can drive westward along the coast (Route 2), turning left just beyond Yauco on to Route 116 which you follow till you come to the signpost pointing left to Parguera. This is an attractive little fishing village and it has become well-known in tourist circles because there is a bay near it whose water is phosphorescent, and it is quite an experience to go boating there at night. This also is a good place to spend the night.

You now proceed northward to the delightful small town of San German, which was first settled in 1573 and for a century or so rivalled San Juan in importance. A town bearing the name San German was actually built in 1512 on the coast at the mouth of the Guaorabo River, but the inhabitants were so pestered by raiding privateers that they decided to move inland, taking the name of their first settlement with them. San German, though now a favoured tourist spot, is perhaps the most charming of Puerto Rico's old towns and it has a genuine Spanish atmosphere, particularly in the evening when the people who live there stroll about its plaza and near-by streets where there are many attractive, smartly maintained seventeenth- and eighteenth-century houses. On high ground at one end of the plaza is the Porta Coeli church, which, so rumour insists, was founded by Diego Columbus, the son of the explorer. The original date of the restored building you see now, which houses a museum of religious art, is probably a century later than the Columbus era.

From San German you drive along Route 114 to Puerto Rico's third largest city, Mayaguez. Like Ponce on the south coast, this busy port is the main centre in the west of the island's sugar and other agricultural products. Again like Ponce, it has become in recent years an important industrial centre, with, among others, plants producing fertilisers, leather goods, tiles, rum and beer. It is the centre also of Puerto Rico's very considerable needlework industry, which now includes carpet-making and the manufacture of abrasives. It is the site of the University of Puerto Rico Schools of Engineering (there is a nuclear reactor) and Agriculture; and at the Federal Agricultural Experimental Station there is a collection of tropical plants, which, it is claimed, is the largest in the western hemisphere. A great part of Mayaguez was destroyed by an earthquake in 1918, so there is little to be seen in the way of Spanish architecture, but, with its broad avenues and tree-bedecked plazas, it is a pleasant enough city; and it has a hotel of first-class international standard.

From Mayaguez you can continue northward (Route 2) along the coast to Aguada and Aguadilla, each of which claims to be the spot where Columbus's party first went ashore in 1493. In Aguada, allegedly founded as early as 1506, there is a mark denoting the exact place of the Columbus landing; but there is also a monument in Aguadilla claiming the same distinction; so you can take your choice. Aguadilla is the centre of Puerto Rico's straw handicraft industry. From there Route 2 takes you via Arecibo, Vega Baja (where there is an excellent beach for a swim) and the agricultural-industrial town of Bayamon, back to San Juan.

M

Let it be emphasised once again that there are many dozens of interesting places to visit in Puerto Rico which have not been mentioned here—the port of Fajardo, for instance, on the east coast, from which you can go by boat to the offshore Isla de Vieques—but perhaps some idea has been given, as a basis for individual planning, of the sort of things you can expect to see.

HOTELS, RESTAURANTS AND ENTERTAINMENT

The very name Puerto Rico is almost synonymous these days with the word hotel. This was by no means so before the second world war, and it follows, therefore, that quite a lot of the island's hotels are either new or modern conversions of old buildings; and this means that, with few exceptions, whatever category of hotel you chose, you can rely on getting clean and up-to-date accommodation.

In the Condado area of San Juan half a dozen hotels warrant A-plus rating because they have all, or nearly all, the qualifying facilities—nightclubs with floorshows, cocktail lounges, several restaurants, air-conditioning, shopping facilities, private beaches, swimming pools, tennis courts, good food and service. In short, it would be possible to spend a lengthy holiday entirely within the walls of these hotels; they are attractively decorated in a variety of modern styles inside and their generally towering and impressive exteriors are just what you associate with the big hotel names such as Hilton and Sheraton. (There are actually two Hiltons; one, the Caribe Hilton, near the old Fort San Geronimo, is not strictly speaking in the Condado area.) Other top rank hotel names in this part of San Juan include the Condado Beach and the La Concha. In the same area there are several hotels which must be given an A-minus rating because, though some have beach facilities, they are not situated on the ocean front and are generally smaller, though not necessarily less comfortable or less attractively decorated than their opposite numbers on the seaward side of the Avenida Ashford. Among these are the Condado Lagoon, the Da Vinci, the Flambouyan and La Rada.

Small hotels or guest houses also exist in the Condado area and it is perfectly possible to say truthfully when you get back home that you have stayed on the fabulous Condado Beach without having had to pay anything like the high prices with which the area is associated. It seems, however, that these smaller places, mostly converted private houses, are getting fewer and fewer as they are demolished to make way for new buildings.

In the Santurce and Miramar areas of San Juan there are several A-minus hotels—the Pierre and the Miramar Charterhouse are perhaps the two most prominent—which offer first-class accommodation, food and service but which are not holiday hotels in the strict sense of the words, though they do have swimming pools and can cater for most tourist wants. In the B bracket, both plus and minus, there are a dozen or so hotels in the Santurce neighbourhood and I have always found the Capitol to be among those which provide good value for money. There are, of course, quite a lot of C category hotels and guest houses in San Juan, but they are not of much interest to visitors from abroad because the B category hotels offer such a wide choice of reasonably priced accommodation.

In Old San Juan I would very much like to be able to give the Hotel El Convento an A-plus rating because it is unique in Puerto Rico—a charmingly modernised seventeenth-century building right in the centre of the old Spanish town; and its service and food are excellent. It has not got, however, the stipulated A-plus facilities, so it must be content with an A-minus classification. The Palace hotel in Old San Juan has a B-plus rating and there are one or two C category establishments such as you would expect to find in the labyrinthine streets of an old Spanish city.

On the excellent beach near Isla Verde airport, about 15 minutes drive eastward from Santurce, there are three large hotels which might warrant A-plus rating—the Americana, the Holiday Inn and the El San Juan. In the same area, though not on the beach, the Hotel La Posada is in the B category. The hotel at the top of the main Isla Verde airport building warrants a B-plus rating and is a good place to stay if you are merely visiting San Juan for a day or so on business.

Outside the San Juan area there are at least four hotels with A-plus ratings. Two of these, the Dorado Beach (a project of the ubiquitous millionaire, Laurance Rockefeller) and the Dorado Hilton, are on the coast about 20 miles west of the capital and provide all the resort facilities—night entertainment, golf courses, and so on—which the most exacting tourist could want; and both have arrangements for getting you to and from San Juan at a reasonable price. The Mayaguez Hilton is on the west coast just outside Puerto Rico's third largest city and it has all the variegated resort attractions which one associates with the name Hilton. On the south coast, at Ponce, the island's second biggest city, there is El Ponce Intercontinental, which, also as the well-known name suggests, caters for all the normal holiday wants. There are two or three B category hotels in Ponce. At Fajardo, on the east coast, the hotel El Conquistador, with its funicular down to the beach, almost warrants an A-plus rating.

In its smaller towns and villages Puerto Rico offers accommodation of excellent value. At the charming hill town of Barranquitas, some 2,300 ft. above sea level, the Hotel Barranquitas must be classified as A-minus because of the charm of its surroundings and the facilities—tennis, pitch-and-putt golf, horseback riding—which it offers at extremely reasonable prices. The Treasure Island hotel in the hill town of Cidra has similar qualifications and warrants a good B-plus rating. Several of the lesser-known hill towns offer accommodation and facilities of excellent value. Among the hotels in or near the smaller coastal towns, the Hotel Montemar at Aguadilla probably warrants an A-minus classification and the Villa Parguera (near the phosphorescent bay), with its good water sports facilities, gets a good B-plus rating. In the same category is the Copamarina Beach at Guanica. But you will find as you drive round Puerto Rico that there are pleasant little hostelries in many of the remoter villages situated both on the coast and inland; you can also get accommodation in cottage colonies, and there are one or two old Spanish colonial farm houses where you can stay, with all meals included, for as little as $4 or $5 a day. So the choice is wide; and you do not have to make reservations before setting out from San Juan; in fact Puerto Rico is in many ways the ideal place in which to set out on an exploring trip stopping for the night, or longer, at whatever spot takes your fancy.

Each of the A category hotels has one or more restaurants where good food is to be had at both lunch and dinner. Normally included in the menu are Spanish rice dishes such as *arroz con pollo* or *paellas*, lobster and land crab dishes, and the excellent thick *asopao* (soup). Roast suckling pig seems to be a speciality favoured by many Puerto Rican restaurants; and always available, of course, to satisfy the taste of the most choosy expatriate American, is the charcoal-broiled steak. At one or two of the hotels Italian food is available and many of them offer what they call "continental" dishes (what continent?), which usually means a not entirely satisfactory rendition of French cuisine. Nevertheless, these A category hotel restaurants have in the main a reasonably high standard.

An interesting feature of San Juan culinary life (as, indeed, it is of other similar American-dominated tourist centres) is the large number of smaller eating places which have sprung up round the big hotels. This presumably is due to the fact that it is not customary for this type of hotel to quote terms which include all meals. You must, therefore, eat out at least some of the time, and in the Condado area you do not have far to walk before you come across a reasonably cheap and good place of the coffee shop variety where anything from hamburgers to a full meal is available. There are also several good and reasonably priced Spanish-style restaurants in the vicinity.

Indeed the Condado-Santurce-Miramar district of San Juan offers an astonishingly large variety of restaurants ranging from the Swiss Chalet, where the food is of top international standard, down to the dozen or more small and less expensive, but on the whole clean and good, establishments on or near the Avenida Ponce de Leon. In this area too there are several larger modern places of the cafeteria type where you can get a meal of a quality and price which compares very favourably with its equivalent on the U.S. mainland. There are restaurants which specialise in particular types of dishes such as German, Scandinavian, Chinese or seafood. There is at least one quite good French restaurant and the American-Italian style of cuisine is—or was—represented by an establishment which rejoices in the name of *Mama's Little Italy*.

In Old San Juan there are several places of the type one would expect to find in the Soho area of London or the Greenwich Village section of New York. There, also, you find speciality restaurants—Spanish, Italian, American-Puerto Rican, or just plain hamburger–hot dog. The La Zambra seemed to me to be a good example of the Spanish type—so did the La Mallorquina, which claims to be the oldest restaurant in Puerto Rico—and there are several small places where you can get quite a good pizza-type meal. In short, San Juan, both old and new—and this includes the Isla Verde area —is probably the most gastronomically satisfying of all the places mentioned in this book. Even in the country districts outside San Juan you will be unlucky if you cannot find a place to get a good meal, and there are, of course, the A category hotels, such as those at Fajardo, Ponce and Mayaguez, whose restaurants are always reliable.

Night entertainment in San Juan is also of a quality and variety which cannot be equalled—at the moment anyway—in the other islands. You have only to walk along the Avenida Ashford and see the "billboards" advertising the performers in the nightclubs of the plush hotels to realise that many of the top mainland entertainers are recruited for the Puerto Rican circuit; and you can dance till the small hours to the music of first-class bands either, as the guide books like saying, "under the stars" or in the traditional dimly lit nightclub surroundings. There are at least two dozen good quality places to go in the Santurce area where you get less spectacular entertainment than that offered by the hotels, but the floorshows, if only consisting of a single pianist or chanteuse, are generally of a high standard. I have not discovered a discotheque, but I am sure there are several.

In Old San Juan, as you would expect, there are places where you can go and drink wine out of pitchers while listening to guitar music, or there is the more sophisticated atmosphere of the El Convento nightclub where the decor is colourfully Spanish renaissance. Old San Juan is still, after all, very much a seaport and it is natural that there should be a good choice of the smaller type bar or "bistro"—"dives" some of them might be called—where you can dance to jukebox music. Some of these are respectable enough to cater for tourists, but some of them are not. For that matter there are plenty of such "dives" in the modern part of San Juan, and an evening "on the town" can be both varied and colourful. Then, of course, there are the gambling casinos in the big hotels where most normal games of chance are played. In those I have visited the lowest stake at roulette is a dollar, so you do not have to be a millionaire to spend an hour or two at the tables.

But let it not be supposed that evening entertainment in San Juan is restricted to the frivolous. The very competent Ballets de San Juan has a short season each year, and serious stage productions are frequently put on by the Little Theatre group. There are two or three film societies which show the best international productions; there are symphony concerts; and there is the annual Festival Casals at which some of the world's best musicians perform.

SPORT AND RECREATION

One cannot help feeling that many visitors to the A category hotels in San Juan spend much of their time alternating between the swimming pools and the bars, restaurants and entertainment places within, as it were, the four walls of the establishments they are staying in; nor can they be criticised for doing so. There are few more delightful ways of spending a lazy week or so than around the pools and beaches of these ocean-side hotels; the more energetic will find, however, that first-class facilities exist in Puerto Rico for almost all forms of warm-climate sport.

Swimming, either in pools or on beaches, can be enjoyed all over the island and many of the best hotels provide their own facilities for snorkelling, skin-diving and water-skiing. The Condado Beach area, which is exposed to Atlantic breakers, does not seem to be ideal for water sports of this type, however, and the enthusiast would be advised to go to one of the many places where the beach is more protected—Isla Verde, Dorado, Ponce or Fajardo, for example—where the water conditions and the facilities provided by the hotels are excellent. So they are at some of the smaller places, such, for example, as Parguera.

The best place for sailing in Puerto Rico is probably the Fajardo area of the east coast, though there are active yacht clubs in several other places, including San Juan, Ponce, Mayaguez and many of the small coastal towns, at all of which you can rent sailing craft or motorboats by the hour or day. A good place to charter boats of large size for more extensive cruising is the little harbour of Las Croabas, near Fajardo; off this part of the coast there are many islands and islets which make a pleasant cruising area, and on one of them, Cayo Obispo, there is a marina with efficient docking and other facilities needed by yachtsmen.

Deep-sea fishing—marlin, tuna, albacore, bonito, sailfish, tarpin—is an increasingly popular year-round sport in Puerto Rican waters, and the Club Nautico in San Juan sponsors frequent tournaments. You can charter boats in the San Juan area of the north coast, but the south and east coasts possibly provide the best facilities for this sport.

Golf enthusiasts will find one of the world's finest (27 holes) championship courses at the Dorado Beach hotel within easy reach of San Juan; and the nearby Dorado Hilton also has a first-class 18-hole course. What must be one of the most unusual places to play golf in the world is the nine-hole course inside the walls of the El Morro fortress, two of whose holes are in the old moat. There is another nine-hole course at the Berwind Country Club in the Rio Piedras area of San Juan, and there are club courses also at Ponce, Mayaguez and Aguadilla. Most of the A category hotels in Puerto Rico have tennis courts, and the dozen or more private clubs throughout the island usually welcome visitors.

Good facilities for horseback riding are to be found in several of the country hotels and there is a hackney stable at Rio Piedras (San Juan). The shooting of waterfowl and other forms of game is controlled by the Department of Agriculture from whom details of seasons and permits may be obtained.

The most popular sport in Puerto Rico is baseball, but cock-fighting follows it closely. The Canto Gallo pit in Santurce is the most convenient for San Juan visitors, but there are many others all over the island. Horse-racing is held two or three days a week at the modern, beautifully laid out El Commandante track. Bowling enthusiasts will find that their needs are well catered for by an increasing number of *boleras*.

THINGS TO BUY

Compared with the Virgin Islands, the Bahamas and Bermuda, it does not seem to me that Puerto Rico can lay claim to be an outstandingly good place in which to go shopping. It is true that you can buy most things there which you can in a town in the U.S. mainland of equivalent size, plus many "luxury" items which you cannot get in such a town. It is true also that a few items imported from Europe or Latin America can be bought at a cheaper price than in the mainland; but the fact remains that Puerto Rico is not a free-port and, being customswise virtually part of the United States, you cannot expect to pick up outstanding bargains to take home; and this applies also to the visitor from Europe or Latin America. The rum made in Puerto Rico is both excellent and cheap but it seems that federal tax has to be added to the price if it is taken into the mainland United States.

Undoubtedly the best buys in Puerto Rico are the locally made handicraft products. Among the best of these are embroidery and needlework in general; straw goods such as mats, lampshades and hats made from local reeds; and hand-painted materials for dresses. It is worthwhile also having a look at the one or two picture and art galleries—*La Casa del Arte* in Old

San Juan is one of the best—to see what they have to offer in the way of wood carvings, paintings, and ceramic work; and some of these are very good. Locally-made trinkets to take home as souvenirs are obtainable in some of the hotel boutiques and in one or two shops in the Santurce district.

USEFUL FACTS FOR VISITORS

Puerto Rico has an area of 3,345 square miles and is situated about 1,000 miles southeast of Miami and 300 miles south of the Tropic of Cancer. The interior is dominated by two mountain ranges stretching mainly from east to west; the highest point (4,398 ft.) is the Cerro de Punta. Agriculture— predominantly sugar—is mostly confined to the lower coastal areas. There are 45 rivers.

The average temperature is 78·9° F. (26° C.) in summer and 73·4° F. or 22° C. in winter. The mean is somewhat higher on the south coast and in certain mountain areas it can be as much as ten degrees lower. The northeasterly trade winds have a cooling effect throughout the year, and Puerto Rico, though in the tropics, is very much a place for year-round vacationing, though its busiest season corresponds with the winter months of North America and Europe. Average annual rainfall is 64 inches but the variation in different areas is extreme, being as high as 200 inches in the Luquillo rain forest area and as low as 30 inches in the southern coastal plain. There is no well-defined rainy season, but, in general, the heaviest rainfall can be expected between the end of May and December.

The majority of the 2,750,000 inhabitants of Puerto Rico, apart from North Americans who live there, are of Spanish descent, though some are Portuguese, French or Corsican in origin. About 23% have Negro blood and there are still some traces of the Amerindian left. The language is Spanish, though in the areas frequented by tourists English is normally understood; in business circles English is also normally understood and spoken.

About a dozen major airlines call at San Juan's Isla Verde

airport which must have one of the world's biggest purely tourist rates of arrival and departure. There are almost hourly jet flights to and from points in North America, and the carriers include Pan American, Eastern and Delta. B.W.I.A., Caribair and Air France connect with points in the Caribbean and with international services at various points. Iberia and Avianca are among the carriers which serve both Europe and Latin America direct. Charter flights are readily obtainable at Isla Verde.

San Juan is the port of call for many cruise ships, predominantly from North America but some also from Europe. Half a dozen or so freighter-passenger lines call regularly from North American ports at San Juan, Mayaguez and Ponce, but, on the whole, Puerto Rico is better served by air than by sea from the tourist's point of view.

The headquarters of the Commonwealth Department of Tourism is at 22 Avenida Ponce de Leon. There are offices in many cities of the United States and Canada, and in London Puerto Rico's tourist affairs are looked after by the United States Travel Service.

THE ISLANDS OF THE ELEVEN
THOUSAND VIRGINS

The Virgin Islands

"If a plebiscite were held . . ."—Ralph Paiewonsky, Governor of the American Virgin Islands

A morning ritual, which takes place in the harbour of Charlotte Amalie, capital of St. Thomas, in the U.S. Virgin Islands graphically illustrates one of the most important issues which since the 1950's has been facing the inhabitants of this northerly group of Caribbean islands, roughly half of which are American and half British. Shortly after eight o'clock two large motor launches tie up at the wharf near the centre of the town. About an hour later a United States Immigration official arrives, rigs up a sort of temporary desk; and the hundred or more passengers disembark from the launches which have brought them on a two-hour journey through some of the most attractive scenery in the world from the neighbouring British island of Tortola.

The disembarking passengers, almost all of Negro stock, are British citizens coming to seek work in the thriving tourist economy of the American islands; and the issue which they raise is the somewhat sensitive one of whether or not the British islands should become overseas possessions—colonies, virtually—of the United States. (The American islands, St. Thomas, St. Croix and St. John, plus a multitude of much smaller islands, were brought by Washington in 1917 for $25,000,000 from Denmark; the largest British islands are Tortola, Virgin Gorda, Anegada and Jost Van Dyke). Financial statistics suggest a merger would be the most intelligent thing for the British islands to seek. Government revenue in the U.S. Virgin Islands which have a total population of about 42,000 is in excess of $25 million a year and tourist expenditure is in the neighbourhood of $50 million. In the British

Virgin Islands, which have a population of some 7,500, revenue is not much more than $1 million. Annual per capita income in the U.S. Virgin Islands runs at the astonishingly high level of about $1,800. No accurate figure is available for the British islands, but estimates put it at a mere fraction of the U.S. figure. Minimum wages in the U.S. islands are about $60 a month and in the British islands about a third of this.

It is not surprising, therefore, that the British Virgin Islanders—at any rate the younger ones—should have been flocking to work in St. Thomas and St. Croix (St. John, almost two-thirds of which is a U.S. National Park, has a population of not much more than 1,000 and, except in one large hotel, not much work to offer). Though they may not be aware of the fact, tourists in the hotels and restaurants of St. Thomas and St. Croix are mostly waited on and driven around in taxis by British Virgin Islanders, or even by immigrants from the more distant British islands of Antigua, St. Kitts or Nevis. The estimated number of British citizens in the U.S. Virgin Islands is 10,000.

In May, 1965, the Governor of the U.S. islands, Mr. Ralph M. Paiewonsky, said that 30% of all births in St. Thomas and St. Croix hospitals came from British Virgin Island mothers, and he added : "If a plebiscite were held tomorrow, 80% of the British Virgin Islanders would vote for annexation" of their territories by the United States. Mr. Paiewonsky had, some months before, created a stir at the opening ceremony of a luxury beach hotel financed on (British) Virgin Gorda by Mr. Laurance Rockefeller. In the presence of the Administrator of the British Virgin Islands and other dignatories of both nationalities he handed the United States flag to Mr. Rockefeller. The implications of this act were only too obvious.

Flag-waving or not, the fact remains that the British and Americans are living cheek by jowl in a group of islands whose magnificent beaches, yachting facilities and general scenic splendour have only recently become widely known; and there has been—at any rate up till the late sixties—a certain amount of ill-feeling. Some British islanders claimed that the United States immigration laws should be altered to enable those who go to St. Thomas to work on a temporary basis to send their children to the public schools and to get free medical attention. They paid social security money, they said, and why should they not get the benefit of it? The feeling was that they were being exploited. But then the Americans pointed out that nobody asked the British islanders to come in the first place, and the lady superintendent of the hospital in Charlotte Amalie emphasised to me that they, their wives and children created grave problems of overcrowding.

All these problems are well known to the opposite number of the American Governor, the Administrator of the British Virgin Islands, whose offices are in the tiny capital of Tortola, which goes by the unattractive name of Road Town. To improve their economies and create jobs Tortola and the other British islands are trying their best to catch up tourist-wise with their American neighbours. A road leading from one end of Tortola to the other has been completed (cars are still a comparative rarity); hoteliers are being encouraged to come by tax concessions; Rockefeller money is already developing Virgin Gorda; it is hoped soon to enlarge the Tortola airstrip to accommodate larger aircraft; and emphasis is being placed on the fact that, though the British Virgin Islands are part of the sterling area, the U.S. dollar is not only in general use but is also an official currency.

It became clear, too, from talking to Tortolans that Governor Paiewonsky's claim that 80% of the British islanders would vote to become American was not accurate. The figure, I was assured, was nearer 50%, and it was this high for strictly economic reasons. "We are proud to be British", was a phrase I have heard used more than once in Tortola. Another opinion expressed was that there were certain values beyond money, and among these was the British system of justice. A Briton living on one of the small cays off Tortola made the point that he would not necessarily object to Washington taking over the British islands but he would very strongly object to being governed from St. Thomas where some people's sense of integrity in public affairs left much, in his opinion, to be desired.

Nevertheless, in both sections of the Virgin group of islands

N

intelligent people have been expressing the view that the islands possess a magnificent potential for development on a binational basis along the lines, possibly, of the remarkable experiment which has been made in the Bahama islands—particularly Grand Bahama—by a consortium of North American and British investors.

American Virgin Islands

"Gold moved through the streets in wheelbarrows . . ."—
Alexander Hamilton

Possibly nowhere else in the Caribbean is there a better place to stand than on the waterfront of Charlotte Amalie, capital of the U.S. Virgin Islands, and sense the feeling of continued history combined with fantastic present-day change. To begin with, you will notice that, though you are in United States territory, the names of the streets are mostly in Danish. The cars have left-hand drive, but the rule of the road is to keep to the left. There is the brashness which one expects of an American tourist centre—neon-lit bars, hot-dog stands, Coca-Cola signs, and so on—but the buildings in or on which these things are to be found are for the most part dignified and ornate examples of the best type of European colonial architecture. American tourist vulgarity has by no means destroyed the charm of a town which was named after a Danish Queen (wife of King Christian V), has a number of French inhabitants, and was twice under British rule.

In Christiansted, principal city of the island of St. Croix, you get the same feeling—possibly, even, to a greater extent—because the centre of the town, or wharf area, has been made into a National Historic Site and it is possible to stroll through the eighteenth-century arcades and alleys and really savour the atmosphere of the city's prosperous Danish past. Though St. Croix also has cashed in on the post-war tourist boom, its out-

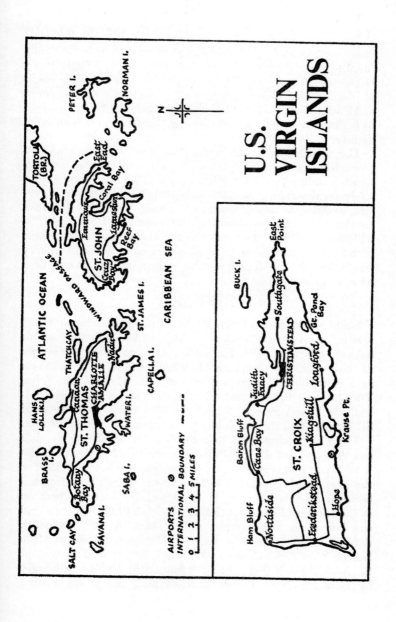

ward neon-light symbols are less evident. Whereas Charlotte Amalie might be described today as being a comparatively fast-moving town geared to cater for the more obvious needs of the tourist, Christiansted has a more dignified, almost residential, tone, and its fine, well-kept colonial buildings seem to be happily browsing and showing themselves off with quiet dignity.

The third main island in the American Virgins group, St. John, has preserved its connections with the past by a policy which is unique in the Caribbean—one of concentrating almost solely on developing its natural beauty. On the whole, therefore, and despite any strictures which might be levelled against the Americans for transforming Alexander Hamilton's gold "in wheelbarrows" into the wealth of the U.S. tourist dollar, these islands can claim to be good examples of how contemporary wealth can be produced without destroying the charm of a more elegant era.

HISTORY

Santa Cruz, now known as St. Croix (pronounced Croy) was among the first lands to be sighted by Columbus on his second voyage in 1493. He landed there to renew his supply of fresh water but found the Caribs so hostile that he sailed on in a northeasterly direction sighting St. Thomas, St. John, Tortola (now British) and other islands. He named them collectively "Las Virgines", reportedly after the 11,000 virgins of St. Ursula; and the name has persisted as the Virgin Islands.

The Caribs continued to show hostility so effectively that no colonisation of the islands was possible till after King Charles V of Spain had sent an army and subdued them in 1555. For the next hundred years possession of the islands was disputed between England, France, Holland and Spain chiefly because of the successful sugar cultivation which had been started and was beginning to bring in wealth. Then, in 1671, Denmark decided to get a share of the rich Caribbean trade, and the Danish West India Company began exploiting St. Thomas and St. John through imported slave labour. St. Croix was bought by Denmark from France in 1733 and, except for a brief period of British occupation during the Napoleonic wars, all three islands remained under Danish sovereignty till 1917.

But the early history of the islands is centred mainly on St. Croix, due to the fact that it is the largest of the group and to the fact also that in 1624 a party of Englishmen settled on St. Kitts, about 125 miles to the east, and so broke Spain's colonial monopoly in this part of the Caribbean. For the next 25 years St. Croix was inhabited by a mixed bag of English, French and Dutch freebooters. Then, in 1650, a Spanish expedition from Puerto Rico seized the island and drove out all settlers; but a few months later a French force from St. Kitts (by then captured from the English) defeated the Spanish garrison and took possession of the island.

It was the French who altered the name, naturally enough, from Santa Cruz to St. Croix, or Holy Cross. In 1651 they sold the island to the Knights of Malta who, apparently being unsuccessful in their efforts to develop it profitably, re-sold it in 1665 to the French West India Company. Nine years later it became a French colony; and it is recorded that, in 1696, no less than 800 colonists of St. Croix were transported to what is now Haiti by King Louis XIV to help develop that territory. Though French colonisation of St. Croix ceased after this, France continued to claim possession of the island, and the result was that it remained largely uninhabited till 1733, when the King of France sold it to the Danish West India and Guinea Company. St. Croix, St. Thomas and St. John thus became a Danish economic and political entity in the Caribbean and the prosperous years began.

During the next 20 years the Danes went all out to attract settlers to St. Croix by offering them land at "bargain" prices. The high mortality rate on the island was overcome by the influx of European immigrants and by pouring in African slaves. By 1755 the population had already risen to 10,200, including nearly 9,000 slaves. Most of the island's fertile land was now under cultivation and, though some cotton was grown, sugar was king in the Danish islands, as it was throughout the Lesser Antilles in the eighteenth century. In 1755 St. Croix, St. Thomas and St. John were sold by the Danish West India

Company to the King of Denmark and for the next 70 or so years the islands had great prosperity.

Due largely to Denmark's policy of neutrality during the European wars of this period, the capital of St. Thomas, Charlotte Amalie, became one of the richest ports and commercial centres in the western hemisphere. It was the largest slave market in the hemisphere and it was a free-port whose jam-packed warehouses were patronised by traders, buccaneers and seafaring men from Spain, France, Holland and England, as well as from the New England coast. Rare goods from all over Europe and the Orient were for sale, and Alexander Hamilton, who was employed as a clerk by a St. Croix merchant from 1766 to 1772, when he visited Charlotte Amalie, made the comment quoted earlier : "Gold moved through the streets in wheelbarrows."

During this period Charlotte Amalie had developed an aristocracy of traders and ship-owners, and it is to them that the island owes its treasure of fine, somewhat ornate, buildings constructed, rather like those of similar communities in the Baltic, from the wealth produced from shipping and trading. In St. Croix, and to a lesser extent in St. John, the wealth was in the hands of the landed aristocracy as can be seen from the estate Great Houses which still exist, and from the impressive stone windmill towers.

Two brief interludes of British rule in St. Thomas occurred during the Napoleonic wars, from which Denmark was not entirely successful in excluding herself. British forces captured St. Thomas in 1801 and remained there for a year. Again in 1807 the island was captured by the British but was finally restored to Denmark in 1815.

After about 1820—that is, a few years after the end of the Napoleonic wars—there was a considerable drop in the price of sugar, and this brought economic distress to St. Croix. The swashbuckling years of wartime boom trading were also over in St. Thomas. In St. Croix and St. John many planters lost their estates through mortgage foreclosures and much land was converted from sugar production to cattle raising. Discontent among the slaves became rife and, with the deeping of the sugar depression, the demands for emancipation were ever more forceful.

In 1847, the King of Denmark issued a proclamation which promised the slaves emancipation in 1859; they were not prepared to wait, however, and, following riots and disturbances, the Governor-General, on 3 July 1848, proclaimed the emancipation of all the "unfree" in the Danish West Indies. But, shortly before this proclamation, rebellious slaves were able to hold the island of St. John for six months. After the revolt was quelled, the slaves, so tradition maintains, killed themselves rather than face the penalties of revolt. About three hundred are supposed to have joined hands and jumped off a cliff on the northern shores of St. John. (It is interesting how similar —almost identical—legends concerning rebellious slaves exist in other Caribbean islands.)

After the freeing of the slaves there was a marked decline in business in the three Danish islands, and prosperity seemed to be a thing of the past. St. Croix's competitive position in the world sugar market got worse owing to the increased cost of production. Discontent spread, and relations between the planters and their labourers became embittered over demands for higher wages. In 1878 there were riots in which the town of Frederiksted was burnt and many plantations were damaged or destroyed. By the end of the nineteenth century St. Croix was little more than a marginal sugar producer, the brisk trade of St. Thomas was little more than a memory, and the forests had largely taken over once again in St. John.

As far back as 1865, the United States, which had been embarrassed by the lack of a naval base in the Caribbean during the Civil War, had made overtures to Denmark concerning the possible sale of the three islands; and negotiations were sporadically carried on over many years. During the 1914-18 war fear that Germany might get possession of the islands provided the final impetus towards their purchase by the U.S. The transfer was completed in 1917, two weeks after the U.S. had entered the war, and the price was $25 million.

The Danish legal code was to a great extent retained after the islands became part of the U.S. but they were administered by the Navy, with naval Governors appointed by the President, till 1931 when the Department of the Interior became responsible and the first civilian Governor was appointed. Under the Revised Organic Act of 1954 the Congress authorised the setting up of distinct executive, legislative and judicial branches in the islands' government. The Governor is still appointed by the President and functions under the supervision of the Secretary of the Interior. There is single-chamber legislature elected for two-year terms.

Latest moves have been to introduce legislation to enable the Virgin Islanders (who have U.S. citizenship) to elect their own Governor, to send an elected delegate to the Congress in Washington, and to vote in national elections for the President of the United States.

ECONOMY

The inhabitants of the U.S. Virgin Islands made a living in the past mostly from agriculture, and a great deal of this was concentrated in St. Croix because the topography of St. Thomas and St. John is such that farming must be limited to the valleys and hillside terraces. Today a new pattern of prosperity has been created by the establishment of small businesses and industries and particularly by the phenomenal growth of tourism. Even in St. Croix, which is more suited to agriculture, much of the arable land is now devoted to cattle-raising, sugar cultivation having been "phased out" as part of a government plan for making better use of the land. Increasing success, however, is being achieved in the production of food crops for export to the winter market of the mainland U.S.A. The rum distilling industry provides one of the islands' main exports and is now being encouraged by the Virgin Islands Rum Council in co-operation with the government; but this is virtually all that remains of the islands' (particularly St. Croix's) sugar plantation economy of bygone days.

Tourism is now by far the most important industry of the U.S. Virgin Islands, contributing more than $50 million annually to their economies. The islands are virtually a free-port and thus attract many shoppers from the mainland; and it is significant that most of the business developments of recent years have had some connection with the tourist industry. Tax incentives exist to encourage the construction of hotels, guest houses, housing projects and industrial concerns in general. Duty-free entry into the mainland U.S. is permitted for articles grown or produced in the islands from either local or U.S. material and also for all products or manufactures of the islands which do not contain, by value, more than 50% of foreign materials.

The Virgin Islands Corporation, wholly owned by the Federal government, plays an important part in the islands' economy in such fields as agriculture, land management, electric power production and distribution, operation of the St. Thomas airport and in the desalination of sea-water for public use. The charter of the Corporation, which was granted in the depression years of the thirties to help stabilise the islands' economy, expires in 1969. The Virgin Islands participate in such federally supported programmes as public housing, urban renewal and various health and educational activities on much the same basis as operates on the mainland. Residents in the islands pay the same federal income tax as do residents of the mainland, but local taxes—the equivalent or State, County, City taxes, etc.—are lower.

All in all the economic picture of the U.S. Virgin Islands is similar to those of other islands in the Caribbean area—the Bahamas, for instance, or Barbados—where the tourist influx has created, and is continuing to create—a new pattern of prosperous living.

The U.S. dollar is the currency of the islands.

St. Thomas

SIGHTSEEING

A woman who made her home in Trinidad shortly after the first world war, but who was born, educated and spent her youth in St. Thomas, has told me some fascinating stories about life there in the final days of Danish rule. In one of them she described a ball which she attended at the Grand Hotel which was then the centre of social life in Charlotte Amalie, but which now, though still a charming, dignified, colonial-style building (completed in 1841), which dominates the north side of the town centre at Emancipation Park, is somewhat decrepit and by no means an hotel of the first order. A junior member of the Danish Royal Family, she said, had arrived on board a warship with his wife, and they both stood receiving their guests at the top of the (still impressive) main staircase of the hotel at the entrance to the grand gallery, a large, beautifully proportioned room (it still is) ablaze with chandeliers. Women with tiaras, long white gloves and flowing skirts; men in colourful uniforms bedecked with orders; flunkeys in tailcoats and knee-breeches. It was the era of the waltz, and my informant told me that "she could have danced all night" because of the beauty (glamour is perhaps the modern word) of the setting—and in the distance, through the deep French windows, could be seen the lights of the Danish warship "dressed overall."

Today, one of the official brochures on the U.S. Virgin Islands has this to say about the Grand Hotel : "there are 18 rooms which can accommodate as many as 50 guests;" that is, almost three to each room. The contrast between then and now is worth noting because it illustrates how, in a comparatively short space of time, the locale of quality shifts. There are plenty of places in Charlotte Amalie where the setting is conducive to dancing all night (that is one reason why so many tourists go there) and it is doubtless true that the town is more attractive, in the sense of having more to offer, in the second half of the twentieth century than it was in the first half; but the story well illustrates the change which has taken place. And one of the reasons why it is fascinating to wander round the town is that one can look at the many lovely old buildings and speculate about what went on in them years ago.

Within a stone's throw, almost, of the Grand Hotel is Fort Christian (1671) which was the main guard centre of the harbour but is now used as a police station. Next to it is the eighteenth-century building which now houses the legislature, but which was formerly the barracks for Danish troops. The elegant and gracefully proportioned Senate Building nearby is one of the finest examples of Danish colonial architecture. On higher ground near the top of the "Street of the Ninety-nine Steps" (much of Charlotte Amalie is built on a hill sloping down to the harbour) is Government House which has a charming period wrought-iron balcony and contains some attractive replicas of Danish colonial furniture. On the same street up more steps is the Hotel 1829, a delightful early nineteenth-century building which began life as a private mansion. Other buildings in the vicinity worth looking at because of their attractive colonial architecture include the former German Consulate, now a government office and oddly named "Quarters B"; and the Danish Consulate, once the private residence of a Danish Governor.

The remains of two towers on hills to the west and east of Charlotte Amalie are of considerable romantic-historic interest. The western one, Blackbeard's castle, dates from 1674, and John Teach, the famous pirate known as Blackbeard, is said to have lived in it. Bluebeard's Castle, now part of a hotel of that name on the eastern hill, was built in 1689 and was used as a fort (Frederiksfort) until 1735. It was sold early in the nineteenth century to a private individual, and the story goes that a manuscript was found in it believed to be the memoirs of the famous Barbary Coast pirate, Musa Ben Hassen, who is supposed to have had seven wives (Blackbeard reportedly had fourteen).

Other early buildings include the Dutch Reformed Church; the Lutheran Church and Parsonage; the Jewish Synagogue, which is one of the oldest in the western hemisphere; and the Nisky Moravian Mission to the west of the town. Also to the west of the town is Cha Cha Village inhabited by descendants of settlers from the French island of St. Barthelemy. The name Cha Cha is supposed to be derived from the expressions of annoyance which the people used to make and this story is substantiated by equivalent expressions which still exist in Caribbean islands with French connections where they make a curious lip formation and utter a word which can approximately be written as "cheeoops".

An interesting feature of Charlotte Amalie is the area to the west of Emancipation Gardens between Main Street, where some of the best shops are, and the Waterfront. Running at right angles to these two streets is a series of lanes or alleys lined by what were originally solidly-built warehouses whose massive, wooden doors have impressive wrought-iron fittings. In the old days these were obviously the business places of the rich Danish (and other) merchants. Today a great many of them have been skillfully modernised and now contain shops, offices, bars and restaurants. Hibiscus Alley, which leads into Beretta Center, is the most distinctive of these alleys and contains the best shops, but there are others through which it is equally pleasant to wander because they still look more or less like what they must have been almost two centuries ago. While in this part of the town it is worth having a look at the Virgin Islands' Museum on Jasmine Lane which has some interesting colonial furniture, coins, and early historical documents. Further west along Main Street—if you are interested in "touristmanship" you can use its original name, Droningens Gade; and the original name for Waterfront, Kronprinsen's Gade—past some pleasant colonial-style buildings, you come to the market which has the usual tourist-beloved fruit stalls presided over by women in colourful costumes.

A trip round St. Thomas by car can be made in a morning or afternoon, though it is probably worth devoting a leisurely whole day to it, as the north coast has some spectacular panoramic scenery and you can pause for lunch on the way. Setting out in an easterly direction, the taxi driver takes you round the eastern tip of the island past Redhook Bay (from which boats take you to St. John) and on to Sapphire Bay which has one of the finest beaches in the island and an excellent water sports centre. The island of Thatch Cay soon becomes visible on your right as you continue, slightly inland, along the north coast. The road begins to climb steeply as you come in sight of Magens Bay with its lovely circular white sand beach which is open to the public. It is certainly one of the finest bays in the Caribbean, and from the road high above it you can see some of the British Virgin Islands in the distance.

At a high point in the road you come to a spot called Drake's Seat where the famous British Admiral and explorer, Sir Francis Drake, is said to have contemplated the ocean and dreamed of new lands to discover. A little beyond is Mafolie, originally a French settlement, with its pleasant little church; and then you come to the Mountain Top Hotel, near the summit of Signal Hill (1,400 feet) with its magnificent view of Magens Bay and the Atlantic Ocean. You continue past the Agricultural Experimental Station at Estate Dorothea on the slopes of Crown Mountain (1,500 feet) and turn left to descend the southern slopes of the central range, pausing again, if you like, at the Shibui Hotel where you get a fine view of the south coast; and so back to Charlotte Amalie.

It is also worth going on one of the regular boat trips round Charlotte Amalie harbour, which is one of the most pleasant from the scenic point of view in the Caribbean; and you can spend the day on Water Island where there is a good hotel and beach.

St. Croix

SIGHTSEEING

The largest of the three main U.S. Virgin Islands and in some ways the most attractive is St. Croix. If you are in St. Thomas the way to get there is by the small, twin-engined amphibian which makes several scheduled flights daily from Charlotte Amalie harbour to Christiansted. It is about a 20 minute flight, and so it is possible to make the return trip in a day.

The best thing to do is to begin by taking a walk round the city-centre which has, like that of Charlotte Amalie, a series of charming arcades in which some of the best shops are situated whose goods are offered at almost free-port prices. The whole area around the wharf at Christiansted has been transformed into a National Historic Site under the administration of the U.S. National Park Service and the six main buildings inside the area are in a first-class state of preservation.

Fort Christiansvaern was originally built in 1744-49 as a garrison for the Danish army, but several later additions were made. It is now the site of various government offices. Government House, dating back to 1747, was built as a merchant's residence, but it was bought by the government in 1771 and used by the Governor-General. It was remodelled and repaired several times in the nineteenth century. It was severely damaged by fire in 1936 when it was again reconstructed and a third storey added. It nevertheless still contains traces of eighteenth-century elegance.

The Steeple Building is a "must" for any visitor to Christiansted. It was built in 1750-53 as the State Lutheran church, but in 1831 the Lutherans moved elsewhere and the building passed through various ownerships and for a period was closed altogether. After extensive and expert restoration had been completed, it was reopened in 1964 as the official St. Croix museum. The Library Building was completed in 1751 as a Customs House. It was modified in 1830 and is now used as a Post Office. The Old Seale House was originally an adjunct to the Customs House and it still, as the name implies, contains the old scales used for weighing sugar, cotton, rum and other exports. It now houses on the ground floor the Tourist Bureau and, above, the Harbour Master's office and the Chamber of Commerce. The present Post Office building, which has an attractive inner courtyard, was completed in 1749 as a warehouse for the Danish West India and Guinea Company. Other buildings worth looking at outside the Historic Site area include the Penthery Building, which was once, like Charlotte Amalie's Grand Hotel, the leading and most fashionable hotel in St. Croix; and the Alexander Hamilton store.

To get a good overall picture of Christiansted you should cross to the little island in the harbour called Protestant Cay. This used to be the home of the Danish Harbour Master. His house still stands on the island and it is pleasant to sit on the balcony and survey the city's waterfront area. Another worthwhile excursion while in Christiansted is that to Buck Island. Boats leave normally every morning from the municipal wharf and return in the afternoon. The island, which consists of 850 acres, was declared a National Monument by President Kennedy in 1961 because of the magnificent barrier reef surrounding its eastern half which forms a lagoon full of marine life.

A little way out from Christiansted the boat passes the ruins of Fort Louise Augusta, now a radio station, and, further on, Green Cay Island. You anchor first off the west shore of Buck Island where a wide sandy beach and clear water provide a good setting for swimming and lying in the sun before lunch. If you are not an expert with snorkels and flippers you can also put in a little practice before tackling the underwater trail. Equipment is supplied on the boats and the skippers are well qualified to explain its use. After lunch the boat takes you southeastward to the famous Buck Island underwater trail. You can either follow your guide in mask and snorkel or be towed along the trail in a glass-bottomed float; which ever you chose, you see a magnificent expanse of underwater life of fantastic colours and shapes, and underwater signs help you identify the things you see.

St. Croix's second city, Frederiksted, is on the western shore of the island. It has a number of buildings of considerable architectural merit including the old Customs House on the wharf, Victoria House at the corner of Market and Strand Streets, Liberty Hall, Benjamin House, and Apothecary Hall. Fort Frederick, a late seventeenth-century building, is of some historical interest because it was from its ramparts that the Danish Governor, Von Scholten, on 3 July 1848, read the proclamation which began : "All unfree in the Danish West Indies are from today free." It is a charming town and has the same atmosphere of peace and good humour as Christiansted. It was severely damaged by fire and rioting in 1878 at a time when the whole island was going through a period of depression and there was little money to rebuild it. The graceful colonnade of stone arches on Strand Street, however, survived the fire and is a good example of the city's former elegance.

St. Croix is blessed with a highly efficient office of the United States Virgin Islands Department of Tourism and Trade, and the staff there can tell you all about guided trips and excursions. The following extracts, however, are taken, for the benefit of those who like to do their own sightseeing, from the Department's own booklet which is well-informed and reliable :

The East End of St. Croix is its most arid section, with cacti the predominant vegetation. A circular trip from Christiansted, out by Tide Village and along the South Shore and back by the East End Road, will give a good picture of this area, which rejoices in being the most easterly point of the United States. Beyond Grapetree Bay, where the South Shore Road joins the East End Road, a turn east will take you to Cramer Park where there is an excellent public beach.

Turning back along the East End Road, you pass the St. Croix Yacht Club, where "sailfish" racing is a favourite sport. A few miles further on, you get an excellent view of Buck Island to the north. About half way to Christiansted, the road passes close to Estate Green Cay and you can get quite a good view of the impressively ruined estate house and buildings.

Setting out in a westerly direction from Christiansted, you come to the Estates of Judith's Fancy, headquarters of the Knights of Malta in the seventeenth century. The main ruins, which once housed the largest sugar and rum industry on St. Croix, have been excavated and cleared so that one can get a very vivid picture of the sugar manufacturing process three centuries ago. The estates overlook Sugar Bay and the mouth of Salt River, where Columbus landed in 1493.

Continuing along the North Shore Road past Morningstar Night Club, a righthand turn into Salt River Road presents a choice of two fascinating routes. The North Shore Road follows Salt River to its mouth and turns westward along the north coast, a steep, rocky, surf-battered shore contrasting sharply with the quiet beaches found elsewhere on the island. On this route you get an impressive view of Mount Eagle, St. Croix's highest peak.

The Scenic Route, reached by taking the second left turn after you enter Salt River Road, follows the highest ridge along

13.   Ruins of a Danish sugar-mill on St. John

14. King's Alley in Christiansted, St. Croix, is one of the most delightful shopping areas in the Caribbean

the length of the island and crosses Mount Eagle close to its peak. Although unfinished and somewhat overgrown in places, it offers spectacular views in all directions. No other single route shows more vividly the great variety of terrain that comprises St. Croix.

Mahogany and Creque Dam Roads at the western end of St. Croix are in sharp contrast with the east end of the island. Here you drive through a tropical rain forest where the sun penetrates only in spots even at high noon. The air smells lush and damp; lianas hang down to the road; you are surrounded by tropical trees—mango, papaya, mahogany, turpentine, breadfruit, cacao. At Annaly, a privately owned estate at the northeast end of Creque Dam Road, there is an old sugar mill which has been converted into a residence and landscaped with representative tropical plants.

The West Shore Road now hugs the coast line and takes you past such fine old estates as Butler Bay and Sprat Hall before entering Frederiksted, where you can pause for refreshment and to have a look at the delightful old town. Just south of Frederiksted, on the southwestern tip of the island, is a good beach at Sandy Point, where another stop can be made. Centerline, the road which takes you back to Christiansted, passes some of the most interesting historic sights on the island. Whim Great House, about a mile and a half east of Frederiksted, was built about 1794 and recently restored by the St. Croix Landmarks Society. Behind it is the Whim Plantation Museum which contains many interesting relics of the great days of sugar. Diamond Distillery, just off Centerline to the south, is the place where Cruzan (pronounced Crooshan) rum is made. Next comes Golden Grove, an old estate house where the St. Croix Branch of the College of the Virgin Islands is situated. Just beyond the Agricultural Experimental Station, to the north of Centerline, is the Bethlehem Sugar Factory, and to the south is Kingshill, formerly a barracks but now a home for the aged. Slob (despite its name) is a charming and picturesque little village to the north of the road just beyond Kingshill; and Estate Grange, where Alexander Hamilton's mother is buried, is the site of the Hamilton Memorial.

o

But anyone who takes a drive round St. Croix cannot help being fascinated by the place names, and the temptation to turn off the main route and have a look is great. Here are some of them in the neighbourhood of Centerline : William's Delight, Betty's Hope, Jealousy, Barren Spot, Blessing, Profit, Peter's Rest, Work and Rest, Humbug—all names which are redolent of minor events in history. And so you return to Christiansted, passing on your right, a place with the apt name of Contentment.

In some months of the year—certainly in February and March—it is possible to get even further insight into St. Croix's past by going on one of the Open House Tours, sponsored by the St. Croix Landmarks Society, which take you inside some of the old Great Houses which are privately owned. To get a complete picture of how the Danish old has been ably blended with the American new in St. Croix such a tour should, if possible, be made.

St. John

SIGHTSEEING

The 19·2 square miles of land which constitute the island of St. John are a paradise for nature-lovers. In fact today the island, which is 85% covered by tropical vegetation, might be said to be orientated almost entirely to satisfying the desires of visitors who seek this form of relaxation.

Under Danish rule a considerable amount of sugar was grown on the island and this necessitated the cutting down of some of the virgin forests, but, with the abandonment of these plantations in the middle of the nineteenth century, the landscape once again returned to tropical growth. Today, except for the ruins of Danish sugar mills, the visitor will see little evidence of the use of land on St. John for agriculture. Nor is it likely that the island will change in the foreseeable future from its present natural state because of an event, unique in Caribbean history, which occurred in 1954.

In November of that year a non-profit making conservation and educational organisation set up by the American Rockefeller family and known as Jackson Hole Preserve, Inc., began to buy land on St. John with the aim of ultimately turning it over to the U.S. National Park Service. Some 5,000 acres were acquired and the Park was formerly established at a ceremony at Cruz Bay, the main settlement on St. John, on 1 December 1956. In subsequent years several gifts were made by Jackson Hole Preserve to the Park Service for buying privately owned land within the Park boundaries and in support of various Park projects such as research and marine studies. Today, in effect, St. John is the Park, which encompasses two-thirds of the island's acreage as well as several offshore rocks and cays.

A Visitor Center (or Centre for the British) has been established at Cruz Bay, the principal gateway to the Park, and much excellent work has been done in preserving historic ruins on the island, providing camping grounds and cottages, clearing trails and instituting nature walks and lectures. A remarkable underwater snorkelling trail has been established at Trunk Bay. In the Park there are nearly a hundred bird species, but relatively few, apparently, are water birds; herons, egrets, pelicans, ducks, gulls, frigate birds and terns, however, can be seen along the shores. Hummingbirds, doves, hawks and warblers are common, and parakeets have been seen. The only native land mammals are six forms of bats. The red fig-eating bat, recently rediscovered, was known previously from a single collected specimen. Several introduced mammals, notably the mongoose, have become established. Native land vertebrates include toads, lizards, snakes and turtles.

Apart from the National Park, the most remarkable development which has taken place on St. John in recent years is the Caneel Bay Plantation Hotel built by Mr. Laurance Rockefeller. It is a large beach resort of considerable charm and beauty surrounded by green hills and white sand beaches, and it takes its name from an eighteenth-century Danish sugar plantation house, the ruins of which are still there. It is on the northwest tip of St. John and only 20 minutes by motor launch from Red Hook Landing on St. Thomas.

The history and objects of the Caneel Bay development are interesting. It was first opened in the 1930's by the West Indies Company and, after a succession of different ownerships, it was offered for sale in 1952 by the Rhode Island Charity Trust and bought by Mr. Rockefeller. All of the stock of Caneel Bay Plantation Inc. was given by him to Jackson Hole Preserve, together with funds for its enlargement and improvement in order that it might serve visitors to St. John and the Virgin Islands National Park. The extensive programme of construction, modernisation and renovation included the building of additional rooms and cottages, a 1,200,000-gallon water catchment, a reservoir and a sea-water distillation plant, an auxiliary power plant, dining terraces and lounges. The programme has required many years work and the expenditure of several million dollars.

The hotel and resort area are owned by Caneel Bay Plantation Inc., and, though they are within the boundaries of the Virgin Islands National Park, are operated independently of the National Park Service. All income is devoted to the operation, maintenance and improvement of the resort and to aid in the conservation purposes of Jackson Hole Preserve, which gave the land and made possible the establishment of the National Park. In addition to providing employment for island residents, Caneel Bay Plantation has underwritten the cost of laying a submarine cable to bring electricity to St. John, supported and helped equip the medical services on the island and assisted in developing native crafts, community programmes and vocational education. Both the hotel and the National Park with which it is connected are outstanding examples of the sort of work which can be done—with, admittedly, a lot of money—both to preserve and make the best use of the beauty of the Caribbean islands.

It was not, perhaps, surprising that the National Park Service Ranger, who drove me round the Park after lunch in his jeep, should have remarked that he would like to see some, or all, of the British Virgin Islands incorporated in the U.S. National Park scheme. It seemed to be certainly an idea worth considering. Conceivably, even the possibility should not be ruled out of starting an even wider National Park project involving United States, British, Dutch and French islands linked with jointly planned hotel and tourist development schemes on the lines initiated by Mr. Rockefeller.

In short, both the Caneel Bay development and the National Park form the major part of the very considerable attractions which St. John has to offer the sightseer, and no visit to the U.S. Virgin Islands is complete without paying the island a visit at least as a day excursion from St. Thomas.

St. Thomas

HOTELS, RESTAURANTS AND ENTERTAINMENT

St. Thomas has pretty well everything to offer the visitor in the way of hotels. Right at the top of the scale in the A-plus bracket is the Virgin Isle Hilton. Even more than most Hiltons in the Caribbean, this one seems to offer the visitor an astonishingly full life within its stately portals on top of a hill overlooking Charlotte Amalie and its harbour. It has its own private beach; there is nightly entertainment, from turtle races to bingo; there is a salt-water swimming pool, tennis courts, shops, a masseur, and one or two really luxurious penthouses on the roof. Ideal for honeymoons; but you have to be well-heeled, at any rate in the season. Bluebeard's Castle is another A-plus hotel on top of a hill the other side of the town, and the seventeenth-century tower of the original castle has been expertly fitted into the modern building. Here again, there are facilities for doing practically everything a visitor could want, including a private beach, Bluebeard's Beach Club, at Great Bay on St. Thomas's eastern tip. The Beach Club also has waterfront cabana rooms. I know from experience that the buffet lunch at the Castle is excellent and the view over the town and harbour is superb.

One of the attractions of St. Thomas is that there are so many hotels of good quality in the brackets just below the top.

Two A-minus examples are the Caribbean Beach Hotel and the Mountain Top Hotel. The first is just outside Charlotte Amalie and has a private beach on which excellent meals of the barbecue type are served. The second, as the name implies, is perched some 1,500 feet on top of Signal Hill roughly in the middle of the island; and from its glass-enclosed restaurant and bar you get a magnificent view over Magens Bay, where the hotel has a private island for guests to picnic on. A classic drink here—and again I speak from experience—is the banana daiquiri.

An interesting place to stay in the B-plus category is the Shibui Hotel which is on a hillside overlooking the south coast. It consists of a group of cottages designed in the Japanese style (there is a parallel in the Caribbean at Nevis) centred on a "Japanese Teahouse", with a swimming pool. The Morning Star Beach Resort, also in this category, is on the attractive beach of the same name just outside Charlotte Amalie, and the Island Beachcomber is distinctive because it offers studio apartments on Lindbergh Bay beach where you can do your own cooking.

The Hotel 1829, also in the B-plus category, is one of the most charming hotels in the Caribbean, with its massive Danish brickwork kitchen converted into a bar. It is conveniently situated near the centre of town. There are plenty of places to stay in or near Charlotte Amalie of the B-minus and C classes, and people with a bent for nostalgia should certainly visit the Grand Hotel. (In view of its past glory, it shall remain unclassified.) This, anyway, is just a sample of the wide variety of places to stay in St. Thomas which cater for both the well-filled and the thinly stocked purse.

Restaurant and night life in St. Thomas are just what one would expect in an island which has become a playground for American mainland tourists. In the various eating places of the top quality hotels the food is generally of a high standard. Both there and in some of the smaller downtown restaurants efforts are made to provide dishes which are unobtainable in the mainland United States. There is at least one restaurant just off Main Street where reasonable French cooking is to be found and it is possible in several restaurants to get seafood dishes of the highest quality. Around the Waterfront area there are several open-air "cafés" which cater for the hamburger type of customer, but the atmosphere is generally very pleasant and the quality of the "sandwich" meal, plus coffee—for which the Americans must surely go down in history as being the greatest experts—is high. You can, of course, get just as good a "charcoal-broiled steak and French fried potatoes" in Charlotte Amalie as anywhere else in the U.S.A. For sandwiches a good place to go is the Castaways underneath the Grand Hotel, where there is an almost infinite variety; the Left Bank restaurant has some interesting Haitian and French dishes; and for Italian food the place to go is The Gate, an attractive old building near the centre of town which is also a small hotel. Top Of The Isle Bar is a pleasant place for snacks and drinks on a hilltop, served by a funicular railway called the St. Thomas Tramway, from which there is a magnificent view.

Night entertainment is also of the varied type which one would expect. The big hotels follow the normal practice in having special "nightclub" rooms where there are floorshows and dancing. The Pirate's Parlour at Bluebeard's Castle is one of the best. There are often "big name" bands at the Hilton. At others the attraction is the steel band and the calypso. Jazz is a feature of night spots such as The Fallen Angel (a charmingly converted old warehouse); and at Sebastian's, on the Waterfront, you can dance all night in a modern setting overlooking the harbour. There are all sorts of little bars with attractive decors in which you can drink, talk and dance to jukebox music. If you are in Charlotte Amalie at Carnival time (good, though nothing like as spontaneous and colourful as the Trinidad carnival) you can dance in the streets. In short, as befits a prosperous tourist resort, night entertainment in St. Thomas is varied and copious—but there are no gambling casinos.

St. Croix

HOTELS, RESTAURANTS AND ENTERTAINMENT

An interesting feature of the accommodation offered to visitors in St. Croix is the number of cottages and apartments which can be rented by the week or by the month and which are essentially geared to accommodating the whole family. These are mostly of the cottage-colony type and some of them make a point of stressing that baby-sitters are available at all times. A lot of them have completely equipped kitchens, with maid service, plus the alternative of eating in a central restaurant. There are also a number of good quality hotels of the more conventional type. As St. Croix is a comparatively large island, with resort areas distributed round the coast, it is simplest to enumerate a cross-section of the places to stay in the different areas.

In the Christiansted area is the Buccaneer Hotel (A-minus) situated in a 200-acre estate about two miles east of the town. It is large and provides most things that the discerning tourist wants—tennis, fishing, beach parties, snorkelling, and so on. In about the same class, though smaller, is the Tamarind Reef Hotel, three miles further away from Christiansted, which also has a marina. Going in a westerly direction from Christiansted you might pause at the Pelican Cove beach which, with its two cottages accommodating four people each, is an excellent example of what St. Croix has to offer in the way of family vacations. It is actually a private club, with excellent facilities for children. A bit further on is St. Croix By-The-Sea, a largish hotel which again has special facilities for children and evening entertainment for the adults.

About half way between Christiansted and Frederiksted is Cane Bay Plantation (small, with three cottages) which commands a magnificent view of the Caribbean. Clover Crest Hotel is on the northwest point of the island, and this is one of the best places to go if you are interested in nature walks and exploring. On the west coast, not far from Frederiksted, is Sprat Hall Hotel, formerly a plantation Great House, which specialises in providing almost every form of sport, including horses for riding. In Frederiksted itself the Royal Dane is a charming, smallish hotel in the old part of the town.

Estate Good Hope is the most westerly of the south coast hotels, just under three miles from Frederiksted, and is a good example of the best St. Croix has to offer in the way of tastefully luxurious seaside living. Between there and the eastern point of the island there is not much in the way of accommodation (though there are a number of pleasant places where house sites are for sale) until you come to the St. Croix Beach Hotel which specialises in beach-front suites with living room, terrace and kitchenette. There is also a central restaurant. A little further on is the Grapetree Bay Hotel which claims, with some justification, to be St. Croix's largest and most complete resort hotel. It consists of attractively decorated and furnished cottages set in an estate of some 400 acres, with two beaches, its own sailing boats for hire, tennis, dancing, movie shows, floor shows—the lot, as the British say.

All the hotels and resorts mentioned are either in category A-minus or B, with the exception of Grapetree Bay, which must qualify for an A-plus. There are many others in the top categories which have not been mentioned purely for reasons of space; the object has been to convey the impression that St. Croix is remarkable as a tourist resort because it has so many places to stay which satisfy the needs—for want of better words —of the discerning upper middle class; and it is an extremely friendly and clean place almost entirely lacking, as has been said before, the somewhat brash atmosphere of St. Thomas. Perhaps for this reason it is becoming more and more popular as a place for retired Americans with reasonable, but not lavish, incomes to go and live.

Apart from the hotels, there are one or two reasonably good restaurants in Christiansted, but you would be mistaken if you went there in the hope of getting dishes which are unobtainable in many towns of the mainland U.S.A. Places like the Mahogany Inn, Hamilton House, the King Christian Restaurant and one or two others talk about their "continental cuisine"; and the food is certainly of good quality served in clean and often beautiful surroundings—courtyards, tree-shaded patios, and so on—but the continent from which it comes, for the most part, is the North American one. And the same applies to the two or three restaurants in Frederiksted of good quality such as The Seven Flags, though La Terrasse has some genuine French dishes. Anyway, it is all very neat, clean and pleasant.

Night life, in the strict sense of the words, is limited in St. Croix, though the bigger hotels do offer good entertainment of the floor show type; and there is a handful of bars where you can spend a pleasant enough "off-beat" evening. But the thing to remember about St. Croix is that the key-words are pleasant respectability.

St. John
HOTELS, RESTAURANTS AND ENTERTAINMENT

Caneel Bay Plantation Hotel is in the A-plus category. All the rooms are furnished in contemporary Danish style and the effect is most pleasing. It is run in the best traditions of international hotel management and offers a wide range of activities to visitors—swimming and snorkelling in the unusually clear water, deep-sea fishing, boating, hiking, nature walks, guided jeep trips through the National Park, day trips to near-by cays and islands for seeing underwater gardens, excursions to nearby Tortola in the British Virgin Islands, and shopping excursions to the duty-free ports of some of the other Virgin Islands. There is evening entertainment.

Accommodation in St. John, apart from Caneel Bay, is limited. Gallows Point Cottages, on a private peninsular in Cruz Bay, offer units with housekeeping facilities and so do Holiday Homes and Cruz Bay Cottages. Little Maho, within the National Park boundaries, has cottages where guests look after themselves for breakfast and lunch but have the evening meal together on the main terrace.

There are a couple of small places to eat in Cruz Bay. Night life, unless you go to Caneel Bay Plantation, is non-existent.

SPORT AND RECREATION

Yachting and fishing are the two sports of unusually high quality which the U.S. Virgin Islands have to offer. With the exception, possibly, of the Bahamas and certain groups of South Sea islands, the waters round these islands (including the British ones) are the most attractive anywhere in the world for leisurely sailing in medium-sized boats (large if you can afford them) because they are protected for the most part from the rough weather of the open ocean and provide unsurpassed scenery.

Game fishing has recently become a big attraction in the waters round the U.S. Virgin Islands. Blue marlin, wahoo, tuna, tarpon, kingfish and bonefish are taken all the year round; sailfish and white marlin can be caught during most months. In 1964 a blue marlin of world record size (814 lb.) was caught in Virgin Islands waters. At the other extreme, you can spend a leisurely few hours drifting around the cays and catching lobsters by hand. Boats of various sizes can be hired in St. Thomas, St. Croix and St. John, but the best place from which to set out on a prolonged fishing trip is probably St. Thomas. The hotel people will tell you how best to rent the type of equipment you want. If you just want to meander along with a group of people you can take a trip on the glass-bottomed boat from the Charlotte Amalie waterfront to the "marine gardens". Regular trips of longer duration—up to a whole day—with meals and drinks included—can also be made.

Snorkelling and skin-diving enthusiasts will find everything they want in St. Thomas and St. Croix (even a special school for beginners) and an experience which should not be missed is a visit to the famous underwater trail and gardens of Buck Island, just off Christiansted (see page 193). The beaches and reefs of St. John have a more off-the-beaten-track charm for underwater exploring and it is fun to peer at the wreckage off Salt Island of a large French ship which sank about a hundred years ago. All three islands have excellent white sand beaches for just swimming, lazing and lying in the sun.

Some of the hotels in St. Thomas and St. Croix have tennis courts (there are public courts at Charlotte Amalie). There is a nine-hole municipal golf course in St. Thomas and an 18-hole championship course has just been opened in St. Croix. The National Park at St. John is ideal for horseback riding, and good facilities for this also exist in St. Croix. In St. John you can also go donkey-riding. The main organised sport of St. Thomas and St. Croix is baseball and, curiously enough, like many other Caribbean islands, cockfighting is popular.

THINGS TO BUY

St. Thomas and St. Croix are ideal places for both Europeans and North Americans to buy things at prices considerably less than those at home. Virtual free-port facilities exist in both the islands, as they do in St. John, though the facilities for buying there are much more limited. It would be pointless to seek to enumerate the low-priced goods which can be bought in these islands—from Swiss watches to English china; from Danish furniture to French perfume; from a Tibetan necklace to shoes from England, Italy or France; from Indian fabrics to shirts made in Hong Kong. Liquor and wine of all sorts can be bought at very reasonable prices.

The thing to do is to browse through the main shopping areas of Charlotte Amalie, Christiansted or Frederiksted and look at the well-arranged shop windows. This can be both a pleasant and a profitable operation because the U.S. Virgin Islands are equalled only by the islands of the Netherlands Antilles in the facilities which they offer for making astonishingly cheap purchases.

USEFUL FACTS FOR VISITORS

The United States Virgin Islands consist of some 50 islands and cays of volcanic origin and form, with their British neighbours (some 30 similar islands and cays), part of the Antilles group which divides the Caribbean Sea from the Atlantic Ocean. They are 40 nautical miles east of Puerto Rico and about 1,435 miles southeast of New York. Only three have any size or population of significance—St. Thomas, St. Croix and St. John. Most of the other islands are uninhabited and uninhabitable. The total area of the three islands is about 140 square miles, of which St. Croix accounts for about two-thirds. St. Thomas and St. John rise out of the same plateau, their mountain peaks reaching a maximum height of 1,500 feet above sea level.

Each of the islands has an equable climate with temperatures ranging from 70° to 90° F. (21° to 32·2° C.) the year round. The average temperature is 78° F. (25° C.) and at all times of the year the trade winds minimise humidity. Rainfall averages 45 inches a year and there is no well-defined rainy season, though the wettest months are normally September and October.

Some 42,000 people live in the islands and more than 80% are wholly or partly Negro, being mostly descendants of the African slaves who worked the plantations in the days of Danish rule. A small group of French people have lived in St. Thomas for many generations, and people of Danish, Scots, Spanish and Portuguese descent form other minority groups. There is, in addition, an increasingly large group of residents from the United States mainland and from nearby Puerto Rico. As a result of the employment created by the present tourist boom, there has been a considerable influx of workers, mostly Negro stock, from the neighbouring British Virgin Islands and from as far afield as the Leeward Islands.

The language of the islands is English, though French is still spoken by the people of French descent in St. Thomas; and, chiefly in St. Croix, there are Spanish-speaking groups who have come from Puerto Rico.

By the end of the sixties decade St. Thomas will have an airport capable of handling large jet aircraft but until then visitors from North America and Europe normally go by jet to Puerto Rico and on from there by frequent (almost hourly during the day) services operated by Caribair. Comparatively inexpensive charter flights can also be arranged from Puerto Rico. St. Thomas is also served by scheduled L.I.A.T flights originating in Antigua, from which point there are regular international flights by B.O.A.C., Pan American, Air Canada, and B.W.I.A.

St. Croix is served by regular Pan American jet flights non-stop from New York which continue south to other Caribbean islands. A locally run amphibian service operates between St. Croix and St. Thomas. Because of its hilly terrain, St. John has no landing strip and cannot be reached by air except by the same amphibian service which operates between St. Thomas and St. Croix.

There is a regular $4\frac{1}{2}$-day shipping service between New York and San Juan and on from there to St. Thomas by smaller vessels. From New Orleans it is possible to go direct by sea to St. Thomas; and Alcoa operate freighters with limited passenger accommodation from New York to St. Thomas. There are also a number of other passenger-freighters which make calls at St. Thomas or St. Croix on international routes. Both St. Thomas and St. Croix are well-served by cruise ships. On the whole, the matter of sea transport to the U.S. Virgin Islands is best discussed with a knowledgeable travel agent; the vast majority of visitors, apart from cruise passengers, go there by air.

To go to St. John it is best to take a taxi from Charlotte Amalie to Red Hook Landing, about nine miles away, from where scheduled boat services operate to Cruz Bay (about 30 minutes).

General information regarding the islands can be obtained from :

> Chamber of Commerce,
> St. Thomas,
> Virgin Islands

> Department of Commerce,
> Division of Tourism,
> St. Thomas, V.I.

Department of Commerce,
Virgin Islands Visitors Bureau,
Christiansted,
St. Croix, V.I.

There is a Virgin Islands Tourist Information Office in New York and one or two other North American cities. In London you can contact the United States Travel Service.

British Virgin Islands

"Yo-ho-ho and a bottle of rum!"—Robert Louis Stevenson

Easily the best way to get to the British Virgin Islands is by sea from St. Thomas in one of the four or five motor launches which make scheduled daily trips. The cost of the return voyage is something over $5, but it is worth double that sum because scenically the trip it quite outstanding.

After getting out of Charlotte Amalie harbour the boat turns gradually to a northeasterly course and passes through a narrow passage between great St. James Island and St. Thomas which seems to be a mass of eddies and whirlpools. The safe channel can only be a few yards wide; but you are through and into the broad Pillsbury Sound which separates St. John from St. Thomas. It is almost an inland waterway cut off from the Atlantic to the north by a group of small islands— Gran Cay, Mingo Cay, Lovango Cay, and others which are inhabited, if at all, by a few sheep and goats. You pass through the Windward Passage and enter The Narrows which separate the American from the British Virgin Islands, the biggest of which, Tortola, lies ahead.

Leaving the small (British) islands of Great Thatch to the north and Little Thatch to the south, the launch enters Tortola's most westerly harbour, the bay of which has the entrancing name of Soper's Hole and the township the rather dull one of West End. (A new coast road has just been opened linking

West End with Tortola's capital, Road Town). A few passengers and goods are disembarked and the launch continues on its way into the Sir Francis Drake Channel, a broad expanse of water two to four miles wide which is sheltered to the north by Tortola and to the south by a chain of smaller islands with such intriguing names as Dead Chest, Ginger Island, Round Rock, Broken Jerusalem, and Fallen Jerusalem. Dead Chest, incidentally, is supposed to be the site of Robert Louis Stevenson's bit of doggerel in *Treasure Island*—"Fifteen men on a dead man's chest, Yo-ho-ho and a bottle of rum." Ahead, to the northeast, the larger island of Virgin Gorda is just visible, with its smaller neighbours, Great Dog, West Dog, George Dog, Cockroach Island and other oddly named rocks and cays. Before turning north and heading for the jetty at Road Town you will probably have passed in the St. Francis Drake Channel half a dozen white-hulled yachts, ketches, yawls, or schooners, because this part of the Caribbean is becoming known as a yachtsman's paradise.

HISTORY

In 1672, shortly after Denmark claimed St. Thomas, Colonel Stapleton, Governor of the Leeward Islands, drove out the Dutch buccaneers who had been using Tortola as a base, and annexed the island to the British Crown. Eight years later several English planters and their families settled on Virgin Gorda. Meanwhile more pirates and buccaneers had established themselves on Tortola where their activities were not wholly directed to leading the peaceful life of planters. Further groups of planters, however, arrived in 1700, and by 1717 a census of the population showed that there were 317 whites on Virgin Gorda and 159 on Tortola. Cotton, rather than sugar, seems to have been the staple crop of these early days.

In 1756 the planters petitioned unsuccessfully for civil government and constitutional courts of justice. A second petition in 1773 was successful, and constitutional government was established with a completely elected House of Assembly (12 members) and a partly elected, partly nominated, Legisla-

15. This young Tortolan has returned from the well with water for his mother. One of the famous Tortolan sloops is under construction in the background

16. The market square at Road Town, Tortola

BRITISH VIRGIN ISLANDS

ANEGADA

ATLANTIC OCEAN

BRITISH VIRGIN IS.
U.S. VIRGIN IS.
PUERTO RICO
ATLANTIC OCEAN
CARIBBEAN SEA
GUADELOUPE
MARTINIQUE
Windward Islands
Leeward Islands
BARBADOS
TOBAGO
TRINIDAD
SOUTH AMERICA

Virgin Gorda Peak

VIRGIN GORDA

Spanish Town

INTERNATIONAL BOUNDARY - - - -
LAND OVER 500 FT.

0 1 2 3 4 5 MILES

GT. CAMANOE

SCRUB I.

BEEF I.

GUANA I.

TORTOLA

Airfield
Padrua
Town

GINGER I.

Fahie Hill

Brewer's Bay

ROADTOWN

Leonard's

COOPER I.

SALT I.

JOST VAN DYKE

Cane Garden Bay

Cactot Bay

Sea Cow Bay

PETER I.

West End

NORMAN I.

GT. TOBAGO I.

GT. THATCH I.

LITTLE TOBAGO I.

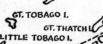

ST. JOHN (U.S.A.)

CARIBBEAN SEA

tive Council or "Board". The Legislative Assembly of the Virgin Islands met for the first time on 1 February 1774.

As a result of the abolition of slavery (1834) the sugar and cotton plantations became increasingly uneconomic and the white land-owning families gradually withdrew. Their estates were mostly broken up into small lots and sold to the liberated slaves. The ruling class having thus largely departed, the islands surrendered their constitution in 1867 when the Assembly and Council were abolished and a Legislative Council of two official and three nominated unofficial members was substituted. Even this limited form of government was abrogated in 1902 when the legislature was abolished and the power to make laws for the Virgin Islands was given to the Leeward Islands Legislature. This state of affairs continued for nearly 50 years during which time the islanders lived somewhat primitively from an economic point of view and in a state of almost complete isolation from the rest of the world.

In 1947 the question arose as to whether the Virgin Islands should be linked with the proposed Federation of the Leewards and Windwards and, later, whether they should join the West Indies Federation. The inhabitants were against both proposals. In fact, links between the British Virgin Islands and the other British Caribbean islands were so tenuous as to be almost non-existent; links with the much closer American Virgin Islands, however, had become closer, partly due to the development of tourism.

A Legislative Council, partly elected and partly nominated, was again given to the islands in 1950, and in 1954 a new ordinance abolished property and income qualifications for candidates, as well as the literary test for voters, and the number of elected members was increased from four to six. These changes indicated that some political progress was being made by this out-of-the-way group of islands, but in view of the fact that a ministerial system of government had been granted to Antigua and St. Kitts, the nearest British islands, and that the American Virgin islands were progressing economically and constitutionally, the demand for further changes became increasingly articulate.

In July 1956, the British Leeward Islands group was broken up and the Virgin Islands became a separate colony. In 1960 the office of Governor of the Leeward Islands was abolished and the Administrator of the British Virgin Islands became directly responsible to the Secretary of State for the Colonies in London. This was followed in 1965 and 1966 by new proposals for the introduction of a ministerial system of administration and—perhaps more important—by a planned scheme to develop the islands' tourist potential.

ECONOMY

Because of the severe limitations imposed by rugged topography, steep slopes, meagre soil resources and unreliable water supply, agriculture is difficult in the British Virgin Islands. Many crops have been tried—sugar-cane, cotton, tobacco and others—but production has always been marginal and cultivation has been abandoned at the first sign of adversity. Such cultivation as is possible is confined almost exclusively to ground provisions for home consumption, the surplus being exported to St. Thomas. In recent years agricultural production markedly declined largely because there were fewer people to work on the land due to the attraction of going to work in St. Thomas. The islands are generally well suited for the cultivation of grass, and for some years there was a thriving livestock industry. Recently, however, even this has tended to decline.

The size of the islands and the absence of flat land contributed to the decline of estate agriculture and its replacement by small-holdings worked, with few exceptions, by the owner-occupier. Being always near to the sea and often in need of ready cash, the small-holder is often a fisherman as well. While the economy of the islands is still largely centred around the livestock industry and remittances from people working in St. Thomas, with a minor contribution from subsistence ground provision production and fishing, the part played by the tourist industry is rapidly increasing, and it is the Government's declared policy to encourage investment in the islands, particularly the construction of hotels and of houses whose owners, when not living there, would rent them to visitors. Customs and tax concessions are granted to this end. Government's annual revenue is not much more than $1 million and something over half of this comes from British Government grants.

The islands are part of the sterling area, but three currencies may be legally used : U.S. dollars, Eastern Caribbean dollars, and Jamaican pounds. The U.S. dollar is normally used.

SIGHTSEEING AND HOTELS

If you arrive at Road Town by sea from St. Thomas you will appreciate the fact that sightseeing in the British Virgin Islands is essentially something that must be done by boat. If you arrive by air, the first thing you should do is to make arrangements for getting a boat. Tortola itself is still very much a sleepy and in many ways primitive island.* You can now drive from West End to East End by car, but the white sand beaches on the north coast—Belmont Bay, Long Bay, Apple Bay, Cane Garden Bay, Josiah's Bay—can only be reached by walking or on horseback. There is not much for the tourist to do in Road Town other than consider the fact that he is in the (as yet undeveloped and in many ways nicer for that reason) centre of an area which, by reason of its maritime scenic beauty, has one of the greatest tourist potentials in the Caribbean.

In Road Town there are three hotels of the B-minus category, though there should soon be at least one in the A category. The Fort Burt Hotel is about a mile from the centre of

* By 1968, however, it became evident that Tortola was emerging from the doldrums of the past. The Fort Burt hotel has now been very considerably enlarged, a new hotel is going up at Slaney Point, and a British syndicate is developing Wickham Key, the reclaimed waterfront of Road Town, into a hotel and resort area. And the same syndicate has acquired and is developing as a hotel and resort area a large tract of land on the coral island of Anegada which hitherto has been inhabited almost solely by a few itinerant fishermen. By the seventies decade the British Virgin Islands should be well on their way to entering the big league tourist business which was formerly the monopoly of their American neighbours.

the town and is built on the remains of an old fort which dates from buccaneer times. It commands an excellent view of Road Town harbour and Drake's Channel. Treasure Isle Hotel is an attractive spot in pleasant surroundings at the opposite end of the town from Fort Burt where occasional dances to steel band music are held. The Lagoon Plaza is, as the name implies, on a lagoon in the heart of Road Town.

At Long Bay on the northwest coast of the island is a cottage-settlement type of hotel called Long Bay Estate. Each cottage has a lounge and patio, two double bedrooms, and a modern kitchen and bathroom. Restaurant and bar facilities are provided in a central building, but maid service is provided in the cottages, so visitors can either eat out or look after themselves. Supplies of food, drink and other requirements are provided from the Long Bay Estate Commissary.

There are half a dozen or so C class guest houses in Tortola, four of which are in Road Town. One, called Harbour View, in Cave Garden Bay, has a good beach nearby; and Maya Cove Guest House specialises in organising trips for guests to the out islands.

One of the most interesting places to visit is Marina Cay, a six-acre island to the northeast of Tortola which has been developed by an English couple, Jean and Allan Batham, into one of the most charming cottage colonies in the Caribbean. There is an air of comfort and informality about the place which is limited to 20 guests accommodated in cottages with twin beds and shower. The away-from-it-all atmosphere is hard to beat as you sit in the early evening with a drink in the central open-air bar and look out over the panorama of small islands which ring the Sir Francis Drake Channel. Batham, who was in the British Navy during the war, is an expert in all forms of water sport, and every facility is available for snorkelling or skin-diving on the reefs which surround Marina Cay. He has gradually built up a fleet of boats of all sizes which can be seen riding at anchor off the island and can be used by guests.

Not far from Marina Cay on Beef Island, which is the site of the airstrip and is now connected by a bridge to Tortola itself, there is a delightful little club-cum-hotel known as the Trellis Bay Club. It has accommodation for about a dozen people in the main building and there are one or two furnished cottages for rent. Marina Cay warrants an A-minus rating and Trellis Bay is in the good B-plus category.

Guana Island, off the northeast tip of Tortola, is a privately owned 750-acre club. It has no less than five beaches which provide first-class bathing and there are facilities for snorkelling, fishing, sailing, tennis, golf and croquet. Rooms are sometimes available when not occupied by members.

The second most important of the British Virgin Islands is Virgin Gorda (population about 600). It has several excellent beaches—Devil's Bay, Spring Bay and Trunk Bay. At Coppermine Point there are remains of copper workings. But the main tourist attraction is the recently opened Little Dix Bay Hotel (A-plus rating) which caters for the richer type of North American tourist. It has 50 attractive beachside rooms, each with its own private terrace and its own path to the beach. There is a "central pavilion" where excellent food is served, an unusually attractive bar built out of steel drums, and a gift shop. During the season there are film shows, beach parties and dancing to steelbands. The hotel specialises in package plan family holidays which include : a half-day cruise off Virgin Gorda and down the Sir Francis Drake Channel; two hours of horseback riding; one half-hour of water-skiing with instruction included; a jeep tour and sightseeing trip of the island. The hotel also caters for all needs of visiting yachtsmen—box lunches, ice, bait for fishing, fuel, cocktail and beach parties; and stenographer services are available in English, Spanish, German and French.

The remaining British Virgin Islands have not yet been developed for other than the more adventurous visitors. They are nevertheless full of charm. Four, at the least, are worth a visit :

Anegada (population about 300) has beautiful beaches on its northern and western coastlines. Its waters abound with fish and there are a number of unexplored wrecks, some of which are alleged to contain treasure.

Jost Van Dyke (population about 200) is rugged and mountainous with two fine beaches on the southern coastline, White Bay and Great Harbour Bay.

Little Tobago is a small island near Jost Van Dyke and close to where the world's largest blue marlin was caught.

Salt Island, where about 40 people live, has salt ponds which are interesting to visit at reaping time during April and May.

SPORTS

Being as yet largely undeveloped from the tourist point of view, the sporting attractions of the British Virgin Islands are those associated with beaches and the sea. Places like Little Dix Bay and Marina Cay have everything in the way of swimming, fishing, snorkelling and sailing which the visitor could desire. The waters round these islands are a yachtsman's paradise. Tortola in particular abounds with trails for horseback riding and the mountains are ideal for hiking.

THINGS TO BUY

Obviously these unspoilt islands have not yet become places where many goods are offered for sale to the visitor; but in Road Town such items as liquor, perfume, English cloth and straw goods can be obtained at prices which compare favourably with those of other islands where free-port facilities exist.

USEFUL FACTS FOR VISITORS

The British Virgin Islands have a total area of 59 square miles and consist of something over 40 islands, islets and rocks. They can be divided into four groups. To the south, extending overall for some 20 miles in a northeasterly direction, is the series of cays which terminates in the island of Virgin Gorda. This group is separated by the Sir Francis Drake Channel from the parallel group of Great Thatch, Tortola and Beef Island, which extends for about 15 miles. To the northwest of the Tortola group, and again separated by a shallow channel, lie the Tobago Cays and Great and Little Jost Van Dyke. The Dogs form a connecting link between the first and second groups. Anegada forms a fourth unit lying about 30 miles north of Virgin Gorda and to the northeast of Tortola.

All the islands, except Anegada, are volcanic and hilly and their soils are probably among the stoniest and rockiest in the world. Anegada is flat, with extensive beaches at the western end.

The islands lie within the trade wind belt and have a pleasant sub-tropical climate. Maximum summer temperatures are usually about 87° F. (30° C.) and in winter the minimum is about 67° F. (20° C.). Sea breezes temper the summer heat, and usually there is a fall of up to 10° at night. On Tortola's lower land, where records have been kept since 1901, the annual rainfall average is 53 inches.

The population of the British Virgin Islands is about 7,300, of which about 6,500 live in Tortola. Apart from 150-odd people of European stock resident in the islands (discounting tourists and visitors) the population is of African descent. The language is English.

L.I.A.T. has scheduled flights to Tortola from Antigua where connections can be made by B.O.A.C., Pan American, Air France and Air Canada with Europe, North America and South America. Chartered planes are available from St. Thomas, St. Croix and San Juan.

Regular passenger services are operated between St. Thomas and Road Town by diesel-engined launches and there are freight services between Puerto Rico, St. Thomas and Tortola. An occasional cruise liner calls at Tortola.

Further information can be had from The Tourist Board, Tortola, British Virgin Islands. In New York the best thing to do is to contact The Caribbean Tourist Association, and in London the Colonial Office.

SOME OTHER BOOKS TO READ

GENERAL

Aspinall, Sir Algernon. *Pocket Guide to the West Indies*. Methuen, London, 1954

Burns, Sir Alan. *History of the British West Indies*. Allen & Unwin, London, 1966

Fermor, P. Leigh. *The Traveller's Tree*. John Murray, London, 1950

Macpherson, John. *Caribbean Lands: A Geography of the West Indies*. Longmans Green, London, 1962

Mittleholzer, Edgar. *With a Carib Eye*. Secker & Warburg, London, 1958

Naipaul, V. S. *The Middle Passage*. Andre Deutsch, London, 1962

Nicole, Christophe. *The West Indies—Their People and History*. Hutchinson, London, 1965

Parry, J. M. and Sherlock, Philip. *A Short History of the West Indies*. Macmillan, London, 1963

Sherlock, Philip. *The West Indies*. Thames and Hudson, London, 1966

Williams, Dr. Eric. *Capitalism and Slavery*. Andre Deutsch, London, 1964

BAHAMAS

Craton, Michael. *History of the Bahamas*. Collins, London, 1962. New Edition 1967

Contemporary titles that really help the visitor:

Hannau, H. W. *Nassau in the Bahamas, a Pictorial Guide*. Panorama Books, 1965

The Bahamas Handbook. Issued annually

The Yachtsman's Guide to the Bahamas

Sun and Sixpence. A Guide to Nassau and the Bahama Resort Islands

BARBADOS

Connell, Neville. *Short History of Barbados*. Barbados Museum and Historical Society, 1966

Hoyos, F. A. *Barbados—Our Island Home*. Macmillan, London, 1962

Lynch, Louis. *The Barbados Book*. Andre Deutsch, London, 1964

BERMUDA

Bermuda Today

Panorama Book of Bermuda. Hannau, 1965

Tucker, Terry. *The Bermuda Story*

de Chantel Kennedy, Sister Jean. *Biography of a Colonial Town*

Geography of Bermuda. Ed. Prof. W. Watson. Collins, Glasgow, 1965

EL DORADO AND GUYANA

Swan, Michael. *British Guiana: Lands of Six Peoples*. H.M.S.O., London, 1957

Swan, Michael. *The Marches of Eldorado*. Cape, London, 1958

Smith, Raymond. *British Guyana*. O.U.P., London, 1962

Newman, Peter. *British Guyana*. O.U.P., London

219

Simms, Peter. *Trouble in Guyana*. Unwin, London
Smith, Raymond. *The Negro Family in British Guiana*. Routledge, London
Durrell, G. *Three Singles to Adventure*. Hart-Davis, London, 1958
Attenborough, D. *Zoo Quest to Guyana*. Lutterworth Press, London, 1956
Guppy, N. *Wai-Wai*. John Murray, London, 1958
Jagan, Dr. C. *West on Trial*. Joseph, London, 1958
Cummings, L. P. *Geography of Guyana*. Collins, Glasgow and London, 1965

HISPANIOLA—HAITI
Stephen, Alexis, *Black Liberator—The Life of Toussaint L'Ouverture*. Ernest Benn, London, 1949
Cole, Hubert. *Christophe: King of Haiti*. Eyre & Spottiswoode, London, 1967
Metraux, Alfred. *Haiti: Black Peasants and their Religion* (translated from the French). Harrap, London, 1960
Rodman, Selden. *Haiti: The Black Republic*. Devin-Adair, New York, 1954

HISPANIOLA—DOMINICAN REPUBLIC
Harding, Bertita. *Land Columbus Loved: The Dominican Republic*. Coward-McCann, New York, 1949
Rodman, Selden. *Quisquaya: a History of the Dominican Republic*. University of Washington Press, 1964

JAMAICA
Bennett, Louise. *Jamaica Labrish*. Ed. Rex Nettleford. Sangster, Kingston, 1966
Black, Clinton. *Story of Jamaica*. Collins, London, 1965
Cargill, Morris, Ed. *Ian Fleming Introduces Jamaica*. Andre Deutsch, London, 1965
Cassidy, Frederick. *Jamaica Talk—300 Years of the English Language in Jamaica*. Macmillan, London, 1961
Clarke, Edith. *My Mother Who Fathered Me*. Allen & Unwin, London, 1960
Kerr, Dr. Madeline. *Personality and Conflict in Jamaica*. Collins-Sangster, London, 1962

PUERTO RICO
Page, Homer. *Puerto Rico: The Quiet Revolution*. Viking Press, New York, 1963
Lewis, Gordon, K. *Puerto Rico: Freedom and Power in the Caribbean*. MR Press, 1963
McGuire, Edna. *Puerto Rico: Bridge to Freedom*. Macmillan, New York, 1962
Senior, C. *Our Citizens from the Caribbean*. McGraw Hill, New York, 1965

TRINIDAD AND TOBAGO
Carmichael, Gertrude. *History of the West Indian Islands of Trinidad and Tobago*. Alvin Redman, London, 1960
Williams, Dr. Eric. *History of the People of Trinidad and Tobago*. Andre Deutsch, London, 1964

INDEX

Florida

Bahama
Is.

FRUIT PINEAPPLES
SALT
LUMBER FISHING

GULF OF MEXICO

FISHING

TOBACCO

Cuba
SUGAR SUGAR COFFEE

SISAL
CATTLE

Mexico

Cayman Is.

FISHING

Haiti

Jamaica

SUGAR
CITRUS

Br. Honduras

BANANAS
TIMBER
FISHING

Honduras

SUGAR RUM
COFFEE COCOA
BANANAS CITRUS
TOBACCO PIMENTOES

CARIBBEAN

SUGAR

CATTLE SISAL

CATTLE

COFFEE

COCOA

Nicaragua

COFFEE SUGAR

Panama

Costa Rica

BANANAS COCONUTS
COCOA FISHING

FISHING

TOBACCO

COFFEE

Columbia

COFFEE

PACIFIC OCEAN

COFFEE

Florida

GULF OF MEXICO

Bahama Is

PINEAPPLES
FRUIT
SALT
LUMBER
FISHING

FISHING

TOBACCO

Cuba

SUGAR
SUGAR
COFFEE

Haiti

SISAL
CATTLE

Mexico

Cayman Is.
FISHING

Jamaica
SUGAR RUM
COFFEE COCOA
BANANAS CITRUS
TOBACCO PIMENTOES

SUGAR
CITRUS

BANANAS
TIMBER

Br. Honduras
FISHING

Honduras

SUGAR

CARIBBEAN

CATTLE
SISAL
CATTLE

Nicaragua

COFFEE
COCOA

COFFEE
SUGAR

Panama

TOBACCO

Costa Rica

BANANAS
COCOA FISHING

COCONUTS

FISHING

COFFEE

Columbia

COFFEE

PACIFIC OCEAN

COFFEE